reworded 5/6/10 ꞒoꞒq

794.109   Schonberg, Harold C.
            Grandmasters of
            chess. 1973

7/61 Sand in cong

JUN 25 $\frac{09}{11}$ $\frac{10}{1}$

$\frac{00}{1}$ $\frac{03}{1}$

        $\frac{01}{1}$ $\frac{02}{11}$

$\frac{74}{11}$ $\frac{78}{1}$ $\frac{86}{1}$ $\frac{82}{1}$ $\frac{83}{111}$ $\frac{90}{11}$

$\frac{75}{1111}$ $\frac{88}{1}$ $\frac{84}{11}$ $\frac{91}{1}$ $\frac{84}{11}$ $\frac{95}{11}$

$\frac{74}{11}$ ILL MAY 02

        $\frac{92}{1}$ ILL OCT 01 $\frac{94}{11}$ $\frac{96}{11}$

Grandmasters
of Chess

Other Books by the Same Author

The Great Pianists
The Great Conductors
The Lives of the Great Composers

Grandmasters of Chess

by Harold C. Schonberg

J. B. LIPPINCOTT COMPANY
Philadelphia and New York

Portions of this book have appeared in
Harper's Magazine and *The New York Times Magazine.*

The passages from the *Times Magazine* are © 1971/1972
by The New York Times Company. Reprinted by permission.

U.S. Library of Congress Cataloging in Publication Data

Schonberg, Harold C
    Grandmasters of chess.

    Bibliography: p.
        1.   Chess—History.   2.   Chess—Biography.
    I.   Title.
    GV1317.S33   794.1′09   73–10391
    ISBN–0–397–01004–4

To the memory of my Dad,
who taught me the moves

Front End Papers

"The Match Between France and England"—William Staunton of England *(left)* facing Pierre Saint-Amant in Paris, 1843. Staunton won.

Back End Papers

The St. Petersburg Chess Tournament, 1914.

Front row, left to right: Gunsberg, Blackburne, Lasker, Tarrasch, Burn, Prof. Dr. R. Gebhardt (President of the German Chess Association), Rubinstein, Bernstein, Capablanca, and Janowski.

Second row: Weinstein, Marshall, Alekhine, N. J. Maxinov,* B. J. Malintin (President of the St. Petersburg Chess Society), P. P. Sabonroff,* E. Talvik,* J. O. Sossnitzky * (Vice-President of the St. Petersburg Chess Society), V. Robinov (Vice-President of the German Chess Association), Lochvitzky, and E. A. Znosko-Borovsky.

Back row: Nimzovich, N. H. Znosko-Borovsky, and D. D. Korolev (President of the Financial and Commercial Society and Hon. Member of the Congress).

* Members of the Tournament Committee

Acknowledgments

To the New York Public Library, and the libraries of the Manhattan Chess Club and the Marshall Chess Club.

To Anne Sunnucks for her *Encyclopaedia of Chess,* that industrious compilation to which all researchers in chess are in debt. I have used many fascinating tidbits from the Sunnucks *Encyclopaedia.*

To Reuben Fine for his pithy comments in *The World's Great Chess Games.* Dr. Fine says in one phrase what other analysts take pages to express.

To David O. Lawson for his long article on Paul Morphy in *Chessworld* of January–February, 1964. It is the best article ever written on Morphy, and I have drawn liberally from it.

To Edward Lasker and the late Hans Kmoch for much stimulating conversation on chess and chess players. Both of these great veterans supplied me with material and anecdotes.

To *The New York Times* for its microfilm facilities and for permission to use parts of two articles on Bobby Fischer that appeared in the Magazine issues of November 14, 1971, and September 3, 1972.

To *Harper's Magazine* for permission to use part of an article on Bobby Fischer that appeared in the July, 1972, issue.

To Janet Chenery for locating many of the illustrations herein.

To Alice N. Loranth, curator of the chess iconography at the Cleveland Public Library, who unselfishly made all the material available.

To Ed Burlingame and Carolyn Blakemore of Lippincott, who
dreamed up the idea of this book.

To Burt Hochberg, who read the manuscript and straightened
out some questionable statistics.

To my wife, Rosalyn, who read the manuscript and had many
valuable suggestions to offer.

Picture Credits

Grateful acknowledgment is made to the following sources for
pictures appearing on the indicated pages:

The Bettmann Archive, Inc.: 167

Collection of the John G. White Department, Cleveland Public
Library (Studio Boris): 33, 43, 56, 57, 69, 87, 97 (top), 101,
114, 117, 121, 125, 145, 151, 161 (bottom left), 217

General Research and Humanities Division, The New York
Public Library, Astor, Lenox and Tilden Foundations: 97
(bottom), 107, 139

Courtesy Burt Hochberg: 161 (bottom right), 191, 207

Manhattan Chess Club: 203, endpapers

The New York Times: 259, 262, 279, 284

Halldor Petursson: 297

TASS From SovFoto: 183, 227, 239, 244, 253

WIDE WORLD PHOTOS: 233

Contents

Grandmasters
of Chess

1 ♛

Game? Sport? Art? Science?

In 1914, Nicholas II, Czar of all the Russias, was host to a great chess tournament instigated by the St. Petersburg Chess Society. Nicholas himself subscribed 1000 rubles toward the prize fund. That may have been a factor in inducing Emanuel Lasker, the chess champion of the world, to participate—his first tournament appearance since 1909. The world's most important players took part. There was José Raúl Capablanca from Cuba, who only a few years previously had made a spectacular entry into international chess, winning the strong San Sebastian Tournament in 1911. Akiba Rubinstein was there—Rubinstein, the end-game artist, the quiet man from the Polish ghetto who had won five successive tournaments and who—many thought—was the strongest player then alive. Frank Marshall, the romantic throwback from America, was on hand. So were Siegbert Tarrasch, the German didact; and Aron Nimzovich, the Latvian-born Danish avant-gardist; and Joseph Henry Blackburne from England, the feared attacking player; and the old-timers David Janowski from France and Isidore Gunsberg from England. Ossip Bernstein and the young Alexander Alekhine, both from Russia, upheld the national pride.

Lasker won, coming in a half point over Capablanca. The brilliant Cuban was in the lead until the eighteenth of the twenty-one rounds. But he lost to Lasker, and that demoralized him. He blundered away a won position against Tarrasch in the next round, giving Lasker the lead. With that went his chances.

Alekhine surprised everybody by coming in third, followed by Tarrasch and Marshall. At the banquet concluding the match, the Czar named those five players "Grandmasters of Chess." Lasker, Capablanca, Alekhine, Tarrasch, and Marshall—the original grandmasters of history.

The term seems to have been used shortly after the turn of the century, and after St. Petersburg 1914 the great players were always referred to as grandmasters, but the coinage would have been unknown to the great players of the previous century. They were known merely as "masters." Today, of course, we would call such titans as Wilhelm Steinitz and Paul Morphy "grandmasters" without question; they were so by any definition; they were the best of their time. The same might be said of ar-Razi, the Persian who defeated al-'Adli in A.D. 847 in the shining presence of the caliph al-Mutawakkil' and his court.

But chess in A.D. 847 was altogether different from chess today. The game is old, very old, and its practice retreats perhaps back to prehistory. In ancient tombs pieces are found which archaeologists assure us constituted a form of chess. A more modern version came out of India in the seventh century A.D. Originally it was a game of war. There it was called *chaturanga,* and it rapidly made its way to Persia and Arabia. Some of the Arab terminology remains to this day. Take the word "checkmate." It comes from the Persian *sháh mát, sháh* meaning "king" and *mát* meaning "helpless" or "lost." From *sháh* also comes the name of the game in many languages: *scacchi* (Italian), *Schach* (German), *échecs* (French), *chess* (English).

By the eleventh century the game was known throughout Europe, and in medieval times a literature about it began to develop. One long poem, written in 1513 by Marcus Hieronymus Vida, later Bishop of Alba, is named *Scacchia Ludus,* and it describes a game of chess played between Apollo and Mercury. The poem shows that the game by then had approached the modern form. Oliver Goldsmith made a translation in hearty Georgian couplets. One section goes:

> But the fierce Queen, whom dangers ne'er dismay,
> The strength and terror of the bloody day,
> In a straight line spreads her destruction wide,

To left or right, before, behind, astride.
Yet may she never with a circling course
Sweep to the battle like the fretful Horse.

As for the King:

He moves on slow, with reverence profound
His faithful troops encompass him around,
And oft, to break some instant fatal scheme,
Rush to their fate, their sov'reign to redeem.

Manuals began to be written. These generally contained the rules, opening moves, and in some cases practical advice to the player. Thus in Lucena's *Repeticion de Amores e Arte de Axedres,* published in Spain in 1497, there is an invaluable tip demonstrating that while the rules may have changed through the centuries, certain things in chess have remained a constant: "If you play by day," the good cleric suggests, "place your opponent facing the light, which gives you a great advantage. Also, try to play your adversary when he has just eaten and drunk freely." Other authors in the early days of European chess were Damiano (Rome, 1512) and Ruy López (Spain, 1561). Lopez was a cleric who developed the most famous opening in chess history. The Ruy Lopez, still among the most frequently played openings, is named after him.

The early history of chess is a complicated subject that demands the ministrations of an Orientalist, historian, linguist, philologist, and chess player. Those interested can consult the standard work in English, H. J. R. Murray's monumental *History of Chess* (Oxford, 1913). There is an equivalent study in German—*Geschichte und Literatur des Schachspiels* by A. van der Linde (Berlin, 1874–1875). And there are any number of shorter, less-detailed studies, going back to the first one in English by Thomas Hyde, published in 1694.

With the development of European chess close to the form practiced today came chess players—the grandmasters as well as the amateurs and patzers (from the German verb *patzen,* to make a mess of). Chess playing on a high level requires a certain type of mind—though exactly what kind the psychologists have not yet determined—and the grandmaster through the ages, ever since ar-Razi defeated al-'Adli, is capable of certain intellectual feats, a certain kind of synthesis, that to the patzer or layman can border on black magic. It was soon discovered that people would pay money to see those prodigies of the human intellect in action, that there was a living to be made out of chess. Starting in the sixteenth century, chess professionals began to emerge, first in Italy and Spain, then through the Continent. Lucena, Lopez, Damiano, Gioacchino Greco, Paolo Boi, Giovanni Leonardo, Giulio Polerio, Carrera, Alessandro Salvio are some of the sixteenth- and seventeenth-century heroes. (The last in that line was Domenico Ponziani, who died in 1792. Since then Italy has not produced a chess player of grandmaster caliber.) Specimens of their play exist. By modern standards the playing is, of course, primitive.

These players started a little international circuit. They wrote books, they traveled, they gave exhibitions, they played for large stakes. Leonardo (1542–?1587), who was born in Calabria, heard about the exceptional powers of Lopez and actually went to the Spanish court to challenge his great rival. He lost, in a match played before Philip II. Leonardo's pride was somewhat salvaged when he proceeded to Portugal and trounced El Morro, the strongest player there. Leonardo returned to Italy and died in Naples. He is believed to have been poisoned by jealous rivals. Greco (c. 1600–1634) developed into the greatest player of his day. Apparently a man of little education—chess and education have nothing in common, as witness Bobby Fischer —he traveled widely (going even to the West Indies), wrote chess treatises that were in use for generations, and made a great deal of money playing high-stakes chess (he won 5000 crowns at the Duke of Lorraine's court alone). There were even international matches. The first one on record took place between Spain and Italy in 1575, at the Spanish court. Lopez and Alfonso Ceron played against Boi and Leonardo. The Italians won.

One of the tricks of those early grandmasters, as it was of the later ones, was to startle the bourgeoisie with exhibitions of blindfold play. Blindfold play does not mean literally blindfolded; it means that one player does not have sight of the boards. He may be sitting with his back to them, or be in another room. Moves are relayed to him and he responds. As early as

1226 there was blindfold play; one Buzzeca, a Sicilian, took on two simultaneous opponents while blindfolded, and at the same time he played a third opponent over the board. Damiano wrote a treatise on the subject: *The Elements of the Art of Playing Without Seeing the Board*. Robert Lambe, in his *History of Chess* (1764), mentions that "The Spaniards play by memory at it on horseback: and so do the Moors, who, by the confession of the Spaniards themselves, are much better players at it." To the layman this ability is an inexplicable gift bordering on witchcraft; obviously the practitioners have to be helped by diabolical intervention. When Philidor in 1783 revived the practice and played two boards simultaneously in London, it was described in the *World* as "a phenomenon in the history of man." But many great chess players, and some not so great, have had this ability. It comes as naturally to them as spelling out a chord away from the piano comes to those with absolute pitch, or as mentally solving complicated equations was to Gauss. Through the years the records at blindfold play have been broken. Morphy could play eight simultaneous games, Pillsbury twenty-two, Réti twenty-nine, Alekhine thirty-two; and in 1960 a Hungarian named János Flesch took on fifty-two in a twelve-hour session, winning thirty-one, losing three, and drawing the rest. Recent unconfirmed reports from Budapest claim that Flesch, around 1970, pushed his world record up to sixty-two simultaneous blindfold games.

Through the centuries chess continued to intrigue, delight, and exasperate people. In 1291 John Peckham, the Archbishop of Canterbury, threatened to put the prior and canons of Coxford in Norfolk on a diet of bread and water unless they desisted from chess playing. It also developed that chess players, hungry for action, did not necessarily have to meet each other face to face. Correspondence chess evolved. Lambe tells the story of "two persons of distinction, the one at Madrid, the other at Rome, who played a game at Chess, at that distance. They began when they were young; and though they lived to a very old age, Tradition tells us, that the game was far from being finished. The first, who died, appointed his Executor to go on with the game: And if we consider the distance, though they kept couriers to convey their correspondence, we should not wonder that the game is

not finished at this hour; which began, perhaps, 100 years ago."
Today there are correspondence games all over the world, and
there are those who complain that the postal service of the United
States is seeing to it that games last as long as those between the
persons of distinction in Madrid and in Rome.

Little by little the rules of chess became standardized, and
it arrived at very much like its present form toward the end of
the eighteenth century through the exertions of the first of the
great modern players, François André Danican Philidor, chess
master and also composer of music. (The term "composer" in chess
has a special meaning; it refers to those who create chess problems
and end-game studies. In the world of chess, the greatest of all
composers, the very Bach and Beethoven rolled together, was Sam
Loyd.) Chess appropriated its own Muse; she was created in a
poem named *Caïssa*, written in 1763 by Sir William Jones. *Caïssa*,
clearly inspired by Vida's *Scacchia Ludus*, tells of the invention
of chess by Mars, and describes the moves. At the end of the poem,
Mars

> . . . fram'd a tablet of celestial mold
> Inlay'd with squares of silver and of gold;
> Then of two metals form'd the warlike band,
> That here compact in show of battle stand;
> He taught the rules that guide the pensive game,
> And call'd it Caïssa from the dryad's name.
> Whence Albion's sons, who most its praise confess,
> Approved the play, and named it thoughtful Chess.

Ever since then Caïssa has spread her protective mantle over
chess and chess players, and has also inspired poem after poem
more dreadful even than Sir William Jones's couplets. No respect-
able chess publication was complete without an ode of some sort
inspired by Caïssa. The *British Chess Magazine* in the 1880's
used to run one in almost every issue. A typical example would
be the heartbreaking poem entitled "Claribel and Her Chess
Queen":

> To play at Chess with Claribel,
> Though you in drawing rooms play well,
> Is dangerous to your game;

When you to strategy should rise,
Her white hand, arm, and piercing eyes
Distract you in your game.

Love blooms over the chessboard. The lover plays with
Claribel. But love does not triumph—not for this poor, smitten
wretch of a chess player, anyway. Claribel is not interested in him;
he plays too rough; and the poem ends with advice to all chess
players in love:

O Claribel! I must confess
I loved thee better than my Chess,
    Most true my love hath been.
Vain words!—she's married to a Don,
With whom she played and always won—
    He never took her Queen.

With Philidor's supremacy, and a powerful group of players
who succeeded him, France was the world leader in chess. Then
the action shifted to England and Howard Staunton, the world's
best player in the 1840's. Paul Morphy brought America to the
fore, and briefly dazzled the world in 1858 and 1859. Then the
Central Europeans took over. The nineteenth century saw chess
put on a solid basis, with regularly scheduled tournaments and
matches, and an acknowledged world champion. Chess clubs
sprang up everywhere. Chess columns began to appear in magazines and newspapers; the first was a column in the Liverpool
Mercury in 1813. (The first in the United States appeared in
1845 in New York's *Spirit of the Times,* a daily newspaper.)
Chess literature grew enormously; it suddenly seemed that armies
of analysts were putting every game through a sieve, codifying
the openings, enumerating untold numbers of variations, testing
every move made by the masters. The theory of chess became
a necessary tool for an aspiring player; he no longer could rely
on instinct. "Book chess," the memorization of hundreds upon
hundreds of openings and all variations within them, became
part of the game. Emanuel Lasker once said that when he was
young, all a player needed was talent and common sense. But in
twentieth-century chess, Lasker continued, a player had to have
memorized thousands of variations. One slip and he was in a lost

position, the prey of a player who had more "book."

For chess is an accretion of knowledge, and every new move made by a master goes into the general fund. Out of an infinite number of possibilities, certain responses have been proved to be more accurate than others. James Mason, in his *Principles of Chess* (1893), estimated the number of possibilities of playing the first ten moves as 169,518,829,100,544,000,000,000,000,000,000. This is an inconceivably large number; and yet inconceivably larger than *that* is the approximate number of possibilities in a forty-move game. Maurice Kraitchik, in his *Mathematical Recreations*, figures it as 25×10^{115}—that is, 25 times 10 followed by 115 zeros. Astronomical numbers are "miserably dwarfish" to this, Kraitchik says. If a computer could be programmed so that it would make a choice, at a microsecond per move (one millionth of one millionth of a second), it would take 10^{90} years to exhaust the possibilities of a forty-move game. Thus the computer might reach only the middle game in a thousand billion *generations*. But all this is, in truth, a numbers game that has nothing to do with chess. Of the billions and billions of possibilities, most are demonstrably wrong. A chess opening or a chess game works on a certain kind of logic; it has a specific theme that must be developed, much as a composer develops a theme, and anybody departing from the logic of that theme will immediately be punished. That is why a weak player has no chance against a master. Of the finite (as opposed to the mythical infinite) possibilities at any move, the master knows more than the amateur; he has the book knowledge; he can capitalize on the tiniest error. In modern grandmaster play the entire action is a subtle jockeying for minute positional advantage. Many chess games may run thirty or forty moves with one player in a permanently lost position because of a miscalculation in the opening. Analysts nod knowingly. "He was lost after the eighth move," they will say.

It is this ability to see and foresee, to conceive of a game as a unity, to make the best choice among many alternatives, that makes chess what it is. Even before the nineteenth century it was realized that chess was more than a mere game. Ben Franklin, for one, saw chess as a moral force, and the great moralizer drew the appropriate conclusions. Chess, wrote Franklin, is not merely an idle amusement. Life is a kind of chess, with struggle, competition, good and ill events. Chess can teach *"Foresight,* which looks a little into futurity . . . *Circumspection,* which surveys the whole chessboard . . . *Caution,* not to make our moves too hastily . . . and, lastly, we learn by chess the habit of *not being discouraged by present bad appearances in the state of our affairs,* the habit of *hoping for a favorable change,* and that of *persevering in the search of resources."*

Franklin goes on to give rules for ethical players. Would that the world were full of Franklin's kind of gentlemen! "If your adversary is long in playing you ought not to hurry him or express any uneasiness at his delay. You should not sing, nor whistle, nor look at your watch, nor take up a book to read, nor make a tapping with your feet on the floor, or with your fingers on the table, nor do anything that may disturb his attention. . . ." This in 1779. But players do all of that today, and some unscrupulous types will do much more than anything in Franklin's innocent list of devices to rattle an opponent. They will mutter to themselves, sip liquid noisily, eat something with great smacks of the lip, blow smoke toward the opposite player, sneeze in his face, stare at him until he becomes uncomfortable, squirm constantly, belch, pick at the nose. Nose-picking has been found to be specially effective; such a sight drives some squeamish players up the wall and makes it impossible for them to concentrate on their game. Some players, after all, are more high-pitched than others; the least little thing bothers them. Bobby Fischer is famous for his low boiling point, and he has his emulators. In December of 1972 the Brazilian star Henrique Mecking came right out and accused Tigran Petrosian, the ex-champion of the world, of cheating. Mecking and Petrosian had just finished playing in Church's "Fried Chicken" Tournament in San Antonio, and Petrosian's actions infuriated the short-tempered Brazilian. Petrosian, charged Mecking, "was only quiet when it was his turn to move. All the time I was thinking he was kicking the table and elbowing the board to make it shake. If this was not enough to upset me, Petrosian kept making noises, stirring his cup of coffee, all the time varying the rhythm, and rolling a coin across the table." What seemed to enrage Mecking worst of all was that no counterattack was possible. When

Mecking tried to retaliate, Petrosian simply turned off his hearing aid. Petrosian won that game.

If Franklin saw the morality of chess, others have seen the game in a different light. Samuel Johnson, in his *Dictionary*, called chess "a nice and abstruse game, in which two sets of puppets are moved in opposition to each other." William Cluley, in his *Philosophy of Chess* (1857), wrote that "Chess may be briefly stated to be an agreeable and invigorating mental exercise, a wholesome discipline of the passions, leading to the acquirement of a skill which is susceptible of the most practical application." Lasker called chess, even more briefly, "a fight." Boris Spassky has called chess "a sport." Some claim it is a science. Some insist it is an art. The fact is, of course, that all these elements are present. And if we are to believe the Freudians, chess contains archetypal elements that reach deep into the psyche. Reuben Fine, one of the world's great players during the 1930's, became a psychologist and psychoanalyst, and in 1956 he wrote a treatise on chess psychology. All analysts seem to agree, said Fine, that "a combination of homosexual and hostile elements are sublimated in chess." The King on the chessboard is "indispensable, all-important, irreplaceable, yet weak and requiring protection." The King therefore symbolizes a boy's penis in the phallic stage, with attendant castration complex. "The Pawns symbolize children, particularly little boys." The Queen is of course the woman-figure. "Put together, the chessboard as a whole may symbolize the family situation." Fine goes on to discuss the profuse phallic symbolism of chess, and concludes that the game is an outlet for hostile feelings. Checkmate is equated with castration and the destruction of the father. To win a game is to beat the father. Ben Karpman, in the *Psychoanalytic Review* of January, 1937, had come to the same conclusion. Chess is a substitute for the art of work, and behind it all is the motive of father murder. The game of chess, says Karpman, reflects an anal-sadistic character. Karl Menninger put it grimly indeed: chess players are silently "plotting (and attempting to execute) murderous campaigns of patricide, matricide, fratricide, regicide and mayhem." By far the most famous psychiatric study of a chess player came in 1931 when Ernest Jones, Sigmund Freud's associate and biographer, wrote a long paper on Paul Morphy.

By the time Jones finished with Morphy's anal-sadistic fantasies, the reader was looking at the King and Queen on the chessboard with a new surmise.

Some take this more seriously than others. But whether or not chess has a psychosexual meaning, it most certainly contains elements of psychic murder. Chess is a confrontation of two minds, one trying to dominate and, if necessary, crush the other. Some players—Alekhine, Fischer—achieve psychic gratification this way. Over the board they can triumph and live out their fantasy life. Fortunately, the brutal side of chess is counteracted by an opposed ideal of truth and beauty. For chess has its own built-in morality, its own stringent truth, its own integrity. "On the chessboard," wrote Emanuel Lasker in his *Manual of Chess,* "lies and hypocrisy do not survive long. The creative combination lays bare the presumption of a lie; the merciless fact, culminating in a checkmate, contradicts the hypocrite." What Lasker is saying is that all creative chess players aim only for Truth over the chessboard—truth as manifested in the integrity of a combination to which there is no answer; truth as manifested in the creation of an elegant sequence of moves that is as inevitable and as flawless as the flow of a Shakespeare sonnet; truth as manifested in such a high order of creation that sheer beauty is the result.

On its highest level, chess, as played by a handful of exponents, is as much a search for perfection as mathematics, art, or any other undertaking of the creative mind. Instead of using notes on ruled paper, or oils, or stone, or words, or formulae, the chess player uses the pieces at his disposal. These are his raw materials. His aim is to take these raw materials and from them forge a continuity that expresses his own personality. What can result is a conception that has a high level of expression and imagination and creativity, and it involves the ability to see, or sense, possibilities hidden to less refined minds. It is this ability to synthesize and come up with an unexpected, unflawed sequence that separates the great chess player from all others. It is much the same thing that separated Mozart from Karl Ditters von Dittersdorf, or Manet from Rosa Bonheur. The chess genius, like the mathematical or musical genius, sees certain inherent positions in a situation that less gifted intellects cannot begin to envisage. The chess genius thinks differently from others. All of a sudden comes the unexpected thrust, the flash of vision, and it is a moment of intellectual and aesthetic beauty. As such, the chess genius is allied to genius in any art form. He aims for beauty; he takes a situation that is composed of materials available to everybody and by sheer imagination creates something unique and perfect, something that nobody else could duplicate. Whether this beauty is expressed in musical notes, or in a formula, or with chess pieces, it is a symbol of man's desire for order expressed in an original, unforgettable manner. Dr. Fine has said much the same: "The most important gift that a great chess player must have is, in my opinion, a fertile imagination. He must be able to retire from the world of obtrusive realities into a realm of strange shapes and forms which he combines to create novel situations. And, in a sense, does not the musical composer do the same?"

No aesthetician or psychologist or creator himself has been able to explain these strokes of genius, but there it is—that combination of logic plus technique plus intuition leading to a *coup de maître* that stands in unflawed perfection. And, as in the other arts, these masterpieces are a reflection of style. Chess has its romantics, its classicists, its avant-gardists, its eclectics. As Fine suggests, there is indeed a strong relation between chess and music. The three standard elements of a chess game—opening, middle game, and end game—bear a certain relationship to the three elements of a sonata movement—exposition, development, and recapitulation. Chess, like music, is basically an art of development, combination, and continuation. And both demand total dedication from their acolytes. Caïssa is a stern Muse. Chess players are like pianists, spending six or more daily hours in practice, to the point where it becomes obsessive. They constantly analyze and study, read annotated games published in magazines the world over, memorize openings, become familiar with end-game studies. For them, standard reading materials are such books as *Modern Chess Openings* and *The Art of Sacrifice in Chess*. They know these pages, and many others, as intimately as a pianist knows the *Well-Tempered Clavier* or the Chopin *Études*. Just as a superior musician has at his finger tips the entire standard repertoire, so the superior chess player has in his mind a working knowledge of Keres on the Double King Pawn openings, Boleslavsky on the semiopen games, Florian on the Schliemann Variation of the Ruy Lopez, Gipslis on the Rubinstein Variation, Gligorić on the Sicilian, Harding and Wade on the Velimirović Attack, Levy on the Sicilian Dragon, Wade on the Accelerated Dragon, Zeuthen and Jarlnaes on the French Poisoned Pawn—and hundreds of other books. These are his bread and butter. He also has his five-finger exercises—rapid transit, at ten seconds a move; or blitz, where the moves must be made immediately; or, most popular of all, clock chess at five or seven minutes for the entire game. Young players indulge themselves in thousands upon thousands of hours of rapid chess; if they have no talent for it, they will never develop into major players. Bobby Fischer is the greatest fast player who ever lived.

And in one case, at least, the actual physical movements of the expert chess player bear an amusing relationship to the polished finger movements of a great instrumentalist. Observe an expert chess player at the moment he captures a piece. He takes up his own piece daintily, between thumb and first finger of the right hand. Observe how his arm comes down with a swoop of finality toward the piece to be captured. Observe the slight anticipatory tremble of the third and fourth fingers as they approach their goal. If fingers can ever be said to salivate, these fingers do. Observe how, in one blurred swoop, as elegant as Heifetz in fingered octaves, the wrist pronates, the third and fourth fingers snatch the captured piece out of the way while, simultaneously, the player's own piece now occupies the captured square.

Like musicians, chess players have extraordinary memories—in their field. The memory does not seem to carry over into other things. A few psychologists have studied chess players, and have come to no conclusions at all. But there are a few objective things on which to make some generalizations.

Most chess players start serious study when young (between the ages of ten and twelve), and a few have started before that, thus meeting all the requirements of the authentic prodigy. Mathematics and music are the only other fields in which prodigies are common. The four greatest prodigies in chess history have been Morphy, Capablanca, Reshevsky, and Fischer. But many others are almost in that class. Paul Keres learned the moves at four and was a strong player not long after that. Arturo (or Arturito, as he was then called) Pomar was the champion of the Balearic Islands at eleven and was playing in international tournaments at fourteen. Max Euwe won a tournament when he was ten. Henrique Mecking was Champion of Brazil at thirteen, and at fourteen tied for the championship of South America. Thus all important players have an aptitude that shows up early. If a player these days has not made a reputation by the time he is twenty, he will never do so. For chess is a young man's game, and the peak years are from twenty-five to thirty-five.

Physiological reasons enter into this. Older people find it increasingly hard to memorize, conceptualize, and assimilate. They find themselves prey to hungry kids up on the latest theory. There also is the matter of body conditioning. It takes a healthy, youthful body to stand up to the rigors of match or tournament play—those five-hour sessions of concentrated brain-boiling, of playing off adjourned games the next day and of going without sleep while the mind races through variation after variation. (Tournament games average forty moves in five hours for both players, but they can run much longer. The longest won game in the annals took place between Wolf and Duras at Carlsbad 1907—one hundred sixty-eight moves over a twenty-two-and-a-half-hour period. The longest draw was between Pilnik and Czerniak at Mar del Plata 1953—one hundred ninety-one moves over twenty hours.) The pure intellectual and physical effort of staring at a chessboard without being able to touch it, trying to capture all possibilities and anticipate all future situations, is brainwork on a rarefied level, and there is a heavy drain on the body. In the December, 1971, issue of *Chess Life and Review* there was a study of physiological changes during tournament chess. Breathing rate was up, and systolic blood pressure significantly increased. Researchers at Temple University, in another test, came to the conclusion that chess drained as much energy as did a comparable session of boxing or football. No wonder many players actually go into physical training before an important match or tournament. Bobby Fischer's comment is: "I gotta stay in shape or it's all over." Gideon Stahlberg, the late Swedish grandmaster, has written about the necessity of sharp physical reflexes: "Of what avail is an unlimited imagination and a wealth of ideas when, after a struggle lasting many hours, the brain suddenly seems to stop working?"

Memory. Technique. Imagination. Intuition. A healthy body. Relative youth. What else goes into the great chess player? A team of Russian psychologists found no relationship between chess and general intelligence, but did come to the conclusion that a high degree of visual imagery was basic to a strong chess player. By visual imagery they meant the ability to visualize the changing shape of a chessboard two, three, and more moves in advance. The great Alfred Binet, in a study named *Psychologie des grandes calculateurs et jouers d'échecs* (1894), came to the conclusion that the best players have an "abstract visual memory"; and this, coupled with a superior degree of "spatial ability," is the mark of talent for chess. Otherwise, there seems to be no relationship between chess genius and the players' background, politics, sex life, financial rating, education, and even general intelligence. Some great masters have been next to idiots (not many, admittedly). A genetic factor has been advanced, for Jews have dominated international chess from the beginning of modern (nineteenth-century) play. Another thing players with world championship aspirations must have is an overwhelming will to win. This involves the ego, and the ego of a great chess player is invariably colossal, on the order of the ego of a major operatic tenor or a .400 baseball hitter. The American player William Ewart Napier was once talking about the necessary ingredients of a great chess player to Richard Teichmann, a German grandmaster. "Have you," Teichmann gently said, "given any thought to vanity?" Grandmasters are vain; they hate to lose; it is a psychic shock; their monumental egos are bruised. Nimzovich once lost to a weaker player, whereupon he mounted the table and yelled at the top of his voice, *"Gegen diesen Idioten muss ich verlieren!"* or "That I should lose to this idiot!" Alekhine once resigned, frantic with rage and frustration, by picking up his King and hurling it across the room, nearly braining a referee in the process. (Tournament pieces are weighted with lead; they can be dangerous weapons.) Alekhine would also relieve himself after a loss by going to his hotel room and destroying the furniture.

It interests psychologists that no woman has been able to compete successfully with male chess players on equal terms. Perhaps it is the lack of killer instinct. Perhaps it is the physical inability to stand up against the rigors of tournament chess as well as men do. Whatever it is, no woman has come near the male level. In the entire history of chess, only two women, Vera Menchik and Nona Gaprindashvili, have ever been invited to international tournaments in which men participate. Menchik had talent, and once in a while she did upset a leading player, but she never scored very high in her tournaments. Nona Gaprindashvili, the women's world champion at the point of writing, has appeared in a few major tournaments, though never taking top prize. Bobby Fischer once announced that he could give the odds of a Knight to any woman player alive. The Soviet Chess Federation hastily took him up on the offer, but Fischer loftily refused to reply.

Until recent years the international organization of chess was chaotic. This was especially true as regards the institution of the world championship. The champions of the past defended their title when and if they pleased, selecting their own opponents (and often running away from the strongest ones). Not until 1924 was a worldwide organization created. In that year FIDÉ (the *Fédération Internationale des Échecs*) came into being. It is FIDÉ today that is responsible for the official rules of play, for awarding the title of grandmaster and international master (as in bridge, through rating points; you get to be a grandmaster by beating other grandmasters), and for arranging world championship matches, which are held every three years. FIDÉ has divided the world into ten zones, and the top zonal players meet in an interzonal tournament. Those who survive the interzonal meet in a series of elimination Candidates Matches. The survivor gets to meet the world champion in a twenty-four-game match. (In 1975, however, the rules may be changed; drawn games will no longer count.)

There are about eighty-five active grandmasters in the world, and over one hundred and eighty international masters. Of these, a dozen or so at any given time are the elite of chess—the acknowledged geniuses, the fructifiers, the creators of beautiful games, the theoreticians who change concepts, the ones whose games will be studied, read, replayed, and enjoyed a hundred years in the future. Fischer, Spassky, Botvinnik, Tal—they are the latest in the grand line that extends backward through Alekhine, Capablanca, Lasker, Steinitz, Morphy, Anderssen, Staunton, Philidor. Geniuses all; different in many ways, but geniuses all. Clive Bell, in his *Men of Mathematics,* says of the great mathematicians that they were geniuses of tremendous accomplishment marked off from the majority of their gifted fellow men only by an irresistible urge to do mathematics. Great chess players, by the same token, are geniuses of tremendous accomplishment marked off from the majority of their gifted fellow men by an irresistible impulse to do chess.

2 ♚

The Musician–Chess Player

The Café de la Régence in Paris, still in existence, was a meeting place for politicians and literary figures early in the eighteenth century. These types tend to sleep late, so they would turn up in the evening. The Café de la Régence opened at 8 A.M., and its first visitors were the addicts who thronged to the game rooms. There they could play billiards, cards, checkers, dominoes. And chess. By noon the Café, with its tables close together and with perspiring waiters pushing their way through the throng, was a thick cloud of tobacco smoke mixed with alcoholic fumes. Through the decades everybody could be seen at the Café de la Régence. Voltaire, Rousseau, Diderot, Robespierre, Napoleon (who loved to play chess and was an impulsive, atrocious player with bad manners), Benjamin Franklin, and assorted ministers of state, as well as the general public, would be watching everything and would be watched by everybody.

Paris from about 1750 to the 1830's was the chess capital of the world, and the Café de la Régence was the chess headquarters. The management supplied a chess professional whose job it was to take on any opponent. At first there was M. de Kermar, the Sire de Légal (1702–1792). Légal was one of the two strongest players in the world at that time; his opposite number was a Syrian named Philip Stamma, who held forth in London. Légal would sit in the Café and play for money, the higher the stakes the better. He nearly always won unless he gave odds. Later, Légal was succeeded as professional by such great players as Saint-Amant, la

Bourdonnais, Deschapelles, Kieseritzky, and Harrwitz. The Café de la Régence attracted its quota of eccentrics. One of the most famous was one M. Bonnour, who always came with his little dog, "a queer little animal who always ran before its master in fine weather and ensconced itself in his pocket when it rained, and which, when its master was playing, put its forepaws on the edge of the table, looking fiercely at each move of the adversary, showed its teeth, growled and barked furiously in case the adversary proved victorious." Eccentrics were welcome at the Café de la Régence. They, and chess players, no longer are.

It was this kind of ambience into which young François André Danican Philidor walked in the 1740's. Philidor was born in Dreux in 1726. His father was seventy-nine at the time. The family was distinguished; many were noted musicians. As far back as the 1650's, Philidors had been active in French music. There was Jean Philidor, a musician in the *Grande Écurie,* who begat André, Jacques, and Alexandre, all of whom were court musicians. André begat Anne (a male, despite the name), who was a composer and the founder of the famous *Concert Spirituel* so admired by Mozart on his visit to Paris. Jacques begat Pierre and Michael, both of whom played in the King's private band. Assorted musical Philidors in the King's service also included several named François, Jacques, and Nicolas. François André Danican (Danican was the original family name), the last son of old André, turned out to be the most famous of the entire clan, and in his time he was supreme in two fields.

There was no doubt that François would study music. He was a Philidor. Philidors were ordained by God to be musicians. François was sent off to the chapel choir at Versailles when he was six years old. One of his teachers was the important composer and theoretician, André Campra. François was a good student and was composing at the age of twelve. He was also taught chess by some of the musicians at Versailles, and became so fascinated that he neglected his studies. In 1740 he came to Paris, where he inevitably drifted to the Café de la Régence and took lessons from Légal. It was there that he discovered a flair for blindfold chess, and he startled the clientele by taking on two players simultaneously.

But there was no way to make a living at chess, and Philidor did not wish to develop into a chess bum, hanging around the Café for the odd franc. On the other hand he found it hard to keep going as a musician. He maintained himself by copying music and giving lessons. He also continued to compose music. Soon he was deeply in debt, and he had to flee Paris in 1747. He told his creditors that he was going on a concert tour, which was true, but he did not tell them that he had few, if any, engagements. In Amsterdam he ran out of money and did become a chess bum, playing in cafés for whatever he could get. Chess occupied his next few years, and his reputation grew. He went to London, where he overwhelmed Stamma by an 8 to 1 score, and that despite the fact that he gave Stamma the odds of the move and allowed him to count draws as wins. Philidor then briefly settled in Aachen, where he wrote his famous treatise, *Analyse du Jeu des Échecs.*

Several British peers took an interest in him. Lord Sandwich praised his work, and the Duke of Cumberland invited him to London, where, he assured Philidor, his book would be published. That is what did happen. Philidor went to London, saw his book through the press in 1749, moved in the best circles, listened to the Handel oratorios (Philidor and Handel must have met, though there is no actual record of their having done so), played chess, and became something of a celebrity. The *Analyse* not only achieved instant popularity; it was for generations the most important chess book available, and it went through over a hundred editions in many languages.

For five years Philidor remained in London, where his blindfold exhibitions (up to three players) were considered the wonder of the age. His hangout was Slaughter's Coffee House, at the north end of St. Martin's Lane. He also briefly visited Berlin, where he gave an exhibition before Frederick the Great, and he dropped into Paris to win a match from his former teacher, Légal. During all this his friends in Paris were worried. That a composer of such promise should fritter away his talent playing chess! Philidor was prevailed upon to return to Paris in 1754, and he soon showed the music world that, in one respect at least, his stay in London had not been a total loss. His first composition on his return, the *Motets à grand choeur,* was, because of the pronounced Handelian influence, more rugged than anything he had composed

Aux Français étonnés de ſa Mâle Harmonie,
Il montra dans ſon art des prodiges nouveaux.
Dans ſes délaſsemens admirant ſon Génie,
On voit qu'en ſes jeux même il n'a point de Rivaux.

Par M. Daveſne

François André Danican Philidor, first of the great modern players. As famous a composer of operas as he was a chess player, he was more than a hundred years ahead of his time in chess theory.

up to then. Philidor also wrote a large-scale choral work that, he hoped, would secure for him the patronage of the King. But *Lauda Jerusalem* did not secure for Philidor the job he wanted as superintendent of the King's music. Disappointed, he turned away from music for the court and began to compose for the stage.

That proved to be his real métier. A steady stream of operas came forth. *Blaise le savatier* was a success in 1759, and an even greater hit was his *Sancho Pança dans son isle* (1762). His best-known opera was *Tom Jones* (1765), set to the Fielding novel, which was having an extraordinary vogue in France. Another opera highly regarded in its day was *Ernelinde* (1767). Authorities on Philidor's music state that he had far greater skill and harmonic originality than had any other French opera composer of the time. He broke away from the *da capo* aria, and some of the arias in his operas are actually based on sonata form. He was a fertile harmonist and, as an opera composer, was much more interested in the relationship between words and music than were most of his contemporaries. Their operas tended to be concerts in costume, whereas Philidor in his way was aiming toward music drama. Philidor was also a pioneer in descriptive music. In *Tom Jones* he delightedly introduced onomatopoeic sounds into his orchestra—the hunting horn, the bay of the hounds, the horses' hooves, the crack of whips. This was primitive program music. For many years the operas of Philidor remained in the repertoire, eventually to be elbowed out by Rossini, Auber, and the new romantics. At that, sporadic revivals of Philidor operas are not unknown. *Le soldat magicien* was given in Paris in 1920, and *Sancho Pança* was revived in Paris in 1922 and in Madrid in 1924.

Having become a favorite and famous composer of operas—indeed, the most respected French composer of his time, according to the famous composer André Grétry (who succeeded Philidor as a concocter of favorite operas)—Philidor returned to chess. A club had been founded in 1770 at the Salopian Coffee House in Charing Cross, and Philidor was invited to London to spend the season (February through June) there at an annual retainer. Philidor, thirsty for chess, was glad to go. Fanny Burney watched him play and noted in her diary: "a well-bred, obliging and very sociable man; he is also a good musician." Chess suddenly became more important to Philidor than his music. He returned to the Salopian in 1772 and 1773, and then switched allegiance to the London Chess Club, which met at Parsloe's, a public house in St. James Street. Every year Philidor came for "the season." He was the resident professional; he taught chess, gave exhibitions, met all comers for money. He also taught music on the side.

His friends in Paris again worried. Philidor once more seemed lost to music, even if he did occasionally compete with the new heroes of the Opéra, Grétry and Gluck. But above all, what worried Philidor's friends were those blindfold exhibitions. Three players at a time! No brain could take this for a very long period. Diderot wrote Philidor a letter on April 10, 1782, begging him to desist:

> I should more readily excuse you for these dangerous experiments if you had wagered enough to win five or six hundred guineas. But to risk your talent and your reason for nothing is simply inconceivable. Besides, I have talked about this to M. Légal, and this is his answer: "When I was young, I decided to play a single game of chess without seeing the board, and at the end of that game I found myself so fatigued mentally that it was the first and last time of my life. It is foolish to run the risk of going mad for vanity's sake." Now, when you shall have lost your ability, will the English come forward to rescue your family? Do not believe, Sir, that what has not yet happened to you will not happen. Take my advice, write more fine music for us, write it for many years yet, and do not expose yourself further to the possibility of being an object of scorn, a state to which so many men are born. At most they will say of you, "There is that Philidor creature, he is nothing any more, he lost all the sense he had by pushing little pieces of wood across a chessboard."

Philidor must have been amused with this letter. He of course knew better, and he wrote in a letter to his wife: "I assure you this [blindfold] chess does not fatigue me as much as many people seem to believe. Therefore do not be worried about my health."

London was fascinated with Philidor the chess player, but apparently not very much interested in him as a composer. Or can it be that Philidor at that time was more interested in chess than in music? Among the few performances of his works in London was the *Carmen Seculaire* in 1779. It was a success, and proved to be one of his most enduring pieces (it was performed in Paris as late as 1937). But from all that can be discovered, Philidor never made much of an effort to push his music in London. One wonders why. He needed money and was growing desperate about his financial condition. "It is ridiculous," he wrote to his wife, "that the composer of *Ernelinde* should be obliged to play chess half the year in England in order to keep his family alive." He was allowed to make his annual visits to England after the French Revolution started, but was in London in 1793 when England and France went to war, and he found it impossible to return. Philidor tried to get back to Paris in 1795 and discovered he was on the list of emigrés. To return would have meant death. His family tried to erase his name from the list and finally succeeded—only to learn that he was dead. Philidor died in London on August 31, 1795, alone and destitute—the first of many grandmasters to die a pauper. "On Monday last," a London paper said, "Mr. Philidor, the celebrated chess player, made his last move."

There can be no doubt that Philidor was far and away the greatest chess player of his time. Nobody could give him a real game except at odds; his concept was far too subtle, and his technique much too strong. It was Philidor who was responsible for the famous axiom "The Pawns are the soul of chess." He was the first to set forth certain basic principles, and he had a feeling for position play that was to be fully exploited by players of a much later school. Reuben Fine, in *The World's Great Chess Games,* points out that Philidor's analysis of the ending with Rook and Bishop opposed to Rook, known as Philidor's Position, is still considered sound. "Here, at last," writes Fine, "was a man whose technical skill could for the first time be compared to some degree with that of the moderns." To illustrate Philidor's style, Fine gives a game which he played against one Captain Smith in London, 1790:

	WHITE: CAPT. SMITH	BLACK: PHILIDOR
1.	P-K4	P-K4
2.	B-B4	N-KB3
3.	P-Q3	P-B3

4.	B-KN5	P-KR3
5.	BxN	QxB
6.	N-QB3	P-QN4
7.	B-N3	P-QR4
8.	P-QR3	B-B4
9.	N-B3	P-Q3
10.	Q-Q2	B-K3
11.	BxB	PxB
12.	O-O	P-N4
13.	P-R3	N-Q2
14.	N-KR2	P-R4
15.	P-KN3	K-K2
16.	K-N2	P-Q4
17.	P-B3	N-B1
18.	N-K2	N-N3
19.	P-B3	QR-KN1
20.	P-Q4	B-N3
21.	QPxP	QxP
22.	N-Q4	K-Q2
23.	QR-K1	P-KR5
24.	Q-KB2	B-B2
25.	N-K2	RPxP
26.	QxP	QxQch
27.	NxQ	N-B5ch
28.	K-R1	RxP
29.	R-KN1	RxNch
30.	KxR	R-R1ch
31.	N-R5	RxNch
32.	K-N3	N-R6ch
33.	K-N4	R-R5 mate

Dr. Max Euwe, former world's champion, puts the case for Philidor most elegantly in his *Development of Chess Style*. Philidor, writes Euwe, "laid the first stone in the edifice of modern position play. He took chess out of the narrow confines of Euclidean observation into the boundless realm of Cartesian thought. . . . A full century had to elapse before the Pawn-lore of the great Frenchman was reinstated by Steinitz and refined to its true worth."

3 ♛

Romanticism Plus

Philidor laid the foundation for position play, but the next generation of French masters promptly ignored his teachings. Philidor had the great conception that a game should be *constructed;* that every piece had its value; that the lowly Pawn was there for a reason and was just as important in the over-all pattern of a game as Queen or Rook; that a closed Pawn formation in the middle of the board should be maintained with a view toward queening one of those Pawns in the end game. But along came such players as Alexandre Louis Deschapelles (1780–1847), Charles Mahé de la Bourdonnais (1797–1840), Pierre Saint-Amant (1800–1873), and Lionel Kieseritzky (1806–1853), and they brought an entirely different, and much less scientific, concept to the game.

Perhaps it was the *Zeitgeist*—the new ideas spawned by the American Revolution, the French Revolution, the Industrial Revolution, the new poetry of Wordsworth, Byron, and Goethe, the startlingly free music of Beethoven. Whatever it was, these chess players, and an equivalent group in England, launched the romantic period in chess—and it *was* as romantic as Byron or Berlioz, or the newfangled paintings of Delacroix. Now the idea in chess was attack and combination, a free-for-all over the board, with pieces grandly and recklessly sacrificed in the mad urge to give checkmate. The first player to move (in those days it was not yet standard practice for White invariably to make the first move) offered a gambit Pawn as soon as possible. The opponent was all but obliged to accept the gambit. If he didn't, he was a

38

coward and people talked about him behind his back. From that point the game was a mêlée of attacking pieces, sacrifices, and combinations in depth. Surprisingly few games ended in a draw. Draws were frowned upon. A chess game was war, a battle to the death. This was not very precise chess, but for some seventy-five years the romantic period in chess gave birth to some of the wildest, maddest, most exhilarating, most exciting, most ingenious, and most exasperating games in the literature.

Deschapelles, La Bourdonnais, Saint-Amant, and Kieseritzky were the dreaded foursome at the Café de la Régence, and they upheld French supremacy in chess until Howard Staunton from England put a stop to it. Deschapelles in many respects was the prototype of today's grandmaster. He had an ego big enough to encompass all Europe to the Ural Mountains, with the Caspian Sea thrown in. He was arrogant, self-confident, domineering, a braggart, and a gambler. He also was an authentic war hero. The son of a marshal of France, he lost his right hand fighting the Prussians, during which battle he also received a saber slash on the head. Phrenology was all the rage in the 1800's, and there were philosophers who gazed upon Deschapelles and wondered if that crack on the head had reassorted his brains so that the bump of chess knowledge came to the fore.

"We leave it to the scientific physiologist to say," wrote the chess enthusiast George Walker in 1850, "whether these saber wounds of the head had any share in exciting his brain to that fervent pitch of imagination, without which a genius lives not." As for himself, Walker had no doubt. "The truth of phrenology is strongly borne out by the conformation of Deschapelles's forehead; in which the organ of calculation is more considerably developed than in that of any human being we ever saw. A high and sharp ridge stands forth as the boundary of his fine, square forehead." Deschapelles was not only the foremost chess player of his time; he was also a professional gambler who made a living playing whist (the Deschapelles Coup is famous wherever whist is played), and Walker observed his dexterity with awe: "It is curious to see the veteran collect the cards with his ONE LEFT HAND, sort, play, and gather them in tricks."

Deschapelles claimed that he not only had never studied the theory of chess; he never even knew the moves until, one day, while he was walking in the Palais Royal, he saw some men absorbed "in a game which I had never seen." For two hours Deschapelles intently watched the action. "Its secrets, at first incomprehensible to me, quickly revealed themselves to my mind." Deschapelles challenged the best player, a M. Bernard, to a game the following day. As he describes the memorable occasion, "I bowed, left the place, and to my discredit must confess that until the appointed hour I did not give my challenge a single thought." The next day Deschapelles sat down with M. Bernard and promptly lost two games. Presumably he went home and this time did some thinking about it. Deschapelles's will to win was of an order no lower than Alekhine's or Fischer's was to be. The next day Deschapelles returned, looking for revenge, and beat Bernard in all the games. "I could give him," Deschapelles relates with some complacency, "the odds of a Pawn and two moves. Since that day I have made no progress. In three sessions at most—from my experience—one must know in chess all one can ever learn."

It is a pretty story, and it is a pity that nobody believes it. But there can be no doubt that Deschapelles, with all his big talk, was for many years the strongest player around. His views about the game were altogether uncomplicated, and resembled Marshal Joffre's philosophy of battle some hundred years later: "Our flanks have dissolved? Our center is broken? Very well, gentlemen. Let us attack!" Deschapelles had much the same approach. He could not waste time on the niceties of position play. "For my part," he once said, "I look neither to the right nor to the left; but I simply examine the situation before me, as I would that of two hostile camps, and I do that which I think best to be done. I want to checkmate. I do not want to capture, to defend, or to attack. I want to checkmate, *et voilà tout.*"

Toward the end of his life he almost completely dropped chess. For this there were two major reasons. One was that a new generation of players—among them his pupil, La Bourdonnais—could beat him, and Deschapelles never looked kindly on defeat. The other was that he became a farmer. After the Napoleonic Wars he took to gardening, and his fruit adorned the King's table. That kept him busy. He also composed music, none of which has come down to us. In 1832 he found himself in trouble. Deschapelles, with his loud mouth and strong opinions about everything, was known everywhere as an anti-Bourbonite. When the disturbances in Paris broke out in June of that year, Deschapelles was suspected of being a party to the affair and was held in custody for some weeks. A letter to the King secured his release.

For some reason Deschapelles, in the 1840's, decided to come out of retirement. He issued a challenge to England, even though he had not played chess for about fifteen years. Possibly he wished to uphold the honor of France. The London Chess Club sent its secretary to discuss details. The bemused Mr. Perigal duly returned home and reported. "M. Deschapelles is the greatest chess player in France," he dryly said. "M. Deschapelles is the greatest billiards player in France. M. Deschapelles is the greatest whist player in France. M. Deschapelles is the greatest pumpkin grower in France. M. Deschapelles is the greatest liar in France." The proposed match never did take place.

La Bourdonnais succeeded Deschapelles as the premier player in France. Born into a wealthy family, he drifted into the Café de la Régence and promptly was lost to the world. Chess seized him. La Bourdonnais had a chess appetite that amounted to a fixation. He had his own table at the Régence, and he was at it from noon to midnight seven days a week, willing to play anybody who wanted a game—for a modest stake, of course. Our phrenological friend George Walker has described him: "His frame is large and square, the head presenting a fine study for a phrenologist, bearing the organs of calculation enormously developed. Solid and massive, the head of La Bourdonnais is a true Napoleon front; carved out of marble, and placed on shoulders of granite, like those of Ajax Telamon. That eye is piercing, looks through and through the board, so as to convey the feeling that La Bourdonnais could really see well in the dark."

Not unexpectedly, considering the amount of playing he did, La Bourdonnais did not find it necessary to spend much time on his moves. He was a very fast player. Walker, visiting the Café de la Régence, took him on. "His rapidity to me was positively terrific. You raise your hand to play a move, and up go the Frenchman's fingers in readiness to present his answer, before you have travelled halfway up towards the piece you mean to touch. You move, and your opponent replies, ere your arm has regained its resting place. This bustle tries English nerves sadly."

England at that time was developing a strong school of chess players, the outstanding figure of which was Alexander McDonnell from Ireland. McDonnell, a member of the Westminster Chess Club in London, the most powerful player in England and also a specialist in blindfold play, visited Paris in 1823 to test his skill against the French aces. He played La Bourdonnais and lost several games. Good old George Walker was present at some of these encounters. The two players, he reported, started the games around noon, and they were seldom over before 6:00 or 7:00 P.M. At that point the exhausted McDonnell went back to his quarters. La Bourdonnais remained at his table at the Régence, cheerfully playing anybody who wanted a game, and was amusing himself long past midnight, smoking cigars and drinking punch. He might have played as many as forty games before going home to a few hours of sleep prior to his game with McDonnell the next day. Two years later, La Bourdonnais went to England to see what was going on there. Ebullient, easygoing, a ferocious competitor, La Bourdonnais became very popular in London chess circles, and was a frequent visitor between 1825 and 1830. In 1834 a match between him and McDonnell was arranged.

This was the first important match of modern chess history. In those days matches were held on an informal basis. A purse, generally not a very large one, would be raised by supporters of each player. Dates and location fixed, the players would pay their own way to the destination and square off. There was no such thing as a clock or a time control; a player might take *hours* on a single move. La Bourdonnais and McDonnell met in London for their match, and the ubiquitous Walker has left a peppy account of the battle.

The two men played in the Westminster Chess Club, in an area that was not even roped off. Inconceivable noise surrounded the players, and one wonders how they could concentrate (though any player active at the Régence or the Westminster must have developed a fair immunity to noise). People thronged around the board, loudly discussing the position. La Bourdonnais did not seem to be disturbed in the least, but McDonnell was. Boors would actually interrupt the players, as Walker relates:

La Bourdonnais: from noon to midnight, seven days a week.

I recollect personally witnessing the *entrée* of one of my dear countrymen into the club room while McDonnell and La Bourdonnais were engaged in one of their most trying positions. Our friend shook hands with each of them, and then thrusting his figure between them, took a deliberate survey of the board, resting with his two hands in the middle of the pieces. However, after merely half a dozen questions, such as "Is this your first game today?—That Rook seems in the devil's own mess"—and "Whose move is it?"—he suffered the game kindly to proceed, for which the parties felt doubtless due obligation.

Walker mildly suggests that in future games a space should be roped off with a silk cord or some such protection for the players.

The games were hot and lively. One commentator wrote, "As the contest went on between these renowned artists, it was curious to mark in how much bolder style they played, than in the introductory games. Like two haughty knights, throwing away helm and shield, each appeared to disdain defence, provided he could strike his opponent a home blow with sword and axe." The two men were a study in contrasts. La Bourdonnais spoke no English, McDonnell no French. McDonnell was dour, phlegmatic, very slow to make his moves. La Bourdonnais was impatient, excitable, sometimes laughing with delight at a good move, sometimes cursing in French: "tolerably round oaths in a pretty audible voice when fate ran counter to his chances." At times he lost his temper over McDonnell's slow play.

At the end of the series, eighty-four games were played in a series of five matches. La Bourdonnais won forty-four and lost twenty-seven. Thirteen were drawn. There could be no doubt of La Bourdonnais's superiority. Plans were being made to continue the confrontation when McDonnell developed Bright's Disease and died on September 14, 1835. There is no reason to believe that the Irishman would have done any better had the series been resumed. He was overmatched, and La Bourdonnais's technique was too much for him. A representative example of his play is his neat win in the sixteenth game, where La Bourdonnais demonstrates that McDonnell's attack, starting with Black's fourteenth move, is in reality suicide:

WHITE: LA BOURDONNAIS   BLACK: MCDONNELL

1.	P-Q4	P-Q4
2.	P-QB4	PxP
3.	P-K3	P-K4
4.	BxP	PxP
5.	PxP	N-KB3
6.	N-QB3	B-K2
7.	N-B3	O-O
8.	B-K3	P-B3
9.	P-KR3	QN-Q2
10.	B-N3	N-N3
11.	O-O	KN-Q4
12.	P-QR4	P-QR4
13.	N-K5	B-K3
14.	B-B2	P-KB4
15.	Q-K2	P-B5
16.	B-Q2	Q-K1
17.	QR-K1	B-B2
18.	Q-K4	P-N3
19.	BxP	NxB
20.	QxN	B-B5
21.	Q-R6	BxR
22.	BxP	PxB
23.	NxNP	N-B1
24.	Q-R8ch	K-B2
25.	Q-R7ch	K-B3
26.	N-B4	B-Q6
27.	R-K6ch	K-N4
28.	Q-R6ch	K-B4
29.	P-N4 mate	

But it would be unfair to McDonnell to omit one outstanding example of his play at its best. The fiftieth game of the match was won in fine style by the Irish master. Judging the position accurately, he surrendered a Queen for two pieces, and pushed through to a win. This game is one of the most frequently anthologized in the literature. Fine calls it the first immortal game of chess history:

	WHITE: LA BOURDONNAIS	BLACK: MCDONNELL
1.	P-Q4	P-Q4
2.	P-QB4	PxP
3.	P-K4	P-K4
4.	P-Q5	P-KB4
5.	N-QB3	N-KB3
6.	BxP	B-B4
7.	N-B3	Q-K2
8.	B-N5	BxPch
9.	K-B1	B-N3
10.	Q-K2	P-B5
11.	R-Q1	B-N5
12.	P-Q6	PxP
13.	N-Q5	NxN
14.	BxQ	N-K6ch
15.	K-K1	KxB
16.	Q-Q3	R-Q1
17.	R-Q2	N-B3
18.	P-QN3	B-QR4
19.	P-QR3	QR-B1
20.	R-N1	P-QN4
21.	BxP	BxN
22.	PxB	N-Q5
23.	B-B4	NxPch
24.	K-B2	NxR(7)
25.	RxPch	K-B3
26.	R-B7ch	K-N3
27.	R-N7	N(7)xB
28.	PxN	RxP
29.	Q-N1	B-N3
30.	K-B3	R-B6
31.	Q-R2	N-B5ch
32.	K-N4	R-KN1
33.	RxB	PxR
34.	K-R4	K-B3
35.	Q-K2	R-N3
36.	Q-R5	N-K6
	Resigns	

After the McDonnell match, La Bourdonnais could have been called world's champion had there been any such thing at the time. He accepted the plaudits for his victory and returned to Paris, where in 1836 he founded and edited the first chess journal in history, *La Palamède*. Shortly after that he developed dropsy and was in ill health. Soon he found himself penniless. Thus in 1840, when the Chess Divan in London invited him there as the house professional, he was glad to go. His salary was two guineas a week, and that was enough to keep him alive—barely. He arrived in London with his wife, was cheerful for a few days, then broke down "and was carried to his lodging in a pitiable state of suffering," writes Walker. A physician diagnosed scrotal hernia as well as dropsy. A committee was hastily formed to raise money for the ailing master. "Thanks to British feeling we got up to a hundred pounds immediately." La Bourdonnais struggled out of bed to resume his work, but "The silver cord was fast loosening, and the bowl was breaking at the fountain of life." He died on December 13, 1840, at the age of forty-three.

Pierre Saint-Amant was next in line as the strongest French player, and with him the French domination of international chess came to an end. Never again did France produce a player of grandmaster strength. Saint-Amant's chess career ended in 1847, though he lived many years thereafter. Unlike La Bourdonnais, who was a full-time chess player, Saint-Amant had several careers. Born on September 2, 1800 (some sources say September 12) at Montflanquin, he entered the government service and from 1819 to 1821 was stationed in French Guiana. On his return to Paris he became a regular at the Café de la Régence, along with another talented player, Lionel Kieseritzky from Livonia. Kieseritzky could hold his own with Saint-Amant, and he was one of those players who could work up a dazzling attack but who lacked staying power. He had an unhappy life, went insane, and died a pauper in 1853.

Saint-Amant took lessons with Deschapelles and was soon stronger than his teacher. But he decided there was no future for him in chess, so he tried his hand at journalism (unsuccessfully), acting (unsuccessfully), and the wine business (much better). He married, and his wife had the reputation of being a shrew. Certain it was that Saint-Amant was terrified of "this energetic and somewhat despotic lady." Regulars at the Café de la Régence never failed to be amused at the daily pavane between Saint-Amant and his wife. At a certain hour there would be a tap at the window. "This trifling signal was such an order as he dared not disobey, on pain of losing his beef tea, as also wifely smiles and domestic felicities. He would instantly close his snuffbox, resign his game, go through chairs and tables like an eel; forget to pay; forget, which was a crime, to salute the pretty mistress of the establishment, and scurry home, out of breath."

He visited England in 1836 and beat some of the best players there. Seven years later he returned and did beat the very best, Howard Staunton. In this match Saint-Amant edged out his opponent by one point. The same year saw another Saint-Amant vs. Staunton match, this time in Paris, and Saint-Amant was soundly whipped. Staunton won eleven, lost six, and there were four draws. After this, Saint-Amant played little chess. He had the typical grandmaster ego, and if he could not be the best he would not play at all. Instead, he concentrated on editing *La Palamède,* which he had taken over after the death of La Bourdonnais, and drifted back into government service. His career in government was not hurt by the skillful way he handled himself during the uprising of 1848. He was a captain in the National Guard and (to quote from a British publication) "was at the head of his company when the revolutionary mob assailed the Tuileries." Saint-Amant stood fast and "contrived to change so effectively the mischievous purpose of the populace, that, instead of destroying the Palace, they appointed him Governor, with acclamation." As a government official Saint-Amant was assigned as consul to California in 1851–1852—a pity, for otherwise he might have been prevailed upon to participate in the London 1851 tournament, to which every major player in Europe was invited. After California, Saint-Amant went to live in Algeria. Chess was no longer a part of his life. He lost his life in an accident; he was thrown from his carriage and, on October 29, 1872, died of the injuries he received.

4 ♚

The Age of Staunton

What the Café de la Régence was to chess in France, the Chess Divan in London was to chess in England, and that is where Howard Staunton (1810–1874), the greatest chess player in Europe for about fifteen years, could generally be found. There were many chess clubs in London at mid-century—the City of London Chess Club, St. George's, the Philidorian Chess Rooms, Kilpack's, Raymond's Coffee House, the Westminster Chess Club —but by far the most important was the Divan, in the Strand. For years the chess rooms were on the street floor; in 1847 the club was moved to the second floor and was generally called Simpson's Divan. Simpson was the headwaiter who later took over the premises. It was he who opened Simpson's famous restaurant in 1886, at which time he moved the club to the third floor. That was the start of the decline of the Divan. The new quarters were less commodious, older members did not like to walk up all those flights, and many drifted to the London and Westminster Chess Clubs. The Divan was still used by major players up to the turn of the century, but its great days were over. Today the restaurant exists and is a famous landmark of the Savoy Hotel, but there is no chess playing on the premises.

In its great days, the Divan was more reflective of a club than was the Café de la Régence. Members could lounge on sofas, order coffee, read newspapers and periodicals. In cold weather, huge fires at either end of the room were sure to be blazing. Not only did chess players frequent the Divan, but actors, artists, politicians, and men about town were habitués. Mostly, however, it was chess at the Divan, and the conservative Britishers wanted things to remain as they were in their favorite hangout. Once, when the Divan was being remodeled, the proprietor went to great ends to make it more beautiful. He had stone mosaic chessboards sunk into marble tables. For this he nearly lost his clientele. The general indignation was unbelievable, and nobody wanted to use the new boards. For, it was explained to the proprietor, those marble boards, being flush with the table, encouraged cheating. A dishonest player might easily coax with his sleeve a captured piece or Pawn back again on the board.

Cheating at chess! What of British sportsmanship? But cheating at chess was a regrettable fact of life at the Divan (and, alas, wherever chess is played), and so was poor sportsmanship. Those mid-century enthusiasts took their game seriously. During the match at the Divan between Daniel Harrwitz and Johann Löwenthal in 1853, there was great excitement and no end of dirty dealings. Harrwitz was the Divan's man, a regular there. Löwenthal was not. Feeling ran high and, according to a report by Charles Tomlinson in the *British Chess Magazine,* there developed such an aura of bitterness

> as to lead to very discreditable conduct on the part of some of its inferior members. As the match inclined decidedly in favor of Löwenthal, one man said, in my hearing, that he had sent an organ boy to play before the window, so as to distract the attention of Löwenthal, who was known to be very nervous. He also did not like smoking, and had stipulated beforehand that visitors should not smoke; but some of the Divan party made it a point to smoke as near to Löwenthal as possible, and I even saw one man light his cigar in Löwenthal's candle and puff the smoke into his face.

Harrwitz won the match by a single point.

The lord and master of the Divan and of all English chess was the irascible, unlovable, stubborn, vengeful, disliked, admired Howard Staunton, a man of high principles and low dealings. But he was a great chess analyst ("the most profound opening analyst of all time," Bobby Fischer has written). He proclaimed himself world champion after he defeated Saint-Amant in 1843, and he had a right to that title, for he successfully defended his honor in matches with Harrwitz and Bernhard Horwitz, the two other strongest players in circulation until Anderssen and Morphy appeared. He was a chess author and journalist; he was a Shakespearean scholar whose edition of the plays was highly regarded at one time; he was instrumental, in 1851, in organizing the first international chess tournament the world had ever seen; he traveled and lectured about chess; he gave simultaneous exhibitions. The man was a torrent, and whether or not people liked him, he put his mark on mid-century international chess more than any other man, and he was instrumental in shaping the future.

Staunton was reputedly the illegitimate son of Frederick Howard, fifth Earl of Carlisle. Neglected in his youth, he received little education. The money he got from his father's will he rapidly spent. For a time he tried the stage, and he claimed to have acted Lorenzo to Edmund Kean's Shylock. In the middle 1830's he started to frequent the Divan, Huttman's, and other chess parlors. Apparently he did not learn the moves until he was about twenty years old. But he was intelligent and aggressive, and soon he was able to defeat any player in England. He developed into an important theoretician, thanks to his work as founder and editor of the *Chess Player's Chronicle,* which started coming out in 1841 and which he edited until 1854. He also wrote big textbooks. The *Chess Player's Handbook* (1847) and the *Chess Player's Companion* (1849) made a study of every opening then known and analyzed games; these two books went through edition after edition, replacing Philidor's *Analyse* as the standard work. By the time Staunton had finished his books he had a greater knowledge of theory than any other player who ever lived. In addition, he wrote a column in the *Illustrated London News* from 1844 until his death in 1874. And one other thing: in 1849 he designed a set of chessmen that has been in universal use to this day. No serious chess player would dream of playing a game with anything but Staunton pieces.

Naturally he was an awesome power in chess. He had no hesitation in using his magazine, his newspaper column, and his books to castigate his opponents with whips of nettles. He was The Law and he hurled down judgments from On High. All this in earthy language. His comments on readers' letters in the

Chess Player's Chronicle were monuments of testiness and, some-times, nastiness. His readers were told that they were childish, inattentive, dolts. Why doesn't this one learn the game before he bothers me with a stupid analysis? Why doesn't that one use what little brains God gave him? And this was for the general reader. When Staunton did battle with a real authority, he would affect an infuriatingly lofty pose, or snarl, or twist facts in his favor, and pack his magazine with obviously inspired letters. As he grew older, he grew even more opinionated. And he liked to pretend that he had always been an amateur, a statement hilarious to those who remembered him when he was penniless and glad to play for threepence a game. He carried himself in a pompous manner, displayed armorial bearings wherever he could (including on his sealing wax), and was a striking figure with his gaudy clothes: embroidered satin vest, scarf gold-sprigged with a double pin, the heads of which connected with a gold chain. A tall (five feet, eleven inches), domineering man, he had to be the center of attraction. "He would brook no rival near his throne," said the Reverend George Alcock MacDonnell, a leading player of the day. "He cared for no man's anecdote but his own, and listened with impatience, if not contempt, to the song or joke contributed by any other member of the company to the general amusement."

This social tyrant played, curiously enough, a brand of chess that was not particularly aggressive. Staunton could, like any other top player, seize upon an opponent's tactical or strategic error (strategy in chess is the over-all plan of the game; tactics is the method of putting it into effect), but in his play he did not have the lust for battle characteristic of the romantics of the day. He played soberly and accurately, content to let his superior book knowledge and excellent technique carry him through. The stand-ard of his play on his return match with Saint-Amant at the Café de la Régence was of a high order, as standards of that day are measured. The fifth game of the match can serve as an illustra-tion of Staunton's style. It lasted nine and a half hours at one sitting, in those backbreaking days before chess clocks and time control, and fatigue may well have been responsible for Saint-Amant's blunder on his thirty-ninth move, which leads to a forced win for his opponent. Hence his resignation.

WHITE: SAINT-AMANT   BLACK: STAUNTON

1.	P-K4	P-QB4
2.	P-KB4	P-K3
3.	N-KB3	N-QB3
4.	P-B3	P-Q4
5.	P-K5	Q-N3
6.	B-Q3	B-Q2
7.	B-B2	R-B1
8.	O-O	N-R3
9.	P-KR3	B-K2
10.	K-R2	P-B4
11.	P-R3	P-R4
12.	P-QR4	N-B2
13.	P-Q4	P-R3
14.	R-K1	P-N3
15.	N-R3	PxP
16.	NxP	NxN
17.	PxN	P-N4
18.	N-N5	BxN
19.	PxB	R-B5
20.	B-Q3	R-QB1
21.	B-K2	PxP
22.	R-B1	N-N4
23.	BxP	N-K5
24.	R-B1	RxR
25.	QxR	K-Q2
26.	Q-K3	B-N4
27.	B-Q3	R-KN1
28.	BxN	QPxB
29.	BxB	PxB
30.	Q-QN3	P-N5
31.	R-Q1	PxP
32.	QxP	Q-Q1
33.	P-Q5	K-B1
34.	Q-B3ch	K-N1
35.	P-Q6	P-B5
36.	Q-B5	P-K6
37.	Q-B2	Q-R5ch

38.	K-N1	R-QB1
39.	Q-K2	R-R1
	Resigns	

Perhaps the most important achievement of his career was his idea of the 1851 tournament, in which the world's leading players participated. Staunton did not do very well in it, ending in fourth place, and from that time he played less and less chess. He concentrated on his Shakespearean researches, using that as excuse to avoid a match with Morphy in 1858 and 1859. Between November, 1857, and May, 1860, he issued a new Shakespeare edition published by Routledge, with many illustrations by Sir John Gilbert. These were reissued in four volumes in 1864. The text, scholarly for its day, was a collation of the folio edition and early quartos.

Of Staunton's work on Shakespeare, the *Dictionary of National Biography* comments: "The conjectural emendations, which were unusually sensible, were kept within rather narrow limits and showed much familiarity with Elizabethan literature and modes of speech. The general notes combined common-sense with exhaustive research." Staunton continued his Shakespearean researches to the end of his life, contributing to the literature nineteen learned articles on corruption in Shakespeare texts. He also took time out to write a history of British schools. Friends and foes took note when he died at the age of sixty-four on June 22, 1874, and the British publications (indeed, publications all over the world) were full of extended obituary notices. Most were, of course, laudatory; but not W. N. Potter's estimate in the *City of London Chess Magazine:*

> And now what was Staunton as a man? An old maxim has it that we must speak nothing but good of the dead. That may be all very well for epigraph writers, whose trade it is to engrave lies on marble, but, for ourselves, we repudiate any such doctrine, considering it to be ethically unsound. . . . We have, therefore, very little hesitation in saying that, in our opinion, the deceased often acted, not only with a signal lack of generosity, but also with gross unfairness toward those whom he had suffered defeat, or whom he imagined likely to stand between him and the sun.

Staunton's idea for a great chess tournament was sparked by the Great Exhibition in London 1851. Staunton was put in charge of a committee to make the arrangements and extend invitations. The idea was to operate on the very highest level; to attract players whose games would reflect the current state of the art. That meant every important player in the world was to be invited; and, indeed, every important player was invited. Some, however, found it impossible to accept, among them Carl Jaenisch and Alexander Petroff from Russia (Jaenisch did get to England during the end of the tournament, but of course did not play). Saint-Amant could not come; he was in California. That other chess-playing diplomat, the one who gloried in the name of Baron Tassilo von Heydebrand und von der Lasa, was on a diplomatic mission for the German government and could not make it (a pity, for he was a very strong player). All contestants in the match had to finance their own way to London and pay an entry fee of five pounds. This money went into a general fund, augmented by outside contributions, and the winner's purse came to 183 pounds. Before the match started, word got out that Jószef Szén from Hungary and Adolf Anderssen from Germany had agreed that if either were to win first prize, the winner should give one-third to the other. This caused raised eyebrows and shocked gossip. "An unbecoming arrangement," Staunton huffed. Besides Anderssen and Szén, players from several other countries were present. Johann Löwenthal came from New York and Lionel Kieseritzky from Paris. Staunton represented England, as did Horwitz, who had been living in London for some years. Some of the better British players were also invited to fill out the field of sixteen. The only major missing local player was Harrwitz, who was the chess professional at the London Chess Club, and this club, for some complicated reasons set forth in an impenetrable letter, refused to have anything to do with the tournament.

London 1851 (so tournaments are designated: Hastings 1895, or St. Petersburg 1914, or New York 1924) was designed as a knockout tournament. The players met each other not in rotating games but in a series of matches, and the loser of the match was eliminated from the tournament. Staunton had the misfortune of meeting Anderssen in the third round, as the luck of the draw, and was knocked out. He blamed the loss on poor health

Howard Staunton—analyst, scholar, and tyrant.

(it is a well-known fact that no healthy player in the history of chess ever lost a game) and a weak heart, both incurred by the unbelievable strain of organizing the tournament. The *Chess Player's Chronicle* ran letters that would have made a brass idol weep; all the letters described in harrowing detail Staunton's physical disabilities during London 1851, the invariable conclusion being that Staunton belonged in a hospital bed at the time, not before a chessboard. It is good for a chess player to have his own magazine. Later, in the official book of the tournament, Staunton as the author took the liberty of explaining, in the analyses of his own games, what had happened. His footnote to the first Anderssen

Adolf Anderssen, winner of the first international tournament in history, London 1851.

game is typical: "Let the reader compare this game, which would be discreditable to two third-rate players of a coffee-house, with any of the match games which he [Staunton] has taken part heretofore, and say how far the result of this mockery of Chess is less a proof of the absolute powers of the two men who are called proficients." In game after game Staunton analyzes in his own favor. He always had the better position, but threw it away "through physical exhaustion."

Anderssen won the tournament and went on to his great career. London 1851 was a trail blazer and the first of many more to come. All concerned with it learned a great deal—about organizing a tournament, about taking care of the players, about disputes that were bound to come up, about rules. It became clear during the course of the tournament that many problems had to be straightened out before future tournaments could be held on a satisfactory basis. What to do, for instance, with drawn games? It was the policy then to replay a drawn game, and London 1851 followed that policy, but the practice slowed up the tournament. Everybody had to wait until two players finished off, and there could be several draws in a row, exasperating everybody. Not until 1867 was the problem solved. At the Dundee Tournament that year, draws were scored half a point for each player, and that has been the rule ever since.

Even more urgent was the absolute necessity of doing something about the establishment of some sort of time control. There was no such thing in London 1851. A slow player could drag a game on interminably. (The Germans call this *Sitzfleish*, not altogether admiringly.) Indeed, the impatient and irascible Staunton, playing a countryman named Williams, was so infuriated at the latter's lethargy that he actually resigned the game in disgust. "Mr. Williams' systematic delay over every move," wrote Staunton in the tournament book, "called forth the marked animadversions of the looker-on. When games are prolonged to twelve, thirteen and twenty hours each, *and single moves occupy two hours and a half* [italics added], one effect upon an invalid can well be imagined." (Staunton, of course, was the "invalid" referred to.)

For years after London 1851, chess circles were alive with suggestions about dealing with the situation. In 1852 the Harrwitz-Löwenthal match imposed a limit of twenty minutes a move. That was unsatisfactory; some moves obviously needed more than twenty minutes of thought. A letter published in the *Chess Player's Chronicle* in 1852 made a suggestion: "Let each player have a three hours' sand glass at his elbow and a friend on either side to turn it. While the player is thinking, the sand must be allowed to run; while his opponent is thinking, his glass will be laid horizontally on the table and the running suspended." The player whose sand ran out first would lose the game unless, of course, he previously mated his opponent or was himself mated. Thus games would be limited to six hours, "which is surely quite enough for any man or animal, barring a snail or a hippopotamus."

The same year, 1852, the *Chronicle* published another letter on the subject, this one by the wise von der Lasa. The Baron pointed out that games were running as much as seven or eight hours, and that the situation had become one of universal complaint. Lasa went into an interesting history of efforts to cope with the problem. He cited the Staunton *vs.* Saint-Amant match of 1843, where the suggestion had been made that no move last longer than twenty minutes, and that any player exceeding that time be fined a guinea. But, said Lasa, simple arithmetic would be enough to show that an average game at only ten minutes a move, much less twenty, could last fifteen hours. So, Lasa said, the only solution would be with clocks, one for each player, to be started and stopped on the move.

It took time, but Lasa's idea eventually was adopted. First an hourglass was used, in the match Anderssen-Kolisch 1861. The players were allowed twenty-four moves in two hours. Shortly after, match and tournament directors were experimenting with clocks. The first mechanical chess clock was invented by Thomas Bright Wilson, a member of the Manchester Chess Club, and was used in the London 1883 tournament. In this type of clock, the prototype of those used today, there are two faces, each with hands and a flag. While a player is thinking, his clock runs. When he makes a move he pushes a plunger that stops his clock and starts his opponent's clock. At the end of the allotted time—standard professional tournament practice today is forty moves in two and a half hours—the end of the minute hand engages the flag, and when the flag falls the player's time is exhausted. If by then he has not made his allotted number of moves, he loses the game by forfeit.

This has led to the ghastly specter of time pressure, to which no player is immune. Some players think so deeply, move so slowly, that they often leave themselves with two or three minutes in which to make some twenty moves. One shudders at the number of won games that have been lost "on the clock." It is among the pitiable sights of the universe to see a perspiring, trembling chess player, watching the minute hand of the clock out of the corner of one eye as his moment of doom approaches. But that was for the future. Staunton and his contemporaries never had to worry about time pressure.

5 ♚

The Pleiads, the Professor, and Black Death

By mid-century the lines were beginning to be drawn. From Central and Eastern Europe the chess players were coming. France had permanently receded as a center of chess, in that not a single player there born after Saint-Amant achieved any kind of reputation in international chess circles (though for nearly a century many chess masters from other countries made Paris their home). Italy had produced nobody of importance since the eighteenth century, nor would it do so. Chess activity in England continued high, but here again Staunton was the last player of championship caliber, though Joseph Henry Blackburne turned out to be a redoubtable warrior capable of smashing any living player.

In Germany, chess activity during the early part of the nineteenth century centered in Berlin, where a group known as the Berlin Pleiads held forth. Chess clubs had been founded in Berlin as early as 1803, and the most important one, run by Mendheim, was located in the Blumgarten. There, in the 1830's, the Pleiads made the club one of the foremost chess centers in Europe. Most of the Pleiads were amateur players—learned gentlemen, often famous in other fields, who came together because of a love for chess. They took up where Johann Allgaier had left off. Allgaier (1763–1823) was an Austrian player who published the first chess manual in German, the *Neue Theoretisch-Praktische Anweisung*. The leader of the Pleiads was Dr. Ludwig Bledow (1795–1846), a professor of mathematics at the Berlin Gymnasium, who in 1846 founded the first German chess magazine, the *Deutsche Schach-*

zeitung. Two painters were in the group—Karl Schorn and Bernhard Horwitz. The latter went off to England and was one of the strongest players of the day. He competed, it will be remembered, in London 1851. "Schorn," said the *British Chess Magazine*, "was as much above Horwitz as an artist as he was below him as a Chess-player." Carl Mayet, a lawyer, was one of the original Pleiads, and so was Paul Rudolf von Bilguer, an army man who for years worked on a monumental chess *Handbuch* and left it unfinished at his death in 1840. This book was to the German-speaking people what Staunton's books were to the English. Completed by von der Lasa, it went through edition after edition.

Baron Tassilo von Heydebrand und von der Lasa (1818–1899) was probably the most interesting of the Pleiads. Possibly he had enough talent to take care of any player in the world. One has to say "possibly" because he engaged in little competitive chess. He was not only the strongest player of the Pleiads; he was also a brilliant man who was a working diplomat (Vienna; Rio de Janeiro; Ambassador to Denmark and other countries), a chess historian, an important chess theoretician, the owner of a chess library unparalleled in the world. As a diplomat he had plenty of opportunity for travel, and wherever he was he looked for chess books to add to his library. The few times he did play tournament chess, the great ones would topple. In 1853 Lasa beat Staunton in a close match.

From the Pleiads was funneled a stream of analyses, theoretical observations, and general articles that fertilized all chess players. Ernst Falkbeer from Vienna, who later went to live in London, profited from the pioneer work of the Pleiads. So did that talented popinjay Daniel Harrwitz, who achieved his greatest fame in London and Paris, and who was trounced by Morphy. So did such players of the following generation as Simon Winawer from Poland, and those two great rivals-to-be, Wilhelm Steinitz from Bohemia and Johannes Zukertort from Latvia. Ignatz Kolisch from Hungary absorbed all he could from Pleiad teachings. Another Hungarian, Johann Löwenthal, was also conditioned by the Pleiads before he fled his country in 1848 and went off to the United States.

The greatest of all mid-century Europeans was Adolf Anderssen (1818–1879) from Breslau. Anderssen, who became a professor of mathematics at the Friedrichs Gymnasium in his native city and taught there all his life, became a chess addict when he was nine years old. His father taught him the moves, and he saturated himself with the writings of Greco, Philidor, Allgaier, and whatever other manuals and analyses he could get his hands on. During his holidays he managed to get to Berlin, where he could drop into the chess clubs and test his strength. Without any doubt he sat at the feet of Bledow and the other Pleiads.

He started his tournament career late, at the age of thirty. Up to then he had been too busy with his mathematical studies and his examinations for a teaching license. But when he did enter the international arena the results were explosive. With Anderssen the romantic age in chess came to its bravura climax. The man was an attacking player with a remarkable feeling for combinations. He had the ability to spot weaknesses in an opponent and then clobber him with a virtuosic sacrificial attack unparalleled in the history of chess, except for some of the games of Paul Morphy. It was not for nothing that two of Anderssen's most spectacular victories are named the *Evergreen* and the *Immortal,* and they are among the most anthologized games in chess history. Even his opponents could be as much delighted as overwhelmed when they were the object of one of Anderssen's murderous attacks. Anderssen's play was so ingenious, his combinations so magical, that the players on the receiving end ended up gasping with amazement and pleasure. Kieseritzky, who was Anderssen's opponent in the *Immortal,* was so excited about the game that he hastily sent a copy to his club in Paris "in a surge and fever of delight." Anderssen, incidentally, a tall, gentle, good-natured man who walked with a stoop, was also a wonderful sportsman. He was one chess player who seems to have made no enemies. "He was massive in figure, with an honest voice, a sweet smile, and a countenance as pleasing as it was expressive," wrote the Reverend George MacDonnell. "I never saw more light and sweetness from any eyes than from his."

His chess career started in 1848 with a drawn match against Harrwitz (before the match started, Anderssen, as a warmup, played Harrwitz blindfolded and beat him). Three years later he stunned Staunton and the chess world by winning the London

1851 Tournament. It was in London that Anderssen's *Immortal* was created; he played it against Kieseritzky in an offhand game at the Divan after the tournament:

	WHITE: ANDERSSEN	BLACK: KIESERITZKY
1.	P-K4	P-K4
2.	P-KB4	PxP
3.	B-B4	Q-R5ch
4.	K-B1	P-QN4
5.	BxP	N-KB3
6.	N-KB3	Q-R3
7.	P-Q3	N-R4
8.	N-R4	Q-N4
9.	N-B5	P-QB3
10.	P-KN4	N-B3
11.	R-N1	PxB
12.	P-KR4	Q-N3
13.	P-R5	Q-N4
14.	Q-B3	N-N1
15.	BxP	Q-B3
16.	N-B3	B-B4
17.	N-Q5	QxP
18.	B-Q6	BxR
19.	P-K5	QxRch
20.	K-K2	N-QR3
21.	NxPch	K-Q1
22.	Q-B6ch	NxQ
23.	B-K7 mate	

After his triumph in London, Anderssen considered becoming a professional. But he was a cautious, conservative man, except over the chessboard, and he decided against it, going back to Breslau to take care of his mother and sister. The next few years he played offhand rather than serious international chess. One of his products was the *Evergreen*, played against J. Dufresne in Berlin, 1853. Dufresne does not show much positional judgment, but that should not detract from the ingenuity of Anderssen's conception:

	WHITE: ANDERSSEN	BLACK: DUFRESNE
1.	P-K4	P-K4
2.	N-KB3	N-QB3
3.	B-B4	B-B4
4.	P-QN4	BxP
5.	P-B3	B-R4
6.	P-Q4	PxP
7.	O-O	P-Q6
8.	Q-N3	Q-B3
9.	P-K5	Q-N3
10.	R-K1	KN-K2
11.	B-R3	P-N4
12.	QxP	R-QN1
13.	Q-R4	B-N3
14.	QN-Q2	B-N2
15.	N-K4	Q-B4
16.	BxP	Q-R4
17.	N-B6ch	PxN
18.	PxP	R-N1
19.	QR-Q1	QxN
20.	RxNch	NxR
21.	QxPch	KxQ
22.	B-B5ch	K-K1
23.	B-Q7ch	K-Q1
24.	BxN mate	

Anderssen had a bad tournament at Manchester 1857, and the following year he lost his famous match with Morphy. He bounced back to win a match against Kolisch in 1861, to win first prize at London 1862, and to draw a match with Louis Paulsen the same year. There was no doubt that Anderssen was entitled to be called the champion of the world. That was the position Steinitz took for his match with Anderssen in 1866. When Steinitz won he proclaimed himself the new champion, and nobody disputed the claim.

It was a surprise when Steinitz beat Anderssen; but Morphy, if the world had but realized, had previously pointed at the future in his match with Anderssen. The romantic age was coming to an end. New players with new ideas were arriving, and they sneered at the old boys with their unsound attacks and sacrifices. The new breed ignored the wild sorties of the romantics. Quietly they went ahead building up a solid center and planning long ahead for the end game. The art of position play was being established, and the romantics were like knights in shining armor faced by peasants with gunpowder. They never had a chance, as Anderssen found to his sorrow. In 1871 he lost a match to Zukertort, and in 1876 and 1877 he lost to Paulsen. The fact that Anderssen was much older than his opponents did not help his chances.

But if romanticism was dying, there still were plenty of romantics around. Chess has always had its romantics: Frank Marshall at the turn of the century; or Mikhail Tal in the decades after the 1950's. There are always those temperaments who are impatient with the "rules" and who will take insane chances. Among Anderssen's contemporaries, there was an extremely interesting player named Ignatz Kolisch (1837–1889). Kolisch, born in Hungary, became interested in chess and for a time was secretary to the chess-loving Prince Urusov of Russia. Like so many of his time, Kolisch became, in effect, a chess bum. He drifted to England and made his living as a chess professional. He was very strong. At the age of twenty-four he drew a game with Paulsen; then he beat Harrwitz and Horwitz, showing a wild brand of romantic chess that was very hard for an opponent to contain. Kolisch played Anderssen twice. The first match was a draw, and in the second, in 1861, Anderssen managed to squeak through with only a half-point advantage. While Kolisch was living in Paris—he established residence there after London—there was talk of a Kolisch-Morphy match, but it fell through. Morphy refused to play for a stake and Kolisch would not play without one. Kolisch's great triumph came at Paris 1867. Out of practice, he nevertheless took first prize ahead of Winawer and the new world's champion, Steinitz. Zukertort had great respect for Kolisch's playing and made a tart comparison between him and Steinitz: "Kolisch is a tiger who jumps at your throat, while Steinitz is a pickpocket who steals a Pawn and keeps it."

After 1867 Kolisch no longer played serious chess. Through the Baron Rothschild he became involved with banking, and eventually he became such a tycoon that in 1881 he was created a Baron of the Austrian Empire. One of his obituary notices, in the *Chess-Monthly* of London, somewhat cryptically stated that Kolisch had discovered a flaw in the French banking system and that he made millions as a result. Kolisch had a princely home on the banks of the Danube, entertained lavishly, and sponsored chess tournaments with generosity. There would have been no Baden-Baden 1870 or Vienna 1882 without his financial contribution. It is too bad that Kolisch at the height of his career, in the late 1860's, did not meet Steinitz in a match. There are those who believe that Kolisch was unstoppable during those years, and that not even Steinitz and his newfangled ideas about position play could have held him.

Another of the century's great romantics was Joseph Henry Blackburne of England, who was so feared in international chess play that he was given the nickname of "Black Death"—as much for his black beard, menacing presence, and killer instinct as for the "black" in his name.

England did produce some fine players after Staunton. There was Henry Thomas Buckle, the famous author of a history of civilization, who was not of championship caliber but who could be depended upon to give anybody a strong tussle. There was the Reverend George MacDonnell; and there was George Mackenzie, who emigrated to America and upheld the Stars and Stripes in his chess forays. There was the ultraromantic Henry Bird (1830–1908), accountant and part-time chess player, author of the noble tome entitled *An Analysis of Railways in the United Kingdom*, who invented an opening still in use, who won the first brilliancy prize ever awarded, against James Mason in New York 1876. (In many tournaments chess enthusiasts or patrons put up money to reward players for especially brilliant efforts.) Bird played tournament chess until well into his old age, lived for chess, and would play anybody anywhere, any time, under any conditions. He was the beloved figure of English chess, this wonderful raconteur who loved life and brought joy to all around him. The German master Richard Teichmann was asked to say something about Bird's chess-playing ability for an obituary notice. "Same as his health," said Teichmann. "Always alternating between being dangerously ill and being dangerously well. England will not see his like again." There was Amos Burn, active between 1886 and 1912, whose impressive victory at Cologne 1898 over Charousek, Steinitz, Tchigorin, and Schlechter established him as one of the world's best.

But it was Blackburne (1841–1924) who above all represented British chess and carried on the work started by Staunton. Unlike his British contemporaries, Blackburne was a complete chess professional who entered every tournament he could, hoping for a shot at the prize money. Through his fifty-two-year-long career (his last major tournament was St. Petersburg 1914) he was one of the most glamorous figures of international chess—this man who had known everybody, played against everybody, lived with high joy, who had proved himself time and time again. When he played in 1914 it was almost as though Franz Liszt had come back to earth for a piano recital. Part of the Blackburne mystique stemmed from his character. He was a big, powerful, extroverted man, a *bon vivant* who liked his glass and was a devil-may-care relic of an adventurous age. Blackburne: the winner of Berlin 1881 (ahead of Paulsen, Winawer, Zukertort, Tchigorin). Blackburne: the great blindfold chess player (he could play up to sixteen boards simultaneously). Blackburne: the tricky old devil who could spin a lethal combination out of nothing.

Blackburne brought something new and breezy to English chess. The stiff, formal, class-conscious Staunton would give a simultaneous exhibition wearing a top hat and morning clothes. Not the easygoing Blackburne, who wore old clothes, joked with his opponents, could lose his temper (that too was part of his attraction), and could drink like a sailor on leave after three years at sea. They called him "the giant," "the man with the iron nerves." In 1899 he estimated that he had played, at a minimum, fifty thousand games—and his career still had fifteen years to go. As for his drinking—well, he never made a secret of it. Quite the contrary. In an interview given at the turn of the century he complacently said: "I find that whiskey is a most useful stimulus to mental activity, especially when one is engaged in a stiff and prolonged struggle. All chess players indulge moderately in wines or spirits. Speaking for myself, alcohol clears the brain and I always have a glass or two when playing." It is not entirely by coincidence that this interview appeared in the *Licensing World,* and one can only hope that as a result of it Blackburne received a lifetime pass to every public house in England. The statement created a storm. The Temperance League was up in arms, some of Blackburne's colleagues tut-tutted, and much was made of it. Soon the American newspapers got into the act. "We have never," righteously wrote the Hartford *Times*, "seen Lasker, or Pillsbury, or Tarrasch, or any other player of the front rank sip whiskey when engaged on games to which they attached any importance."

One among many examples of Blackburne's play at its most sparkling is his win against Amos Burn in New York 1889:

	WHITE: BURN	BLACK: BLACKBURNE
1.	P-K4	P-K4
2.	N-KB3	N-QB3
3.	B-N5	N-B3
4.	O-O	P-Q3
5.	P-Q4	PxP
6.	NxP	B-Q2
7.	N-QB3	B-K2
8.	B-K3	O-O
9.	B-K2	R-K1
10.	B-B3	B-KB1
11.	B-N5	P-KR3
12.	B-B1	P-KN4
13.	P-KN3	NxN
14.	QxN	B-N2
15.	Q-Q1	B-B3
16.	R-K1	Q-Q2
17.	B-N2	R-K2
18.	Q-Q3	QR-K1
19.	B-Q2	N-N5
20.	P-B3	N-K4
21.	Q-B1	P-Q4
22.	QR-Q1	PxP
23.	BxP	PxP
24.	B-R1	N-Q6
25.	RxR	B-Q5ch
26.	B-K3	RxR
27.	QxN	RxB
28.	QxB	R-K8ch

Adolf Anderssen, archromantic, perhaps the greatest combination player of all.

Joseph Henry Blackburne, in Spy drawing of 1888 from Vanity Fair. He was known in chess circles as "Black Death."

29.	K-B2	QxQch
30.	RxQ	RxB
31.	R-KR4	R-B8
32.	N-K4	RxPch
33.	KxP	P-B4
	Resigns	

A queen sacrifice is always the most electrifying moment in chess, especially on the grandmaster level. On the twenty-third move of this game, Blackburne offers his Queen. But, as in all well-planned Queen sacrifices, to take it would be fatal. And Blackburne's twenty-fourth move, which puts his Knight *en prise,* was admired by no less an authority than Steinitz, who called it "a splendid master coup of the highest ingenuity." If White accepts the Knight, then RxR causes terrible havoc. No wonder Blackburne was called "Black Death." A man who could create this game need not have been afraid of any player alive. And Blackburne wasn't.

6 ♚

The Pride
and the Sorrow of Chess

The pride: because in his short career of about a year and
a half he was not only the greatest chess player of his time but
very possibly the greatest natural chess player who ever lived.
The sorrow: because he retired early from chess, grew to hate
the game, and died insane. Paul Morphy, who was born in New
Orleans on June 22, 1837, and died there on July 10, 1884, is the
supreme legend of chess history—a mysterious young man of genius
who appeared from nowhere, disappeared into nowhere, created
some of the most beautiful chess games of all time, and yet
was never fully tested as a chess player because he was so insult-
ingly superior to anybody around him that there simply was no
contest. Who can begin to conceive of his real strength? "Morphy," Bobby Fischer has written, "was perhaps the most accurate
chess player who ever lived. . . . In a set match Morphy could
beat anybody alive today." Reuben Fine has put it even more
strikingly: "Imagine Joe Louis at his prime in a country where
his most dangerous opponent was 5'6" and weighed 150 pounds."

It was Morphy who combined the elements of modern positional play with the flashy sensationalism of romantic combination play. Like Philidor, he conceived of a chess game as a logical
construction. The combinations would flow out of a solid position.
"Help your pieces so they can help you," he once said. In vain
did his opponents unleash their attacks on him. Morphy realized
that the wild attack could not succeed against a solid, carefully
prepared position. He let his opponents weaken themselves with

their unsound attacks until he was ready to retaliate. Then, with his position well in hand, he called upon a feeling for combination that could match that of Anderssen, Blackburne, and any of the others. Morphy's chess was pure chess, classical in nature despite the brilliance and violence of his eventual attack. Max Euwe has admirably described the essence of Morphy's style. Morphy, he says in his *Development of Chess Style,* could defend as well as attack; the others could attack but not defend very well—indeed, were not very much interested in defense. Morphy was a position player who was a disciple of Philidor and a forerunner of Stein- itz, and yet he won his games in romantic style *à la* Anderssen. Morphy, concludes Euwe, had a better grasp of total position than any other player of his day.

It was strange that New Orleans should have produced two prodigies within a few years of each other. Louis Moreau Gott- schalk, born in 1829, was a brilliant pianist at ten, was sent to Paris when he was thirteen, and eventually became America's first great pianist, her first American composer of national music, and a matinee idol. Gottschalk died at the age of forty in Brazil while on a concert tour. Morphy's career in many respects paralleled Gottschalk's. He too was a prodigy, a matinee idol, a great tech- nician and a creative thinker.

Paul Morphy was born into a well-to-do family of Irish (the name originally was Murphy), French, and Spanish background. His mother (like Gottschalk's) was Creole French; his father was a judge. There were four children in the family. Paul had an elder brother and sister, and a younger sister. He learned the moves when he was eight years old. Both his father and Uncle Ernest were avid chess players, and the boy learned the game from them. Not much has come down about Morphy's earliest years. He seems to have been a quiet, uncommunicative boy, one of those frightening children who keep their thoughts to them- selves. Uncle Ernest was the talker of the family, and he was very proud of Paul. He spread the word through New Orleans about the child's extraordinary grasp of the game. In 1846, Gen- eral Winfield Scott passed through the city and a game between him and Paul was arranged. Scott fancied himself as a chess player, and did have the reputation of being a strong amateur. An article about the game appeared some time later in the *Eve-*

Paul Morphy, in early photograph taken in London, 1858. He was unsuccessfully chasing after Howard Staunton for a match.

ning Post and was picked up by many other American newspapers:

> One of Scott's passions was for chess. It may be said to have been one of his vanities as well. He was in the front rank of amateurs in his day. After renewing old friendships and talking a little about the war [in Mexico], he turned to Chief Justice Eustis and asked whether he could have a little game of chess in the evening. . . . "Very well," said Justice Eustis, "we can arrange it. At eight o'clock tonight, if that will suit you." At eight o'clock, dinner having been disposed of, the room was full. Gen. Scott, a towering giant, was asked to meet his competitor, a small boy of about ten years of age and not by any means a prepossessing boy, dressed in velvet knickerbockers, with a lace shirt and a big spreading collar of the same material. At first Gen. Scott imagined that it was a sorry jest, and his tremendous dignity rose in protest. It seemed to him that his old friends had committed an incredible and unpardonable impertinence. Then Justice Eustis assured him that his wish had been scrupulously consulted . . . [that Paul] was quite worthy of his notice. So the game began, with Gen. Scott still angry and by no means satisfied.

Paul checkmated General Scott on the tenth move, which did not make the general very happy. Then Paul won another game, "and the General rose, trembling with amazement and indignation." Scott took his awful dignity home. Paul too was taken home, "sullen and silent as usual."

The Morphy family was not reluctant to show off the brilliant child. Paul played everybody in New Orleans, and also began to develop an aptitude for blindfold play. One of his early games, and it is a beauty, took place on his twelfth birthday. Paul played blindfolded against his Uncle Ernest, and as he announced his twentieth move he also added that he must win by force. The game already shows Paul's ability at combination play and his way of seizing upon the slightest error of his opponent:

WHITE: PAUL MORPHY		BLACK: ERNEST MORPHY
1.	P-K4	P-K4
2.	N-KB3	N-QB3

3.	B-B4	B-B4
4.	P-B3	N-B3
5.	P-Q4	PxP
6.	O-O	P-Q3
7.	PxP	B-N3
8.	P-KR3	P-KR3
9.	N-B3	O-O
10.	B-K3	R-K1
11.	P-Q5	BxB
12.	PxN	B-N3
13.	P-K5	QPxP
14.	Q-N3	R-K2
15.	BxPch	RxB
16.	NxP	Q-K1
17.	PxP	BxNP
18.	QR-K1	B-R3
19.	N-N6	Q-Q1
20.	R-K7	Resigns

Paul's next coup occurred when Johann Löwenthal visited New Orleans in 1850. One of the best players of his day, Löwenthal had recently come to the United States from Budapest. He had allied himself with Kossuth during the uprising of 1848, and would have been executed had he remained in his country. Löwenthal was on a chess tour of the United States, giving simultaneous exhibitions and playing matches. An encounter between him and the twelve-year-old Paul was arranged. Three games were played. The first was drawn and Paul won the other two. Later in life Löwenthal did play down Morphy's two victories. His comments in the book he wrote on Morphy's games are still another proof of the axiom that no healthy player has ever lost. "At that early age," Löwenthal writes, "he [Morphy] was victorious in one or two games with the Editor of this work, who was then paying a short visit to New Orleans, and although the latter was at that time depressed in mind and suffering in body, and was also prostrated by the climate. . . ." The evidence is that in New Orleans, Löwenthal, who was really a very nice man, was overwhelmed and predicted that Morphy would develop into the greatest player who ever lived. According to Uncle Ernest, Löwenthal, "a finished, courteous gentleman," sat down for the first game thinking that it would be "a bagatelle." As Löwenthal got into the game, "and felt Paul's force, his startled looks and upraised brows after each move of Paul's was perfectly ludicrous. . . ."

There is every evidence that Paul came to full strength without studying chess at all. During his school days nobody ever saw him with a chess book. The boy went to Jefferson Academy and then to Spring Hill College near Mobile. At college he made a lifelong friend in Charles Maurian, who vouches for the fact that Paul neither talked, studied, nor played chess during his first few years at Spring Hill. "He had neither a chess board nor even a chess book." As a student, Paul was at the top of his class. Toward the end of his college days he did play some chess with Maurian and his classmates, giving them odds of Queen, Rook, or Knight.

But who knows the resources of Paul Morphy's incredible chess mind? He never had a chess book around because it is altogether possible that once having skimmed through a chess book he had it committed to memory. It is known that as a teen-ager he gave away whatever chess books he owned because once he had read them he no longer needed them. One chess book known to have been in his possession was Staunton's on London 1851. The title page read, after Staunton's name, "Author of The Handbook of Chess, Chess-player's Companion, & & &." Paul, who was fifteen at the time, scribbled after it, "and some devilish bad games." Even at that age he knew he could beat Staunton or anybody else.

In 1855, Paul graduated from Spring Hill with the highest honors ever awarded by the college; then he entered the University of Louisiana, receiving his law degree in 1856. His memory worked as well there as in chess; it is said that he could recite most of the Louisiana Civil Code by memory. Legally he was too young to practice law; he was only eighteen, still a minor. He had time on his hands. Uncle Ernest, ever Paul's booster, took an advertisement in Leslie's *Illustrated Newspaper* of August 30, 1856, heading it "Chess Challenge Extraordinary." He challenged anybody in the United States to come to New Orleans and play Paul in a stakes match of $300 a side. There were no takers. Next it was decided that Paul should play in the American

Morphy and Johann Löwenthal, London, 1858. Morphy decisively beat Löwenthal, but they remained close friends.

Chess Congress, to be held in New York in 1857. But then tragedy. Paul's father died suddenly, on November 22, and playing in New York was the last thing on Paul's mind. But the grief did wear off, and his friends persisted, and the pride of New Orleans left for New York in September of the following year, arriving there on October 4, two days before the tournament started.

The American Chess Congress was inspired by the London tournament of 1851. No American-born player had participated, and that rankled a bit. The idea for an equivalent tournament restricted to American players took hold, and the New York Chess Club was the principal sponsor in organizing such an event. "Such an assemblage of American players," wrote Daniel Willard Fiske in his subsequent book about the event, "would serve at once to illustrate and assess the advancement of chess in this country. It would exert a wide and enduring influence upon popular opinion, and, in its ultimate results, would establish our elegant pastime on the same broad footing of public favor which it has so long occupied among the nations of Europe."

A national committee was set up, and news of the Congress was announced in every major city from New York to San Francisco. It was decided to hold the tournament in New York, in Descombe's rooms at 704 Broadway, and no pains were spared to make the surroundings something special. Fiske describes the hall with an air of great satisfaction:

> . . . The peculiar fitness and elegance of the decorations excited general admiration. At the east end of the main Hall, a room eighty feet in length, was a slightly raised platform, over which hung the American flag, draping the bust and bearing the name of Franklin, the first known chess player and chess writer of the New World. Along each side were suspended various national banners in the following order: the French tri-color, adorned with the name of Labourdonnais; the English St. George's, with that of M'Donnell; the German tri-color, with that of Bilguer; the Spanish, with that of Lopez; the Italian, with that of Del Rio; the Neapolitan, with that of Salvio; the Portuguese, with that of Damiano; the Hungarian, with that of Szen; and the Turkish, with that of Stamma. At the foot of the hall were entwined the

French and American colors, and stretching across them was seen the memorable name of Philidor. On scrolls, above the banners, were inscribed in silver and gold typography the names of the leading living professors of the art, including those of Lewis, Staunton, Walker, Von der Lasa, Anderssen, Löwenthal, Harrwitz, Petroff, and Jaenisch. The walls were furthermore ornamented with numerous chess engravings and photographs, much enhancing the general effect. Through the entire length of the hall extended two rows of marble tables, upon which were placed large inlaid boards and the classically designed Staunton chess-men. These were protected from the crowding of spectators by cushioned seats arranged on either side of these rows. A huge telegraphic chess-board, for repeating games of more than ordinary interest, hung at one end of the hall.

Morphy arrived, looked at New York, and New York looked at him. New York saw a short (five feet, four inches), slim man, "with a face like a young girl in her teens," a man with impeccable manners and something of a dandy. His hands were small enough to wear ladies' gloves (he invariably wore gray kid gloves), "and his shoes a child's size into which not one woman in a hundred thousand could have squeezed her feet." He wore a cloak, sported a walking stick and a monocle, and was agreeable to everybody. Morphy was one of sixteen players, and as the games went on, two things were apparent: Morphy was an exceedingly good player, and he was also a scrupulously ethical player. He would sit quietly in front of his opponent, patiently waiting for him to move, never expressing annoyance, never showing glee or despondency, never gloating over a won position. Ben Franklin would have been proud.

His strongest opponent was Louis Paulsen from Dubuque, Iowa. Paulsen, born in Leppe-Detmold, Germany, in 1833, emigrated to the United States at the age of twenty-one and went into business in Dubuque. He was considered the strongest player in the Midwest but, like Morphy, was untried in international play. Later Paulsen was to make a great name for himself as a chess player in Europe. Paulsen and Morphy met in the final section of the tournament—the luck of the draw, for if they had met in the first round, one of them (Paulsen, undoubtedly) would have been eliminated. The New York tournament, like London 1851, was a knockout tournament.

And so the Morphy-Paulsen match would decide the winner. There was considerable excitement, and much comment about the habits of play of the two men. Paulsen was an excruciatingly slow player, as slow as Morphy was fast. It is said that tears of frustration were running down Morphy's face as he waited motionless for Paulsen to make his moves. The longest Morphy took for any move was twelve minutes, on a Queen sacrifice. Paulsen spent seventy-five minutes determining whether or not to accept it, and he would deliberate for a half hour or so on other moves. Toward the end of the Paulsen series, Morphy was so irritated that he told a friend before the game: "Paulsen will never win a game of me while he lives." The final score was five wins, one loss, and a draw for Morphy. He easily won the tournament. Paulsen was second; Theodor Lichtenhein of New York was third, and Dr. B. I. Raphael of Louisville was fourth. The first prize was "an elegant service of plate, consisting of a Silver Pitcher, four Goblets and a Salver, costing $300."

During the tournament the chess players, as chess players will, amused themselves playing skittles (rapid offhand games). Paulsen, who was good at blindfold chess (he achieved a world's record of fifteen simultaneous games in 1859), would take on five players at a time, and once he had the gall to ask Morphy if he would be one of the five. Morphy agreed—on the condition that he too play blindfolded. On his twenty-eighth move, Morphy announced a mate in five. He had said that Paulsen would never win another game from him. Morphy, incidentally, quiet though he may have been, exerted a palpable power over the board. Like Fischer in the next century, he had something about him that scared his opponents. One player in New York later wrote: "When one plays with Morphy, the sensation is as queer as the first electric shock, or first love, or clorophorm, or any entirely novel experience. As you sit down at the board opposite him, a certain sheepishness steals over you."

Morphy's victory was celebrated all over the American press. He was now modestly famous, and many poems were written about him. One fifteen-verse exultation in the *Chess Monthly* of December, 1857, had such moving quatrains as:

> And THOU Caïssa's hope and pride
>   We hailed thy early dawn
> But hope could ne'er have prophesied
>   The glory of the morn.

And such unabashed jingoism as:

> Go forth and bear in other lands
>   Our country's starry shield!
> Go beard the lion where he stands
>   Till England's champion yields.

Returning to New Orleans, Morphy—still waiting to come of age and practice law—did some chess playing. While in New York he had challenged any player in the country to give him, for money or honor, a match at the odds of Pawn and move. He had no takers. Morphy normally disliked playing for money. He considered himself an amateur chess player and a gentleman, not a professional, but in many cases the only way to get professionals to play with him was to put up a stake. (In at least two known cases Morphy, winning a stake match, secretly sent the prize money to his opponent's wife.) Then, possibly inspired by Paulsen's ability, Morphy started playing blindfold chess and pushed the number of simultaneous boards to seven. Morphy may have enjoyed all this, but he had no real competition. So his friends issued a challenge to Staunton. In a long letter dated February 4, 1858, the New Orleans Chess Club invited Staunton to its city, the stakes for a match with Morphy to be $5,000 a side, winner take all. Staunton would be reimbursed for all expenses. Several months later the New Orleans Chess Club had a reasonable answer from Staunton. The British champion said that he had not played much in recent years, that his other duties were taking up all his time, and that he simply could not make the trip. All of which was true. But in his own column in the *Illustrated News,* Staunton was much bitchier. No doubt, he loftily wrote, Morphy could find a strong player or two to meet him if he came to Europe. "But the best players in Europe are not chess professionals, but have other and more serious occupations, the interest of which forbid such an expenditure of time as is required for a voyage to the United States and back again." The inference was that Morphy was a hustler. To a man like Morphy, who prided himself on his amateur standing, this article must have come as a slap in the face. Staunton concluded by saying that Morphy should come to Europe and get himself a reputation before bothering his superiors.

There was nothing left for Morphy to do but go to England and try to meet Staunton on his own grounds. The New Orleans Chess Club offered to pay Morphy's way. Morphy refused. He was no professional; he had enough money to pay his own way. Obviously he was eager to demonstrate that he was the best chess player in the world. He left New Orleans on May 31 and a month later was in England. He celebrated his twenty-first birthday the day he arrived in London, on June 22, 1858.

7

Triumph and Fall

The first thing Morphy did after settling into his hotel was to go to the St. George's Chess Club to meet Staunton. They did get together, and Staunton watched the young American play some informal games, but always found an excuse for not taking on Morphy himself. He needed more time to brush up on his openings and endings. He had an appointment. He was busy with his Shakespeare research. Morphy politely agreed to give Staunton all the time he needed. Meanwhile Morphy's old opponent, Johann Löwenthal, appeared. Now living in England, Löwenthal had done poorly in the 1851 tournament and had then lost a match to Harrwitz, but his game nevertheless was improving, and in 1857 he took first at Manchester ahead of no less than Anderssen. Löwenthal challenged Morphy to a match for a hundred-pound stake. Morphy accepted and beat Löwenthal 9 to 3, with two draws. One of the things that impressed the British, in addition to Morphy's easy win—his opponent, after all, was one of the best players alive—was his speed. The Reverend George MacDonnell watched the match and later wrote of Morphy's play:

> He seldom—in fact, in my presence never—expended more than a minute or two over his best and deepest combinations. I fancy he always discerned the right move at a glance, and only paused before making it partly out of respect for his antagonist

and partly to certify himself of its correctness, to make assurance doubly sure; and to accustom himself to sobriety of demeanor in all circumstances.

Staunton kept dodging a match. Had he come right out and said that he was out of practice, or semiretired, or unwilling to put in the time for preparation, perhaps Morphy would have understood. But Staunton's pride would not let him do that, and he led Morphy to believe that there would indeed be a match.

Considerable correspondence passed between the two men. Staunton, in those letters and in his chess column, kept dangling a promise before Morphy, who vainly pursued it. Morphy even chased Staunton to Birmingham, where Staunton was playing in a tournament (Löwenthal won that one, ahead of Falkbeer and Staunton), and besieged him with letters. Nothing happened. Morphy's secretary, Frederick Edge, later was to say that he did not begrudge Staunton's determination to avoid a match. But Edge deplored Staunton's tactics of leading Morphy on and then running away. "Mr. Staunton's weakness," concluded Edge, "was want of sufficient courage to say, 'He is stronger than I.'" Morphy returned to London to play chess with the best local talent. One of his most beautiful games was against Bird. The impulsive Bird could not resist a premature attack. Morphy played positionally and then, spotting a weakness in Bird's structure, launched a spectacular combination. The Rook sacrifice on Black's seventeenth move, to clear the rank for the Queen to get to Rook 6, is a colossal conception:

	WHITE: BIRD	BLACK: MORPHY
1.	P-K4	P-K4
2.	N-KB3	P-Q3
3.	P-Q4	P-KB4
4.	N-B3	PxKP
5.	QNxP	P-Q4
6.	N-N3	P-K5
7.	N-K5	N-KB3
8.	B-N5	B-Q3
9.	N-R5	O-O

10.	Q-Q2	Q-K1
11.	P-KN4	NxP
12.	NxN	QxN
13.	N-K5	N-B3
14.	B-K2	Q-R6
15.	NxN	PxN
16.	B-K3	R-N1
17.	O-O-O	RxBP
18.	BxR	Q-R6
19.	P-B3	QxRP
20.	P-N4	Q-R8ch
21.	K-B2	Q-R5ch
22.	K-N2	BxNP
23.	PxB	RxPch
24.	QxR	QxQch
25.	K-B2	P-K6
26.	BxP	B-B4ch
27.	R-Q3	Q-B5ch
28.	K-Q2	Q-R7ch
29.	K-Q1	Q-N8ch
	Resigns	

Presumably feeling like Sir Palomides chasing the Questing Beast, Morphy pursued Staunton until he realized that the man just was not willing to play. Morphy then decided to go to Paris and engage the players at the Café de la Régence. He arrived there on August 31, accompanied by Edge. A match with Harrwitz, the professional at the Régence, was immediately arranged, and negotiations with Anderssen were initiated. Anderssen let it be known that he could come to Paris for two weeks and no more. The Harrwitz match began on September 7, and Morphy lost the first two games. Edge says that Morphy spent his time taking in the night life of Paris, did not get to bed until an unseemly hour, and had trouble acclimatizing. Harrwitz was exultant. The beast from America had turned out to be a paper tiger. Harrwitz was one of those players who is insufferable in victory, intolerable in defeat. During the second game he was openly derisive of Morphy's play. At the end, when Morphy resigned, Harrwitz looked around at the crowd, leaned over and felt

Morphy's pulse. "Well," he said. "This is most astonishing. His pulse does not move any faster than if he had won the game." That was the end of Harrwitz. Morphy, walking back to the hotel, said to the French player, Jules Arnous de Rivière, "Will they not be surprised if Harrwitz does not win another game?" Nor did Harrwitz. Morphy took the next five games, with one draw intervening. At this point Harrwitz whined for a delay and then refused to continue the match. Morphy took the stakes and sent the money to Anderssen as expense funds for his trip to Paris.

It was about this time that Morphy received a letter from Staunton that closed out the possibility of a match. Dated October 4, 1858, the letter pleaded pressure of work on the Shakespeare project. Also, Staunton pointed out, the handicap on him was too great. "A combat when one of the contestants must fight under disadvantages so manifest as those I should have to contend against, after many years' retirement from practical chess, with my attention absented, and brain overtaxed by more important pursuits, could never be accounted a fair trial of skill." Staunton never made this letter public. In effect he was conceding that he stood no chance against Morphy. He did invite Morphy to his house. "I may add that, although denied the satisfaction of a set encounter with you at this period, I shall have much pleasure if you will again become my guest, in playing you a few games *sans façon.*"

While waiting for Anderssen to arrive, Morphy gave a blindfold exhibition at the Régence, taking on eight players. The session took about ten hours. At the end, writes Edge, "Morphy stepped from the armchair in which he had been almost immovable for over ten consecutive hours, without having tasted a morsel of anything, even water, during the whole period; yet as fresh, apparently, as when he sat down." There were cheers and a rush by the spectators for Morphy. The waiters were supposed to carry him on their shoulders but could not get near him. It took Morphy an hour before he could get out of the Café. Then there was a near-riot in the street. The Imperial Guard came running out to see if a new revolution had started. The next day Morphy woke Edge up at 7:00 A.M. and dictated the moves of all the games. There is evidence that Morphy considered pushing his blindfold exhibitions up to twenty simul-

Contemporary print of Morphy playing eight simultaneous blindfold games at the Café de la Régence in 1858.

taneous boards, but his friends talked him out of it. They said he would develop brain fever and were appalled at the idea. Morphy really could have done it without much trouble.

Morphy now was the lion of Paris. He dined out in the best society, had his bust sculpted by Eugène Lesquenne (one of his blindfold opponents), and went to the Opéra as often as possible. Morphy loved music, and his memory worked there, too. Once he heard a melody he had it permanently memorized. It was at a performance of Rossini's *Barber of Seville* at the Opéra that he played his most famous game. The Duke of Brunswick had invited him to his box, along with Count Isouard. They challenged him to a game. One can imagine the fixed smile with which Morphy, gentleman that he was, agreed to take on his two titled opponents. While the opera was going on, Morphy, with one part of his mind on the music, scored a pretty win. There are better Morphy games, for he really had no opposition here, but few have this élan:

	WHITE: MORPHY	BLACK: DUKE AND COUNT
1.	P-K4	P-K4
2.	N-KB3	P-Q3
3.	P-Q4	B-N5
4.	PxP	BxN
5.	QxB	PxP
6.	B-QB4	N-KB3
7.	Q-QN3	Q-K2
8.	N-B3	P-B3
9.	B-KN5	P-QN4
10.	NxP	PxN
11.	BxPch	QN-Q2
12.	O-O-O	R-Q1
13.	RxN	RxR
14.	R-Q1	Q-K3
15.	BxRch	NxB
16.	Q-N8ch	NxQ
17.	R-Q8 mate	

During Morphy's stay in Paris, Staunton—despite his private letter of October 4—publicly protested that he really was eager for a match. But Morphy, said Staunton, had not met certain conditions, and he put on an injured pose, giving the impression that Morphy was dodging *him*. The chess column of the *Illlustrated News* was filled with letters attacking the American. Staunton began to call the negotiations "bunkum" and kept insisting that Morphy had not offered the proper terms and stakes. But Morphy, at the moment, had other things on his mind. Anderssen was on his way. He arrived on December 18 to find Morphy ill in bed. The honest Anderssen was reluctant to take advantage of Morphy's condition. But Morphy, knowing that Anderssen had only two weeks before he had to return to his classes in Breslau, insisted on playing immediately. It was decided that the first player to win seven games would win the match. No money was involved; this was for honor. Morphy had great respect for Anderssen. "There," he told Edge while playing through an Anderssen game, "that shows the master."

The match started in Morphy's hotel. Anderssen won the first game. The second was a draw. Then Morphy went on a winning streak, ending with a score of 7 to 2, with two draws. Anderssen was more amazed than put out. He was asked why he wasn't playing as well as he generally did. "Morphy won't let me," Anderssen said. According to Edge, Anderssen stated that "Mr. Morphy always plays not merely the best move but the *very* best move, and if we play the move only approximately correct, we are sure to lose. Nobody can hope to gain more than a game now and then from him." Edge, like everybody else, fell in love with Anderssen and his sportsmanship. "I have never seen a nobler-hearted gentleman than Herr Anderssen. He would sit at the board, examining the frightful positions into which Morphy had forced him, until his whole face was radiant with admiration of his antagonist's strategy, and positively laughing outright, he would recommence resetting the pieces for another game, without a comment."

Thus Frederick Edge, in his book on Morphy's exploits in Europe. Staunton later took issue, writing in his *Chess Praxis* that Anderssen's statements were distorted by Edge; that Edge was, in effect, a liar. In the *Praxis*, Staunton analyzed the Morphy-Anderssen games, and his comments were not those of one good Christian to another. He blames Anderssen's loss not on Morphy's skill but on Anderssen's advancing age and general neglect of chess. The notes to the games are peppered with such comments as: "The purpose of this is so manifest that in his old play Mr. Anderssen would have detected it at a glance." Or, "This is poor work for a player of Mr. Anderssen's former force." Or, when Morphy works out a combination, "A fine conception, but the success of which depended on White's playing badly." Or, "This is described as admirable by certain critics, who affect to fall into ecstasies at the most ordinary move Mr. Morphy makes. In reality it is a very bad play, and properly taken advantage of it would have cost the game." But Anderssen, never petty or malicious, knew better; and in a long, thoughtful letter to Lasa, that Nestor of German chess, Anderssen soberly described what had happened:

> In any case you have evaluated correctly the miraculous talent of the foreign master. I believe, not only that he commands deeper plans of greater strokes than La Bourdonnais, but that he is ahead of him in regard to infallible calculation and solidity. Whoever plays with him should give up all hopes that he might fall into a trap however subtly prepared; to the contrary he should presume that his opponent has it quite clearly before his eyes, so clearly indeed that there cannot be even an idea of a misstep. . . . Even if one has the decisively better position against him, nothing could be more pernicious than to be too cocksure of victory. I have hardly a better way of describing the impression he has made on me than to say: He treats chess with the seriousness and the thoroughness of an artist. . . .

After the Anderssen match, Morphy, according to Edge, seemed to lose his appetite for chess. There was nobody else to beat. In addition he may have been homesick, and he must have known by then that a Staunton match was not to be. His brother-in-law, John Sybrant, arrived in Paris to escort him home. Morphy did issue a challenge to Harrwitz, who was running around saying that Morphy had not really beaten him. Morphy let it be known that on a return match he would give odds to Harrwitz. There was no match. Morphy played a few more games, then returned to London preparatory to going back to New York. There were a few exhibitions in London and a grand farewell banquet at the

St. George's Chess Club. Staunton did not attend. After making a graceful speech, Morphy left England in an aura of good feeling from nearly all sides.

He returned to America on May 11 to find himself famous. If there are those who believe that Bobby Fischer's return from Reykjavik received unprecedented attention from the American press and public, they should look at the American newspapers for May and June of 1859. America went wild over its hero. There were Morphy hats, Morphy cigars, a Morphy baseball club. Morphy had to attend banquet after banquet. He discovered that Americans had been following his deeds much as the country in 1972 followed the Spassky-Fischer match. As the *Chess Monthly* of New York reported even before his return:

> Mr. Morphy's knight-errantry in Europe has made his name familiar to thousands of his countrymen at home who had hardly heard of him before. Nothing so quickly excites the sympathies and enchains the attention of Americans as a rivalry with the old world in any branch of science or art. . . . The best, as well as the most marked, result springing from the éclat of Mr. Morphy's European triumphs is the impetus given to Chess in the Western world. Clubs are everywhere rapidly forming; chess books and chess implements are bought with avidity; the readers of periodical chess publications are largely increasing. Hundreds of people now play chess who, a half-year ago, were utterly ignorant of the moves.

The New York Times on May 25 had a long story on page one about one of the banquets and the presentation to Morphy of a pearl-inlaid chessboard with gold and silver pieces, and also a watch. "The board," said the *Times,* as eager to flood the reader with detail then as it is now, "is so paneled and dovetailed in construction, that no influence of climate or position can possibly affect the integrity of the squares. As a specimen of workmanship, in addition to the felicity of its design, the fact that the most skillful artisans consumed six weeks in its manufacture and another week in polishing it, is pertinent of its superlative excellence. Its cost is not far from $300." At the ceremony following the banquet at which this chessboard was presented to Morphy, Mr. W. J. A. Fuller made a long and boring speech that called forth the full wrath of the *Times* the following day. Mr. Fuller, said the *Times* in an editorial,

> took up the theme of Mr. Morphy's victories in the style of that famous German philosopher who, on being commissioned to write the history of the House of Brunswick, filled seven volumes folio with a preliminary sketch of the Creation of Man and the Temptation in Eden. Mr. Fuller began with Alexander on the Nile, and after tracing the "civilization of Europe," by some process original with himself to the fall of the commerce of Egypt, dismissed ten centuries with a wave of his hand to usher Columbus on the scene, and make him responsible for the foundation in the "cold North" of the Empire whereof in the "order of prominence" New York has become the metropolitan center. Thence Mr. Fuller branched gracefully off into a constitutional history of the United States. . . . He also indulged in prophecy; in physical geography; in disquisition on the "alluvial soil of the Mississippi;" on the classic shades of the elms of New-Haven; on Whitney's invention of the gin; on the merits of Morse as a painter of "female beauty;" on the "electric telegraph;" on the yacht *America* and George Steers; and finally on the American Watch Company and Mr. Morphy himself.

At this point, it would appear, Mr. Fuller first began warming to his subject, and he went on at considerably more length, culminating in a fireworks display of oratory where the genius of Shakespeare, "towering as it does with Alpine height above the other Heaven-piercing peaks in the world of letters stands not so utterly alone as the genius of Morphy." Morphy, who had sat as patiently through this as he had sat before the slow-moving Paulsen, arose, modestly disclaimed this cataract of declamation, and spoke a few quiet words.

But this banquet was as nothing to what went on in Boston on June 1. At an evening ceremony honoring Morphy, Oliver Wendell Holmes was the keynote speaker, James Russell Lowell read a long poem he had written for the occasion, Paul Agassiz was on the stage with Henry Wadsworth Longfellow, Benjamin Peirce, James Walker (the president of Harvard), Mayor Lincoln, and, indeed, an awesome grouping of the Athens of America. For this story *The New York Times* devoted three of its six columns on page one. Lowell's speech was pure flag-waving (and just as turgid as Mr. Fuller's, though the *Times* did not come forth with another editorial). Lowell used the entire handbook of nineteenth-century rhetoric: "Who has tamed the earth, gentlemen, like the American," roared Lowell, "whose instruments of husbandry so far surpassed all others in the day of trial that they reaped not only all the grain before them. . . . Who has tamed the ocean like the American shipbuilder. . . ." After a half hour of this he finally got to Morphy:

> As I stretch my hand above this youthful brow it seems to me that I bear in it a welcome, not of a town or of a province, but of a whole people. One smile, one glow of pride and pleasure, runs all over the land, from the shore which the sun first greets to that which looks upon the ocean where he lets fall the blazing clasp of his dissolving girdle—from the realm of our Northern sister, who looks down from her throne upon the unmelted snows of Katahdin, to hers of the broad river and the still bayou who sits fanning herself among the full-blown roses and listens to the praises of her child as they were wafted to her on every perfumed breeze.
>
> I propose the health of Paul Morphy, the world's chess champion—His peaceful battles have helped to achieve a new revolution; his youthful triumphs have added a new clause to the Declaration of American Independence.

As if this were not bad enough, Lowell's poem went on at almost equivalent length. It could easily lay claim to being the worst poem in the English language, and it contained such passages as:

> Besides, I also had some right to expect
> Met-a-Morphy-sis here which I would not neglect;
> I might come out as a bore, and believe me a scion
> Of the lion's own stock if I drink with the lion.

And the last four lines of the poem, in equally breathless doggerel, are:

> I give you the man who can think out and dare
> His bloodless Marengos on twelve inches square,
> Yet so modest, the conquered all feel that they meet
> With a Morphy—and not mortifying defeat.

Morphy remained in the East for several months, playing some chess and arranging for a column in the *New York Ledger,* which he did write for a year (August 6, 1859, to August 4, 1860). Not until December did he return to New Orleans. The rest of his life was sheer tragedy. He wanted to be a lawyer; the world insisted on regarding him as a chess player. The Civil War broke out and Morphy returned to Paris for a while, going home in 1864. In Paris he played no serious chess. He was fast developing into an eccentric recluse. In New Orleans he had cards printed, setting himself up as a lawyer. His practice was nil. There was, of course, no chess except for some friendly games with his old friend Maurian. He became a highly disturbed man, suffering from what in those days was called melancholia. Today it would be diagnosed as paranoia. Another trip to Paris did not relieve his mind. He was there during the important tournament of 1867 and refused to attend even a single session; chess was repugnant to him. It was not that there was anything wrong with the way his mind functioned at that time. When Staunton died in 1874 Morphy wrote a brief and lucid account of Staunton as a chess player:

> Mr. Staunton's knowledge of the theory of the game was no doubt complete; his powers as an analyst were of the very highest order, his *coup d'oeil* and judgment of position and his general experience of the chess board, great; but all those qualities, which are essential to make a great chess player, do not make him a player of genius. These must be supplemented by imagination and by a certain invention or creative power, which *conceives* positions and brings them about. Of this faculty [I see] no evidence in the published games of Mr. Staunton.

But these were among Morphy's last coherent thoughts. He began to develop delusions of persecution. His brother-in-law, he felt, was stealing his patrimony, and Morphy instituted lawsuit upon lawsuit to stop him. He would see only a few people. His mother took care of him. Nobody was allowed to talk about chess in his presence. When Steinitz was in New Orleans in 1883 he was granted an interview—with the proviso that chess not be mentioned. The meeting lasted an awkward twenty minutes, with both geniuses mumbling inanities. (When the subject of Steinitz's visit was broached, Morphy said something interesting. "I know him. His gambit is not good." Had Morphy on his own, without telling anybody, been keeping up with the world of chess? The remark is tantalizing.) Once Morphy was asked to give his biography for a book on famous Louisianans. His reply was something to the effect that his father had left him $146,162.54 and he had no profession, hence no biography. Every day he walked on Canal Street, talking to himself. People learned to avoid him. A man named C. P. Meredith told why in the *American Chess Journal* of April, 1879: "The least encouragement will result in being compelled to listen for hours to the same old story that everybody knows by heart—that relating to his father's estate. He talks of nothing else and apparently thinks of nothing else."

On July 11, 1884, he suddenly died of an attack of apoplexy. His mother, who died a few months later, found him dead in his bath. The *New York Sun* in its obituary notice had no doubt at all about the reason: blindfold chess had made him insane and then killed him. "The strain in his brain produced a brain fever, from which he never recovered." *The New York Times* had a different diagnosis: melancholia verging on madness. A New Orleans correspondent for the *Times* wrote about Morphy's last days: "For years he has been a conspicuous character upon our streets. Every fair day his trim little figure, clad in the height of snug-fitting fashion, might be seen swinging his little cane on the boulevard, scrutinizing through his glass the fair promenaders. What would have been impertinent in others was pardoned in Paul, and for years he thus passed his useless life away unmolested and unmolesting. As late as yesterday he was seen on Canal street chattering to himself and smiling at his own conceits."

8 ♛

Good Bishops
and Bad Squares

Wilhelm Steinitz from Prague, a contemporary of Blackburne, Anderssen, Morphy, and the other romantic heroes, was the first acknowledged world champion of chess. He completely changed the game as it was played by those romantics, and most likely he was the foundation upon which all modern chess has been built, but that did not prevent him from being the most unpopular chess player who ever lived. He had a grudge against the world, and the world returned it. Short (barely five feet in height) and unprepossessing, born lame, heroic above the torso and a cripple below, reliant on cane and crutches, near-sighted, arthritic, with a squashed-in nose, testy, stubborn, megalomaniacal, he was not everybody's ideal. It was said of him that he was not only a bad loser; he was also a bad winner. His tongue was feared. "The bitterest tongue in Europe," said Robert J. Buckley, reminiscing about Steinitz in the *Chess Amateur*. Snarled Steinitz to an onlooker who failed to understand one of his moves and asked a silly question: "Have you ever seen a monkey examine a watch?" When enraged he became subhuman. During the Paris Tournament of 1867, in a trifling dispute, he spat on his opponent, a British player—some say it was Blackburne—who promptly knocked his head through the window. He quarreled with everybody. "A perfect porcupine," said Buckley. "Wherever you touched him was a sharp point."

He started out a player in the romantic tradition, going all

Early drawing (ca. 1875) of Wilhelm Steinitz, first chess champion of the world.

Steinitz as world champion, ca. 1890.

out for sacrifice and combination. Then he developed a series of concepts that made him all but unbeatable during the twenty-eight years that he was the champion. It was a puzzling, cramped style that he developed, and his opponents kept hurling themselves at it only to pick themselves up dazed and bleeding. The frustrated Henry Bird reflected the attitude of the romantics toward Steinitz when he described the champion's mode of play: "Place the contents of the chessbox in your hat, shake them vigorously, pour them on the board at the height of two feet, and you get the style of Steinitz." Steinitz himself explained it another way. "I was champion of the world for twenty-eight years," he wrote in the September, 1899, issue of the *American Chess Magazine*, "because I was twenty years ahead of my time. I played on certain principles, which neither Zukertort nor any one else of his time understood."

That style involved what he described as "an accumulation of small advantages," and it went back to the forgotten precepts of Philidor and, to a large extent that Steinitz was never prepared to admit, to Morphy. Forget those wild attacks. Prepare a position and follow it through, using the logic of the position itself and not the chimera of a superficial attack. Wait, prepare—and then you *must* attack when the opponent's position is shaky. If at that time you do not attack, you will have lost your advantage. This is somewhat reminiscent of the Morphy approach, except that Morphy preferred clear, open positions, whereas the crabbed style of Steinitz was "unesthetic" and a despair to many of his contemporaries. Steinitz once referred to his style as "trigger chess"—a pulling back of the pieces in order the better to spring. It was a style of the utmost tenacity, based on a profound feeling for position. In this kind of chess, *every* unit on the board, including the King, had attacking possibilities. Steinitz worked out the concept of strong and weak squares (weak squares can be occupied by a hostile piece, so watch your Pawn structure carefully), of good and bad Bishops (the "bad" ones have no mobility), of strong Pawn formations, of close positions. Other players may have had more dash and flair. It made no difference. Steinitz beat them all because of the profundity of his ideas. He always played the board, never the man; he was always looking for the objectively right move. In an interview in the *British Chess Magazine* in 1894 he was asked if he ever played the man. "Certainly not! I am fully and entirely concentrated on the board. I never even consider my opponent's personality. So far as I am concerned my opponent might as well be an abstraction or an automaton."

Born in 1835 or 1836 (the date has never been ascertained), Steinitz was brought up as a Talmudic scholar. But he was introduced to chess at the age of twelve, and it was chess that captured the Talmudist. Like most smart youths from Bohemia, he went to Vienna, ostensibly to study mathematics. Instead he concentrated on chess, making his first international appearance at a tournament in London 1862. He took sixth place, far below Anderssen and Paulsen. Paulsen, whom Morphy had conquered in New York, had developed into a powerful master and a very important theorist. "There is hardly an opening which he has not enriched with original ideas," said the *Chess-Monthly* of London. The *Chess Encyclopaedia* says that Paulsen's ideas were so far ahead of his time that his contemporaries failed to recognize their value, and it was left to another generation to appreciate and exploit them.

Steinitz remained in London as a chess professional. Then came his match with Anderssen in 1866. This encounter was played under a set of rules designed to cope with the interminable play of previous matches. A time limit of twenty moves in two hours was established, the time measured by sand glasses. All games were to be completed at one sitting, without any adjournments except for a fifteen-minute interval after four hours of play. The first player to take eight games would be the winner. Steinitz won, 8 to 6. When Morphy previously had defeated Anderssen it was a chess match, no more. The two men shook hands and departed. But when Steinitz won, he trumpeted the fact everywhere and announced that he was the world's champion. There was no dispute about the claim; no magazines, newspapers, or, indeed, the chess world rose to object. And Steinitz never was hesitant about defending his title. He preferred it that way; he was much better in match than in tournament play. He did come out high in his tournaments—third in Paris 1867;

second at Dundee 1867; first in London 1872 and Vienna 1873—but he never lost a match until his meeting with Lasker in 1894. There was, however, a ten-year period in which he lay fallow. From 1873 to 1882 he played hardly any serious chess, the only exception being a match with Blackburne, whom he demolished 8 to 0. (That was the match in which "alarum time-pieces" were used for the first time, replacing sand glasses.) Steinitz spent those ten years working out his new theories, and he later admitted that Paulsen's innovations had played a major part in his new style. When he returned to the arena, at Vienna 1882, it was a grand re-entry. He came in first above the leading players of the day.

But life was not easy for so tempestuous a man. He was constantly fighting with his colleagues, constantly imagining insults where none were intended. A more touchy, hypersensitive, irascible man never lived. "Every one who knows the great chess player," sighed the *Westminster Papers* (a chess publication in London) in 1875, "knows also that it is his misfortune to be afflicted with a conviction that every mundane matter has some reference to himself." The *Westminster Papers* here referred to a tremendous hassle during which Steinitz in a fury resigned from the London Chess Club over some imagined slight. A few years later his arch rival, Zukertort, was writing in the *Chess-Monthly* (a publication edited by Zukertort himself) about the difficulty of getting on with Steinitz. The article may be biased—Zukertort and Steinitz had no love for each other—but Zukertort was merely echoing the prevalent feeling in international chess circles:

> Every one knows Mr. Steinitz' happy nature. There is not one Tournament in which he has taken part without a protest of some kind. . . . If a man has been twenty years in a country, and has succeeded, like Mr. Steinitz, in alienating his friends and well-wishers, is the whole of the Chess community wrong and is he right? We would ask Mr. Steinitz why he was compelled to resign the Westminster Club? why a note of censure, couched in the strongest terms, was all but passed on his conduct at the City Club? why he was not admitted to Simpson's Chess-rooms for some months, until some of the members petitioned the directors for his

Steinitz at the height of his career: egomaniacal, masterful, and scatological.

readmission? why he was not on speaking terms with Staunton, Wormald, and Boden? why is he not on speaking terms with Messrs. Blackburne, Bird, Duffy, MacDonnell, Potter, Hoffer, Zukertort?

Johannes Zukertort (1842–1888), the author of these lines, was a remarkable man. Born in Riga, educated in Germany, he was the all-time Renaissance man of chess. A linguist, he spoke eleven languages fluently and had, in addition, a working knowledge of Arabic, Turkish, and Sanskrit. He was a physician, with an M.D. from Breslau University in 1865 after studies in chemistry and physiology. He served as a physician with the Prussian army through several campaigns, was a swordsman and a crack shot, and was decorated for gallantry. A fine pianist, he had studied with the renowned Ignaz Moscheles, the composer, conductor, and teacher of Mendelssohn. He was a pioneer social scientist who at one time edited a political magazine and also wrote for Bismarck's *Allgemeine Zeitung.* He was also a music critic for a while. As a chess player, he learned the game late—at the age of eighteen—and then took lessons with Anderssen. His career went up fast. In 1871 he beat Anderssen in a match, amazed everybody with his blindfold exhibitions (up to sixteen boards), edited the *Berliner Schach-Zeitung,* moved to England (where he became a citizen in 1878), and started the *Chess-Monthly.* Steinitz also had his forum—a chess column in *The Field,* starting in 1872. He and Zukertort were automatic enemies; the world was not big enough to contain both of them. The two titans belabored each other in print. Magnificent were the verbal tilts; strong was the language. When Steinitz moved to New York and started the *International Chess Magazine,* the literary duels continued at long range.

Zukertort was not insensitive to the new chess theories in the air, but basically he remained a romantic, unable to cope with the solidity of the Steinitz kind of play. Against his fellow romantics, however, Zukertort was capable of superchess. One of his most famous games was played against Blackburne in London 1883. The climax occurs on White's twenty-eighth move. If Black accepts the Queen, a forced mate in seven moves follows.

Even Steinitz was impressed. "Really a glorious move," he wrote.

	WHITE: ZUKERTORT	BLACK: BLACKBURNE
1.	P-QB4	P-K3
2.	P-K3	N-KB3
3.	N-KB3	P-QN3
4.	B-K2	B-N2
5.	O-O	P-Q4
6.	P-Q4	B-Q3
7.	N-B3	O-O
8.	P-QN3	QN-Q2
9.	B-N2	Q-K2
10.	N-QN5	N-K5
11.	NxB	PxN
12.	N-Q2	QN-B3
13.	P-B3	NxN
14.	QxN	PxP
15.	BxP	P-Q4
16.	B-Q3	KR-B1
17.	QR-K1	R-B2
18.	P-K4	QR-QB1
19.	P-K5	N-K1
20.	P-B4	P-N3
21.	R-K3	P-B4
22.	PxP e.p.	NxP
23.	P-B5	N-K5
24.	BxN	PxB
25.	PxNP	R-B7
26.	PxPch	K-R1
27.	P-Q5ch	P-K4
28.	Q-N4	R(1)-B4
29.	R-B8ch	KxP
30.	QxPch	K-N2
31.	BxPch	KxR
32.	B-N7ch	K-N1
33.	QxQ	Resigns

Those two fiery personalities, Steinitz and Zukertort, had a go at each other in London 1872. It was a massacre. Steinitz won seven games, Zukertort only one. Four were drawn. Zukertort had enough resilience to bounce back, with a tie for first (shared with Winawer) in Paris 1878, and a resounding first in London 1883, where he came in three full points ahead of Steinitz. It probably was that victory which restored Zukertort's confidence and gave him the urge to challenge the champion once again.

But it had to be an overseas challenge. Shortly after the 1883 tournament, Steinitz decided to emigrate to the United States. He had had enough of London. In the United States he probably expected to find El Dorado. Every European knew that the streets of America were paved with gold. If there was any gold, however, poor Steinitz did not find it. He had to work very hard to keep alive. He gave exhibitions, taught, and concentrated on the *International Chess Magazine*, which ran from 1885 to 1891. In that publication is a style of journalism never encountered before or since. The bread-and-butter sections— games, analyses, hard news—were models of conscientious work and brilliant insights. But in his own column, *Personal and General,* Steinitz could be just a wee bit excitable. He was not the man to turn the other cheek. In one of the early issues he mentioned the German poet who wrote: "They are not the worst fruit which are gnawn upon by the wasps." Steinitz's comment on that was: "I thought this a rather soothing philosophy—for the wasps." So he made it clear that he was going to swat the wasps before they had a chance to gnaw on him.

A representative example of the Steinitz wasp-swatting style in its full glory occurs in the April, 1888, issue. Steinitz begins by righteously saying that he holds a sword in one hand and an olive branch in the other. He is a man of reason. "But when the pettifogging, journalistic Yaahoo (take that and choke it down, Mr. Séguin) . . ." Steinitz devotes some time to the unfortunate Mr. Séguin. Then comes the turn of Mr. James A. Russell, that "curious literary cur," from Baltimore. Among the terms that Steinitz directs at Mr. Russell are "snob," "imbecile stupidity," "miserable literary parade dog," "malicious cad." Steinitz next turns his attention to the "shyster" of a writer on the *New Orleans Times-Democrat,* in which the scatological splendor of the master's prose rises to its height: "I shall have to enter on the somewhat unpleasant process of pulling about his shystering nose, and then to rub into it some of his own filth, which he tried to throw at me, and which I shall have to pick up with a dirty glove at a distance."

Perhaps the superhuman effort of maintaining this kind of literary standard prevented Steinitz from engaging in international play. But the United States in 1884 did see the physical presence of the two greatest players of the decade. Zukertort came over for a tour. Whether or not he met Steinitz is not known. The chances are that he would have avoided him, considering how the two men felt about each other. Zukertort sent amusing stories about his experiences in America back to the *Chess-Monthly*. He did not find much activity in the Far West. Denver, he reported, had a club which sported very fine chess tables but hardly any players. He arrived in Cheyenne, capital of the Territory of Wyoming, and looked around. He could find "only one Chessist in the Territory." On his return to London he issued a challenge to Steinitz, and negotiations were started. These were difficult negotiations; an ocean separated the two players, and communications were slow. The *Chess-Monthly* went into great detail about the progress. Of course it gives only the Zukertort party's side of it. The order of invective used by Zukertort, though not as breathtaking as that of Steinitz, carries no mean ring. "We have come to the conclusion that Mr. Steinitz' modesty was a sham. He possessed a certain amount of self-restraint, which steadily waned with advancing age, and since he has grown fat, *un*fair, and *over* forty, he has thrown off the mask and gives full play to the floodgates of his accumulated venom." And:

Since the conclusion of the London Tournament, Mr. Steinitz has considered it his duty to pose as a martyr before the Chess World, persecuted and injured by myself and my friends. He generously reminds me, on every possible and impossible occasion, that I lost a match to him twelve years ago, and asserts that I now carefully avoid another encounter. It is beyond the limits of decorum and parliamentary language to enter into a discussion with an opponent who so prides himself on the scurrility of his speech and his writings. . . .

Months were spent working out the details of the match. Steinitz originally asked for a time limit of twelve moves an hour. Zukertort protested; that was too slow. He wanted twenty moves an hour but would settle for fifteen. Steinitz wanted to play for a stake of $1000 a side, and Zukertort thought that figure was too low. Finally everything was worked out. The stake was $2000 a side. The first to take ten games would be the winner. Draws were not to count. The time control was thirty moves during the first two hours and fifteen moves an hour thereafter. The duration of play was to be a minimum of eight hours on days of play, with an intermission of two hours after four hours of play (provided, of course, that the game had not been settled by then). Double stop-clocks would be the timing mechanism. The match would be divided among the cities of New York, St. Louis, and New Orleans.

Considerable international interest was paid to the Steinitz-Zukertort rematch, which started in New York in 1886. Many foreign magazines and newspapers sent correspondents, and the American press gave the event unusual prominence. Zukertort worked up a strong initial lead in New York, going ahead by a score of 4 to 1. Steinitz was terribly out of practice. The New York press was enchanted with the match. Nothing like this had previously happened in the city. A world championship chess match! Sports reporters were sent to cover it—reporters who did not know the back end of a Pawn from Aunt Nelly's crab-apples. But they outdid themselves in descriptive writing. A sample of the *Times* coverage can serve as an illustration of chess reporting of the day:

> . . . Then Steinitz drew first blood by capturing the white's king's pawn with his knight, and again calling check. The bold black knight was then laid low by a private white soldier, who in turn was slain by a black-mitred prelate, acting under the orders of Steinitz, who presently brought more of his heavy artillery to bear upon this wing.

*Etching made in 1886, after the Sarony photograph of the champion-
ship match between Zukertort (left) and Steinitz.*

Later Zukertort captured a Knight with his Bishop, "who, however, was immediately brained by the crozier wielded by his colored fellow-ecclesiastic."

In St. Louis Steinitz evened the score, and in New Orleans he ran away with the match. The slim, nervous, dapper Zukertort was in grievous shape, a fact duly noted by the correspondent of the *British Chess Magazine*. Toward the end, he reported, Zukertort appeared intellectually, physically, and emotionally crushed, and had trouble concentrating. Zukertort was "nervously weak, his slim, delicate fingers running through his moustache, and pulling at his whiskers. He sat with his legs crossed, frequently clasped his hands together, cast furtive glances around the room, seemed unable to comprehend the combinations . . . would get up, and, after pacing the floor for a while, return to his chair, press his hand to his brow, sip of ice water, and strive to gather up the threads of the labyrinth of moves spread before him." The final score was 10 to 5, with four drawn (which did not count).

Zukertort explained his loss by—of course—ill health. In a speech he made at the London Chess Club on his return, he blamed it all on the changes of climate. "In New York, among the breezes of the Atlantic, I was of course all right, but in St. Louis, in the interior of the continent, I was not so comfortable, and at New Orleans, in the Gulf of Mexico, I simply broke down. At New York my score was 4-1, at St. Louis the score was even, and at New Orleans the score was completely turned against me." Q.E.D. Zukertort ended his speech by expressing the hope for still another match, this one to be held "not for a trial of constitution but for a trial of chess skill."

But that was not to be. Two years later Zukertort was dead. It was an article of faith among chess writers that he died of a broken heart as a result of the second match. "He returned from the United States," said the *British Chess Magazine*, "a broken-down man, his nerves were over-strained, an impediment in his speech was noticeable and became more accentuated, and he had no energy left to rouse himself from a kind of mental torpor." He died on June 20, 1888, and the chess world grieved. Zukertort was a popular man. The *Chess-Monthly*, the following month, published a poem in his memory, the ending of which is:

> ... alive
> To all the varying chances of the game
> We place him high upon the roll of fame.
> He had his foibles, I am bound to say,
> Bound—pleased—exists perfection?—answer Nay.
> And we who knew him well and loved the man
> Hoped in his next fight he would lead the van.
> It could not be—who can control the fate?
> "Check!" There was no reply, and Death cried "Mate!"

The player after Zukertort who created most interest in chess circles was Mikhail Tchigorin, who came out of Russia and started to topple everybody around. Tchigorin came to New York for a tournament in 1889, and a match between him and Steinitz was arranged. Steinitz beat him, 10 to 6. The following year he met the Hungarian-born Isidor Gunsberg, a British citizen, and beat him 6 to 4, with nine draws. By this time in international chess play, draws counted half a point; no longer were they disregarded. There was some byplay in the final game that gives an idea of the working of grandmasters' minds. It was the nineteenth game, and all Steinitz needed was a draw to clinch the match. On his fourteenth move he offered the draw to Gunsberg, who refused. On the forty-second move Guns-berg, unhappy with his position, offered Steinitz the draw. Stein-itz accepted and retained his championship. Then something happened that would not happen today. "Gunsberg proposed to Steinitz that they should finish the game, and the latter assented to his proposal and suggested a small stake, at the same time giving his opponent the odds of a draw." That is, if Gunsberg drew the game it would be counted as a win for him. "On this understanding they continued the game just for pleasure, and after about a dozen moves Gunsberg's position became untenable and he resigned. Steinitz contends that nobody will blame him for having agreed to the draw when he did, because, had he played on before securing the match, he might have made a mistake as he did in the previous day, and this might have cost him the game."

A rematch with Tchigorin took place in Havana in 1892. Tchigorin might have been heartened by the result of the re-

cent cable match he had held with Steinitz in 1890 and 1891.
The two players got into a heated argument about a point of
chess theory and they decided to resolve it by cable—Steinitz in
New York, Tchigorin in Havana. Tchigorin won both games. The
New York police, notified about the cabled messages, came to
arrest Steinitz as a spy who was transmitting information by use
of a code. Havana, always a strong chess center, invited the two
players to hold their rematch there. This time the results were
closer than they had been in 1889. Steinitz won, 12½ to 10½.
Chess was not so easy for him as it used to be; he was getting
old, and he complained about it. "I have been for hours with my
eyes staring open and burning like fire and nothing would bring
sleep. At the close of a contest, I am wrought to such a nervous
tension that for weeks afterwards I am in an almost uncontrollable state, living on champagne or some stimulant that will
bring artificial strength." In addition he had other problems.
His teen-age daughter died in the late 1880's, and that upset him
terribly (she was a child of his second marriage; little is known
about his first wife). And financial problems continued to plague
him.

Yet he was still the strongest player in the world. Some of
the games of the Tchigorin match are as deft and beautifully
organized as anything that ever came from his mind. The fourth
game is cited by Reuben Fine as a case in point, "one which
brings out Steinitz's unique gifts more than any other he ever
played":

	WHITE: STEINITZ	BLACK: TCHIGORIN
1.	P-K4	P-K4
2.	N-KB3	N-QB3
3.	B-N5	N-B3
4.	P-Q3	P-Q3
5.	P-B3	P-KN3
6.	QN-Q2	B-N2
7.	N-B1	O-O
8.	B-R4	N-Q2
9.	N-K3	N-B4
10.	B-B2	N-K3

11.	P-KR4	N-K2
12.	P-R5	P-Q4
13.	RPxP	BPxP
14.	PxP	NxP
15.	NxN	QxN
16.	B-N3	Q-B3
17.	Q-K2	B-Q2
18.	B-K3	K-R1
19.	O-O-O	QR-K1
20.	Q-B1	P-QR4
21.	P-Q4	PxP
22.	NxP	BxN
23.	RxB	NxR
24.	RxPch	KxR
25.	Q-R1ch	K-N2
26.	B-R6ch	K-B3
27.	Q-R4ch	K-K4
28.	QxNch	Resigns

Steinitz's time came, as it must come to all champions, in 1894. The fifty-eight-year-old veteran lost his title to the twenty-five-year-old Emanuel Lasker. Two years later there was a re-match in Moscow, and Steinitz could make no headway against his young opponent. But he did not retire from chess. He had to keep on playing. Somebody asked him why, at his age, he had to continue to exhaust himself with the rigors of tournament play. Had he not enough fame? "I can spare the fame," Steinitz wryly said, "but not the prize money." Mental trouble started to afflict him. After the second Lasker match he had a breakdown and spent forty days in a Moscow sanitorium. Yet even after he lost his championship in 1894 he was able to turn out brilliancies, and he remained an indomitable fighter. He was able, at Hastings 1895, to play a masterpiece against Kurt von Bardeleben, one of the better players at the turn of the century. This is one of the most piquant games on record; it is known as "Steinitz's Gem," and it fully deserved both the brilliancy prize which it received and its appearance in so many anthologies of chess games:

	WHITE: STEINITZ	BLACK: BARDELEBEN
1.	P-K4	P-K4
2.	N-KB3	N-QB3
3.	B-B4	B-B4
4.	P-B3	N-B3
5.	P-Q4	PxP
6.	PxP	B-N5ch
7.	N-B3	P-Q4
8.	PxP	KNxP
9.	O-O	B-K3
10.	B-KN5	B-K2
11.	BxN	QBxB
12.	NxB	QxN
13.	BxB	NxB
14.	R-K1	P-KB3
15.	Q-K2	Q-Q2
16.	QR-B1	P-B3
17.	P-Q5	PxP
18.	N-Q4	K-B2
19.	N-K6	KR-QB1
20.	Q-N4	P-KN3
21.	N-N5ch	K-K1
22.	RxNch	K-B1
23.	R-B7ch	K-N1
24.	R-N7ch	K-R1
25.	RxPch	Resigns

Bardeleben was in a mating net. Had he continued playing, he would have been finished off (as Steinitz announced at the end of the game) in ten forced moves: 25. K-N1; 26. R-N7ch, K-R1; 27. Q-R4ch, KxR; 28. Q-R7ch, K-B1; 29. Q-R8ch, K-K2; 30. Q-N7ch, K-K1; 31. Q-N8ch, K-K2; 32. Q-B7ch, K-Q1; 33. Q-B8ch, Q-K1; 34. N-B7ch, K-Q2; 35. Q-Q6 mate. (There are other ways, depending on Black's cooperation, to win the game. This is the prettiest.)

As if to show that there was nothing he could not do, Steinitz, at the age of sixty-one, began to give exhibitions of blindfold chess. Up to then he had never shown any particular interest in this side of the game, but he needed the money, so in 1897 he took on twenty-two players simultaneously. Two years later he entered the London 1899 Tournament and for the first time in his career did not finish among the leaders. Discouraged, he returned to New York, where his mind failed. He began to believe that he could telephone anybody in the world without wire or equipment, and that he could move chess pieces at will by emitting electric currents from his brain. Behind the house in which he lived at 155 East 103rd Street was a small yard. Every morning, no matter what the weather, Steinitz would carefully get dressed except for shoes and stockings, and hobble barefoot in the yard for an hour or two. Perhaps he thought that he was absorbing electrical energy from the earth. After this he would go inside and experiment with his wireless telephone. For hours he would try to call up various people he knew in Europe. He also tried to get in touch with God; he wanted to challenge the Deity to a match, offering Him odds of Pawn and move. His wife had him committed to Ward's Island. There Steinitz spent his time writing a biographical sketch. It closes with:

> And since 1895 I have been obliged at an advanced age and while I was half crippled to export myself in order to import only a portion of my living for myself and my family, and this portion did not amount to $250 per annum within the last two years when I deduct my travelling expenses and increased cost for staying abroad, although I was chess champion for twenty-eight years!!!

Friends raised a fund to take care of him. His wife opened a little candy store and tried to keep going. Steinitz was released from his misery on August 12, 1900. Many years later, Lasker, analyzing Steinitz's contribution to chess, paid full tribute to his predecessor. He went at length into Steinitz's genius for positional chess, his capacity for divining the combinations of his opponents long before they were on the board, his theoretical ideas.

One weakness, however, Steinitz did have as a chess player. "He was pig-headed," Lasker laconically said.

The London Graphic *of July 17, 1886, captioned this as "The Sixteen Leading Chess Players of the World."* Seated, left to right: *Blackburne, Steinitz, Zukertort, Englisch.* Standing, left to right: *MacKenzie, Kolisch, Winawer, Bird, de Rivière, Rosenthal, Mason, Potter, Schallopp, Paulsen, MacDonnell, and Gunsberg.*

9

The Pragmatist

The man who took the championship away from Steinitz in 1894 was a frail, dapper, serious young fellow with an olive complexion, a silken mustache, and liquid dark eyes over which were placed pince-nez dangling from a black cord. His victory came as more than a surprise to the world of chess. It was a shock. Emanuel Lasker was only twenty-five years old and had participated in a minimum of international chess. Europe had almost forgotten about him, for he had gone to the United States around 1890 and had more or less disappeared. Talented, yes. Everybody would admit that. He had won the Berlin 1889 Tournament; and in London he had won matches against Blackburne, Bird, and a promising young German player named Jacques Mieses.

But to beat the great Steinitz! Nobody could understand it. There had to be some sort of reason, and Leopold Hoffer (Steinitz's old adversary) of the *Chess-Monthly* figured it out to his satisfaction. Steinitz had lost, he wrote, but not *the* Steinitz. Not the Steinitz of Anderssen and Zukertort. "Lasker," added Hoffer, "is not our ideal of a first-class player. Formerly he would have disappeared in the crowd. Is it possible to imagine that with his repertory he could successfully have met Morphy, Kolisch, Anderssen or Zukertort? The great masters have grown old, and our time is anything but prolific in *hors ligne.*"

Die guten alten Zeiten. . . . Hoffer, a representative of the old school, sighed for romantic chess. Lasker's tidy positional chess appeared dull, unenterprising, labored. But Lasker and the new international breed, who suddenly appeared as though a new Cadmus had sowed a cross section of the globe, represented modern chess; and much as the old boys complained, it was modern chess that was to prove demonstrably superior to anything that had gone before. Lasker and Pillsbury, Tarrasch, Maróczy, Marshall (the romantic throwback, though his was a romanticism based on position play), Schlechter, Tartakower, Rubinstein, Mieses, Duras, Spielmann, Capablanca, Alekhine —these men changed chess and made it what it is today. And of all of them, the Lasker who was despised by Hoffer and the romanticists had the longest and most brilliant career. At an age when most players are rocking in a chair mumbling about the exploits of their youth and damning the younger generation, Lasker was winning tournaments over such giants as Alekhine and Capablanca. The man who played Steinitz in 1894 also played Botvinnik and Flohr in Moscow in 1935, and almost won that tournament, coming in just half a point below first place.

He was an interesting man: chess champion, philosopher, mathematician, dramatist, poet, card-player—a Renaissance man of chess. Born in Berlinchen, a province of Brandenburg, on December 24, 1868, the son of a cantor in the local synagogue (Berlinchen had a relatively large Jewish community), he was sent to study mathematics in Berlin when he was eleven. There he lived with his elder brother, who taught him the game. There was no money in the family, and young Lasker found that he could pick up a few pfennigs at the chess clubs. His usual hangout was the Café Kaiserhof, and soon he was winning tournaments there. In his first tournament, Breslau 1889, he took first place in a weaker section of the tournament. Later that year, in Amsterdam, he came in second in a very powerful field. At that point chess won out over mathematics. He went to London in 1890, returned there for tournaments in 1892, crushed Blackburne 6 to 0, then emigrated to the United States. There he challenged Steinitz. Could the champion have known the strength of his young opponent? One somehow doubts it. Steinitz, who so recently had conquered Tchigorin, probably felt that the inexperienced, relatively untried Lasker would pose no problems.

*Emanuel Lasker in 1890.
This lithograph appeared
in the* Chess-Monthly
*of London in 1890
and is one of the
earliest-known portraits
of the future champion.*

*Lasker, ca. 1900,
as world champion:
philosopher,
mathematician,
dramatist, poet,
and card player.*

The New York Times of March 11, 1894, did refer to Lasker as one of the four greatest living players but warned Lasker's admirers not to get their hopes up. "An excellent style may lead to naught if he have to meet an opponent of equal or superior strength." The match was played for $2000 a side, with the first to take ten games declared the winner; three games a week, at fifteen moves an hour, were scheduled. The match started on March 15 at the Union Square Hotel, and Steinitz lost the first game. In an interview that appeared the following day he blamed it on fatigue and overexcitement:

> The public scarcely realizes that the mental strain required for hard match play at chess taxes the physical capacities of the contestants in a greater measure than the heavy athletic exercises. An eminent physician at Havana, whom I consulted during my last match at Havana, said to me: "I overworked myself as an amateur, both at chess and at the gymnasium, and I cannot imagine anything that so afflicts, simultaneously, all the vital organs—brain, heart, kidney and liver—as the excitement of playing board chess under public responsibility.
>
> It cannot, therefore, be wondered at, that the early part of a great chess contest very rarely draws out the best form of both parties, and this was the case with the first game of the present match.

Steinitz went on to claim, as chess players have always claimed, that he had a winning position, blundered, and then missed a draw "under the influence of disappointment." After eight games, with Lasker in the lead, the series shifted to Philadelphia's Cosmopolitan Club for three games. Lasker won all three, and this time Steinitz blamed insomnia for his poor showing. The games were very well attended and, *The New York Times* reported: "One of the prettiest features of the scene was the extraordinarily large number of women, who seemed to follow the game with considerable interest and excitement." Steinitz, five games behind, returned to New York, where he took massages to control his insomnia. Lasker went to Quebec to rest for a week. The match was concluded in Montreal. Steinitz's massage treatment helped at first, and he cut Lasker's lead to three games. Then the challenger went on a winning streak. On May

26, 1894, he won the championship, the final score being 10 to 5, with four draws. Steinitz immediately challenged. He wanted a return match in December. But he did not get one for two years. Lasker never was in a rush to put his championship on the line. At the rematch in 1896 the results were decisive. Lasker won 10 to 2, with five draws. "The thinker," Lasker said, "was conquered by the player." Steinitz's age also had something to do with the results, and Lasker admitted as much many years later, pointing out that a man of Steinitz's venerability could not be expected to stand up to a young and vital player: "That Steinitz at the age of 59 was defeated by me and later by others is due to no defect of his theory. His theory is and forever remains the classical expression of the idea of Chess."

The world of chess soon realized that Lasker had not beaten Steinitz by accident. In 1895, the new champion made a strong showing at Hastings—that near-mythical tournament unexpectedly won by the young American, Harry Nelson Pillsbury—and from that point Lasker never turned back. Despite the fact that he was recovering from an attack of typhoid fever contracted in the United States, Lasker came in third, a point behind Pillsbury and half a point behind Tchigorin. The writer of the Hastings program book described Lasker as a "modest and intelligent gentleman, but frail and delicate in health. . . . Lasker, unlike many experts, has first-class business qualities. . . . Like his great rival [Steinitz], he takes chess and life generally in a very serious way, and there seems to be but little fun in either of their natures. If this means that humor is inimical to chess, so much the worse for the latter. On the other hand, however, there is Dr. Tarrasch, who has plenty of true humor in his nature, and Pillsbury and others are not wanting in that element."

The remark about Lasker's "first-class business qualities" as early as 1895 is interesting. Already Lasker was putting a high price on his services. He was a chess professional, he was the champion of the world, and he expected to be paid accordingly. He never was bashful in letting sponsors of tournaments know that they could not expect to get him for nothing. But, as a matter of fact, Lasker was a terrible businessman. He had the reputation of being shrewd in money matters, but he failed at whatever he did outside of chess. In 1913 he tried farming and made a mess of it. Then he decided to be a pigeon breeder and went bankrupt. (He finally understood that he was in the wrong business when he tried to mate a pair of pigeons, not realizing that both were males.) Hans Kmoch, the Grand Old Man of international chess until his death in 1973, remembered the time when Mieses approached Lasker with the idea of starting a chess magazine. Lasker immediately wanted to buy a paper mill so that they could save money on paper. It was Lasker who, after World War I, had the fine business acumen to invest his money in German marks. Kmoch thought that Lasker had ridiculous views on economic and financial matters, and that Lasker was the most impractical man he had ever met.

It was because Lasker insisted on receiving at least $2000 for an appearance that he was called money-hungry. "I don't want to die like Steinitz or live on charity like a beggar," he once said. Lasker even wanted his games copyrighted, an idea that Fischer was to pursue unsuccessfully in the 1960's. "Publication of the games in a newspaper is a virtual gift of all rights," said Lasker. A few players did try to put his ideas into effect. After Tarrasch and Marshall had a match, they refused to permit indiscriminate publication of their games. Chess editors all over Europe were indignant. Lasker rushed to the defense of Tarrasch and Marshall:

> Have these writers ever thought that even a master must pay his board bill all the year round? And that it might be unfair to ask the master to deliver the proceeds of his activity without compensation? If the complainants will look for an opportunity of serving the "vital interests" of chess, they will find it at their very door. They have hitherto neglected to pay the chessmaster for the game produced, and have pocketed the entire profit of his labor. Would that some people talk less about idealism and show more of it in the way they act.

Although Lasker held the title for twenty-seven years, he defended it only six times after his rematch with Steinitz in 1896. He played Marshall in 1907, Tarrasch in 1908, Janowski in 1909 and 1910, Schlechter in 1910, and Capablanca in 1921. This overprotection of the championship caused resentment in chess circles. Lasker, it seemed apparent to everybody, did not

nichts rührte sich drinnen und niemand trat den verstand den Blick. „Thu' Dich nicht sorge
zen; in der Stube, die er leer fand, steckte er über der Bruder wird den Buben in unsere Kam
ie Fackel in den Ring. Als er sah, daß Eber= damit Du ruhen kannst in der heutigen Nach
Baters wankte, sprang er ihm in den Weg und Stumm nickte Eberwein und ließ sich auf d

Dich, guter Herr, sinken. Ohne Wei
, nur heut' red ihm Schweifer do
r heut' nimmer!" mit trockenem Kl
n Zelle knarrten Moos zu weiche
Lagers, Schritte telte und die zit
cam erschien auf wärmender Kotze
utlitz von gespen= Schweifer einei
en brennend schlürfte er den Di
Eberwein ohne zu merken,
Schweifer. Bruder atmete e
von mir, Becher geleert u
mein Auge Tropfen de
eine fri
und
de

Emanuel Lasker und Wilhelm Steinitz.

Adolf Anderssen.   Paul Morphy.   Joh. Herm. Zukertort.   Louis Paulsen.

Meister des Schachspiels.

nid
blei
Au
Sch
sted
Bra
aus
Kar
hot
sche
rod
Honig, als wä
menstand. Auf i
Bruder Wampo w
genden Armen. S
der Brust bis nie
fleckig, als hätte
Honigtiegel gezog
stand Schweifer
Schnarchenden.
andere Lager leer

klang Eber=
ie Berge...
chwer stützte
r, der ihn
torten in die
ie die Fackel

"Meister des Schachspiels"—Masters of Chess, from an 1894 issue of Die Gartentaube. At top: Lasker (left) and Steinitz face each other. At bottom, left to right: Anderssen, Morphy, Zukertort, and Paulsen.

want to take the risk of losing. Certainly he threw obstacle after obstacle into his negotiations with challengers. He waited until 1903 before discussing terms with his eager challenger, Frank Marshall. This dragged on interminably, and the chess world was infuriated. William E. Napier, the American player and chess journalist, had some acid comments to make in the *British Chess Magazine:* "If Dr. Lasker insists for the remainder of his life on selecting the time and place of meeting, it would seem that any bona-fide challenger would be disqualified by the champion's whim. . . . Dr. Lasker might prefer to play in a balloon, or in the nether recesses of a coal mine, or at Archangel or Timbuctoo." Napier also criticized Lasker for asking for too much money—his usual $2000. Lasker was not the one to take this lying down, and he had something to say about that:

> If the chess world wants to have the pleasure, excitement and instruction which a championship match affords to some hundreds and thousands of chess players, nay even in some degree to the succeeding generations, why should it not pay for it? . . . Why then does the chess world expect *all* the sacrifices from the masters, why does it not create an organization, when the whole question turns round a really paltry amount of money?

Negotiations with Marshall came to a halt. The American grandmaster could not raise his share of the purse. Lasker then looked in the direction of Géza Maróczy from Hungary. Maróczy (1870–1951), an engineer and teacher of mathematics, had come out first at Monte Carlo 1904, Ostend 1905, and Bremen 1905. In those years there was no doubt that he was one of the strongest players alive. An agreement for a Lasker-Maróczy match was actually signed on April 6, 1906, but after a few months Maróczy withdrew. Lasker, in his own publication, *Lasker's Chess Magazine,* which he edited from 1904 to 1909, said the negotiations broke down because the players could not agree on a site. Maróczy wanted Vienna and Lasker wanted New York. When the match fell through, again there was unrest. So in 1907 Lasker returned to Marshall, who still could not raise the $2000. Lasker settled for $1000 a side, sat down to play Marshall in January, 1907, and the result was a catastrophe for the American, who could not take a single game. Lasker won 8 to 0, with seven draws.

Siegbert Tarrasch came next, in 1908. Tarrasch (1862–1934) for some fifteen years had been working up a magnificent tournament record. At one stretch, with seven consecutive tournament wins, he seemed invincible. From 1885 to 1894 he was second in the world only to Steinitz—if, indeed, he *was* second. They never had a match. Then, after 1894, Tarrasch was in the shadow of Lasker. He was a sharp, irascible little man: lame (born with a club foot), a working physician, a dogmatic theorist, the author of learned treatises on chess. The "Praeceptor Germaniae," he was called, and he was to chess in his time what Staunton had been earlier in the century. Tarrasch, more than anybody else, established the chess dogma of the last half of the century. One did certain things because Dr. Tarrasch said they should be done. Occupy the center. Seize open files. Create a strong outpost. Never move a piece twice in the opening. Develop the Knights first, then the Bishops. Tarrasch was one of the great technicians of chess. But it was never in him to be world champion. Perhaps, as Lasker once said, at basis he lacked fighting spirit.

Lasker and Tarrasch detested each other. Lasker, who in his magazine could twist the knife, had delivered himself of some rather nasty remarks about Tarrasch and his ego. In the January, 1906, issue, Lasker said that the only thing that made Tarrasch go was his untold good opinion of himself. "Dr. Tarrasch's strength or weakness—if one likes—is his pronounced amour propre. Without it he would have been a very mediocre chess player; gifted [with self-love] to an abnormal degree he has become a giant. His amour propre is such that he must excel in something. Chess was, as it were, the easier medium for him to choose, and he is very fond of chess, therefore, but most particularly of his own chess." Just before the start of the match Lasker had further thoughts: "Dr. Tarrasch," he wrote, "is a thinker, fond of deep and complex speculation. He will accept the efficacy and usefulness of a move if at the same time he considers it beautiful and theoretically right. But I accept this sort of beauty only if and when it happens to be useful. He admires an idea for its depth, I admire it for its efficacy. My opponent believes in beauty, I believe in strength. I think that by being strong, a move is beautiful too."

Tarrasch saw these articles, and others like them, and was so furious he would not speak to Lasker. In addition, Tarrasch, *echt*-Deutsch (as so many German Jews have been), professed to be disgusted with Lasker's money-grubbing (so he called them) tactics. He himself, a successful physician, a well-to-do bourgeois type, the big man of German chess, the upholder of Chess for the Fatherland, was no mere professional. He played for art, not for money, and he let the world know what he thought of the champion. The match was held in Düsseldorf and Munich. Before the first game, the organizers tried to bring the two enemies together. Lasker was willing. Tarrasch approached the room, got as far as the door, looked at Lasker, clicked his heels, and made a curt bow. "To you, Dr. Lasker," he said, "I have only three words, check and mate." With this immortal *défi*, Tarrasch made another stiff bow and disappeared. Lasker won the match without much trouble—8 to 3, with five draws. Tarrasch blamed his defeat on the fact that he was sensitive to the sea. This the *British Chess Magazine*, with all respect, could not understand. Tarrasch's alibi, the editors said, "does not leave altogether a pleasant flavor in the mouth. Düsseldorf is some 170 miles from the coast. A gift so sensitive to sea influence is not robust enough to carry the world's championship."

Nor did Lasker have any trouble with the Polish-born Janowski in 1910. David Janowski (1868–1927), who was born the same year as Lasker, was a devil-may-care player of the romantic school, and this kind of player was made to order for the champion. Janowski was one of the eccentrics of chess—a violent man always feuding with his colleagues, a psychopathic gambler, a sore loser, but always an exciting, fighting player. "He follows the wrong path with more determination than any man I ever met," said Marshall of him. Reuben Fine remembers Janowski as the great master of the alibi. He invariably lost because the room was too hot or too cold, the windows open too far or not far enough. Always he found something to complain about, and after a match would blame that on his showing. As a chess player he had but two rules: attack, and get the Bishops out. He himself once described his game: "It is like Mary Queen of Scots—beautiful but unfortunate." Others said of him that he knew well how to attack but not *when* to attack. His best years were

THREE LASKER OPPONENTS

Top right: Siegbert Tarrasch. To Lasker he had only three words: "Check and mate."

Bottom left: David Janowski. He described his game as "like Mary Queen of Scots, beautiful but unfortunate."

Bottom right: Karl Schlechter, "The Drawing Master." He nearly took the title from Lasker.

between 1898 and 1905, when he won some important tournaments. Not well educated, with no interests outside of chess and gambling—he would rapidly lose his chess winnings at roulette—he had a raging temper when he lost, and he was one of those detestable players who stubbornly insists on playing out a game even in a dead lost position. Perhaps his opponent would blunder. Janowski always worked on the principle that nobody ever won a game by resigning. His principle worked two ways. With his fighting instinct—*that* Janowski did have—he would desperately try to win drawn games and as a result lost a lot of them. His ego matched anybody's. When he lost to Marshall in 1905 he immediately rechallenged, offering Marshall the odds of a four-point advantage in a ten-point match. Certain weak players had Janowski's number; he could seldom win against them. One was the Anglo-American master James Mason, who drove Janowski frantic. "I don't understand it," Janowski would wail. "I am bewitched when I play Mason. All the time he smokes his bad cigars and spits. I cannot stand it. Every few minutes I have to sprinkle myself with eau de cologne."

Janowski may not have been a popular figure in international chess, but there never was lack of excitement when he was around. In his two matches with Lasker he played true to form, throwing all his artillery at the champion in an all-out gamble for victory. Lasker contemptuously beat him 7 to 1 with two draws in 1909, and 8 to 0 with three draws the following year.

But the match with Karl Schlechter was a cliffhanger. Schlechter, an Austrian, was called "The Drawing Master." He could beat anybody when aroused, but he seldom was. In the seven hundred or so games he played during his tournament career, he drew over 50 per cent. He was a mild, unambitious man who was capable of beautiful chess—he had the technique and knowledge—but did not have the killer instinct. Lasker, in his magazine, had got his hooks into the inoffensive Schlechter also. In 1906, he wrote an article about possible challengers to his title. Tarrasch and Maróczy, he said, had priority. "It is true," Lasker went on, "that the Austrian, Schlechter, also has the ability that would enable him to compete with a good chance for success, but Schlechter has only the ability—nothing more. He is a man who loves Nature and the simple life and who has so little of the devil about him that he could not be wooed to take anything coveted by somebody else."

Taking advantage of Schlechter's placidity, Lasker worked up a set of match conditions that threw everything in his favor. (Some researchers, however, suggest that the match conditions have never been clearly established; the full story of the Lasker-Schlechter match remains to be told.) The match would be declared a draw and Lasker would retain his title unless Schlechter had a clear majority of two points. And if Schlechter was able to overcome this handicap and win, Lasker still was to be considered the champion until a rematch was played. One wonders why Schlechter bothered to play at all under these absurd conditions. But that was the kind of man he was. The ten-game match was held in 1910. At the end of the ninth game, Schlechter had won one game and drawn all the others. Lasker must have been desperate. Certainly he was baffled by Schlechter's imperturbable play. "How can one beat a man," Lasker asked, "who meets offers of success and threats of apparent attack with equal calm?" In the tenth game Schlechter had an easy draw in hand. He picked this moment, of all the games in his career, to go for a win; he *had* to, if the match conditions called for him to win by two points. Three days later, after two adjournments and seventy-one moves, he lost. Lasker never played a match with *him* ever again. Poor Schlechter died from starvation in Vienna shortly after the end of World War I.

Lasker was very strong in match play. But in tournament play he was supreme. Unlike Steinitz, the unbeatable match player, Lasker gloried in the shifting fortunes of tournaments, where different opponents had different styles, and different problems had to be faced every day. In a tournament career that lasted some forty years, Lasker entered twenty major tournaments. Of these he won ten outright, tied for first twice, came in second twice, tied for second twice, and was below third place only three times, two of those when he was sixty-seven years old. His greatest games came in tournaments rather than in his title matches. Typical was his thrilling win over Pillsbury at St. Petersburg 1895:

	WHITE: PILLSBURY	BLACK: LASKER
1.	P-Q4	P-Q4
2.	P-QB4	P-K3
3.	N-QB3	N-KB3
4.	N-B3	P-B4
5.	B-N5	BPxP
6.	QxP	N-B3
7.	Q-R4	B-K2
8.	O-O-O	Q-R4
9.	P-K3	B-Q2
10.	K-N1	P-KR3
11.	PxP	PxP
12.	N-Q4	O-O
13.	BxN	BxB
14.	Q-R5	NxN
15.	PxN	B-K3
16.	P-B4	QR-B1
17.	P-B5	RxN
18.	PxB	R-QR6
19.	PxPch	RxBP
20.	PxR	Q-N3ch
21.	B-N5	QxBch
22.	K-R1	R-B2
23.	R-Q2	R-B5
24.	R(1)-Q1	R-B6
25.	Q-B5	Q-B5
26.	K-N2	RxP
27.	Q-K6ch	K-R2
28.	KxR	Q-B6ch
	Resigns	

The high point of the game is Lasker's Rook sacrifice on his eighteenth move. From that point on, Pillsbury's position was eroded. He had to resign because of a forced mate in four moves. In Marshall's *Chess Masterpieces*, Lasker called this the best game he ever played. "I was able to ward off a furious attack and then succeeded in carrying my own counter-attack through."

Another highlight of Lasker's career was his win over Capablanca at St. Petersburg 1914. The tournament was nearing its end, and Capablanca was in first place, a point ahead of Lasker. They met in the eighteenth round. When, as early as the sixth move, Lasker allowed the Queens to be traded off, Capablanca, the phenomenal technician, must have felt certain of a draw. But Lasker probed and probed, and succeeded in weakening Capablanca's Pawn structure, tearing everything apart on his thirty-fifth move. He showed that he, too, knew something about the technique of the game of chess. "The spectators," Lasker wrote, "had followed the final moves breathlessly. That Black's position was in ruins was obvious to the veriest tyro. And now Capablanca turned over his King. From the several hundred spectators, there came such applause as I have never experienced in all my life as a chess player. It was like the wholly spontaneous applause which thunders forth in the theatre, of which the individual is almost unconscious." Reuben Fine writes of Lasker's fourteenth move: "Lasker now has worked out a complete winning method, which is simplicity itself: he will tie Black's pieces to the defense of the QP (that was impossible before the Pawns were undoubled) and build up his K-side attack via P-KN4-5. He also hopes to plant a Knight on K6":

	WHITE: LASKER	BLACK: CAPABLANCA
1.	P-K4	P-K4
2.	N-KB3	N-QB3
3.	B-N5	P-QR3
4.	BxN	QPxB
5.	P-Q4	PxP
6.	QxP	QxQ
7.	NxQ	B-Q3
8.	N-QB3	N-K2
9.	O-O	O-O
10.	P-B4	R-K1
11.	N-N3	P-B3
12.	P-B5	P-QN3
13.	B-B4	B-N2
14.	BxB	PxB
15.	N-Q4	QR-Q1
16.	N-K6	R-Q2
17.	QR-Q1	N-B1

18.	R-B2	P-QN4
19.	R(2)-Q2	R(2)-K2
20.	P-QN4	K-B2
21.	P-QR3	B-R1
22.	K-B2	R-R2
23.	P-N4	P-R3
24.	R-Q3	P-QR4
25.	P-KR4	PxP
26.	PxP	R(2)-K2
27.	K-B3	R-N1
28.	K-B4	P-N3
29.	R-N3	P-N4ch
30.	K-B3	N-N3
31.	PxP	RPxP
32.	R-R3	R-Q2
33.	K-N3	K-K1
34.	QR-KR1	B-N2
35.	P-K5	QPxP
36.	N-K4	N-Q4
37.	N(6)-B5	B-B1
38.	NxR	BxN
39.	R-R7	R-B1
40.	R-R1	K-Q1
41.	R-R8ch	B-B1
42.	N-B5	Resigns

Lasker compiled his staggering record in tournament chess by sheer will power. Most experts agree that he was not a natural player, and in many respects he was lazy. He seldom studied a chess book, and even average players knew much more about the latest wrinkles in opening theory than he did. When Lasker trained for his match with Tarrasch, he went to the country with the international master Edward Lasker without a chessboard or a chess book. They spent the time playing the Japanese game of *go*.

Lasker represented no school of chess, and he founded no school of chess. If he had any philosophy of the game, it was his idea that chess was a struggle, and in such a struggle the stronger *character* (not necessarily the stronger technician) would win.

Lasker won by outplaying and outpsyching his opponents. With him, psychological chess came into being.

What Lasker often did was make the psychologically best move rather than the objectively best move. A chess-playing psychiatrist, Dr. Ben Karpman, pointed out in Lasker's own day that Lasker "uses the medium of a chess game to fight, above all, his opponent's psyche." In other words, Lasker played the man rather than the board. Richard Réti, the great player of the 1920's, was utterly fascinated with Lasker's procedure and wrote a long analysis of it. More than any other player, Réti said, Lasker had the ability to turn a lost position into a draw or win. Every tournament saw Lasker in a lost position almost every second game. Yet he managed to wriggle out and win in the end. This, Réti decided, could not be a matter of luck; it happened too often. There could be only one answer. "Lasker often plays badly on purpose," and it is the opponent who falls, "as if seized by vertigo." And how did Lasker accomplish this magic? "He studies the games, the manner of playing, the strength and the weak points of the masters whom he is to meet. He is not so much interested in making the objectively best move as he is in making those most disagreeable to his opponent; he turns the game in a direction not suitable to the style of his opponent." The result is frustration for the player facing Lasker; the poor devil "never has a chance of playing a position which suits him."

Every chess analyst has echoed Réti's remark. Fine writes that Lasker's mastery consisted of "an intensive understanding of the human element." He delighted in complicated positions, confident that his opponent would blunder. "There is no master, living or dead, whose maneuvering ability approaches that of Lasker," said Aron Nimzovich. And nobody was a better defensive player. To his opponents, Lasker's play seemed inexplicable. He would be in a lost position; he *had* to lose; there was no play left. But two dozen moves later the opponent would be strangled to death.

There were periods when Lasker was out of chess. Between 1896 and 1899 he concentrated on his mathematical studies and in 1902 received his doctorate from Erlangen University. Dr. Lasker was an algebraist. His headquarters was Berlin, where he made his home in the early 1900's. After the death of his first wife, he remarried in 1911. For a time he taught mathematics and wrote three books of philosophy. His private life was chaotic. Seldom was he in bed before 3:00 A.M. He never carried a watch; he ate when he was hungry and slept when he was sleepy. Intelligent, aggressive, learned, with a wide range of interests, he would argue about relativity with Einstein (who apparently treated him with real respect) or outshout any authority on any subject. His own chess books have a peculiar charm. Not many have read his philosophical systems as outlined in *Kampf* (1907), *Das Begreifen der Welt* (1913), and *Die Philosophie der Unvollendbar* (1917) —but every chess player has studied his analytical books, and those have a double literary standard. In his description of games and in his discussion of theory, Lasker's prose is analytical, precise, and thorough. But every so often, Lasker, who must have fancied himself as a prose stylist, takes off into flights of hysterically exalted Beautiful Writing, as in the section of his *Manual of Chess* where he traces the history of early players:

La Bourdonnais died young in London, and the goddess of Chess, Caïssa, very much grieved, mourned for him and forgot to inspire the masters with her sunny look. A dreary time came over the Chess world. The masters played in a dry style, without enthusiasm, without imagination, without force, and the chess fraternity was full of the wrangles of the mediocrities. It is true, soon the goddess repaired her omission. She flirted—Goddess! pardon me this vulgar expression, but the coarse human language does not know the shades of meaning such as undoubtedly you would be able to express by means of Chess pieces—she flirted, I beg to say, with the English historian Staunton, and prevailed upon him to organize an international chess tournament, in London, 1851, in the days of the great International Exposition. And then—O fickle Goddess—she gave her love to a young German mathematician, the German Anderssen, and inspired him to superb combinations. And then—O weakness—she spied with her great sunny eye in far distant Louisiana a boy, highly talented; she forgot all about Anderssen, guided the steps of the young American, fell in love with him, introduced him to the world and said triumphantly: "Here is the young Paul Morphy, stronger and greater than master ever was." And the world listened and applauded and cried "Hurrah for Paul Morphy, the King of Chess."

Lasker did not mention it in his *Manual of Chess,* but from around 1910 to 1914 Caïssa must have been grinning from ear to ear. The world was suddenly full of wonderful players, all favored by the Goddess, and they were snapping at Lasker's heels. The two most prominent were Akiba Rubinstein and José Raúl Capablanca. But Lasker showed no inclination to meet either one of those two mighty challengers; he kept putting them off until the war came and put everything off. Lasker was talking about a match with Rubinstein in 1914, but only talking. Capablanca ever since 1909 had been chasing Lasker everywhere, demanding a chance at the title. Lasker found excuse after excuse to avoid a meeting with the Cuban. He imposed all kinds of unheard-of conditions for a match. Capablanca, not unreasonably, objected, and wrote a long letter to Lasker calling the negotiations "unfair." Whereupon Lasker, asserting that his honor was wounded, let it be known that Capablanca had insulted him:

> Vain effort! He is a young man whose chess career has been very short. He overrated himself. His record is a match won and one first prize. I have stood for twenty years before the chess world and have won many matches and first prizes. A more modest behavior would have been seemly. I am compelled to accept all challenges. But I have certain rights which protect me. Capablanca has disregarded those rights and must cede the place he has usurped to more worthy aspirants to the world's championship.

After the war, Rubinstein was nowhere near the player he had been, and Capablanca was the logical—indeed, the only— challenger on the scene. The chess world and the public would have it no other way. Capablanca had beaten every player in the world, and the championship would be a travesty until he and Lasker competed. At that, Lasker prolonged the negotiations for two years. But the time came when he could evade Capablanca no longer. Discussions about time, place, and purse were started. Things seemed to be all set in 1920, and *The New York Times* had an editorial about the forthcoming match, contrasting the difference in purses between chess players and prize fighters. Lasker and Capablanca, the *Times* said, stood at the head of the world's chess players, "but they are to contend for and divide,

60–40, only $8000, an amount for which Carpentier and Dempsey would scorn to lift their fists."

Then a bombshell. Lasker bowed out.

The *Times* broke the story on June 26, 1920. Lasker yielded the title to Capablanca without playing. In a letter to the challenger he offered a feeble excuse: "From various facts I must infer that the chess world does not like the conditions of our agreement. I cannot play the match, knowing that its rules are highly unpopular. I therefore resign the title of world's champion in your favor. You have earned the title, not by the formality of a challenge, but by your brilliant mastery. In your further career I wish you much success."

Capablanca, in Havana, was appalled. He said that he would immediately go to see Lasker in Amsterdam and attempt to work out an arrangement agreeable to all. He did not wish to become the world champion this way. Capablanca also had a bit of news that could not make Lasker unhappy. Havana, thanks to Capablanca's enthusiastic backers and the volatile sporting instinct of Latin Americans, had guaranteed a purse not of $8000 but of $20,000—incomparably the largest purse in chess history up to then. Sure enough, the reluctant Lasker was persuaded to play. It takes no great insight into the human mind to see that Lasker was terrified of Capablanca. The proud champion knew that he did not stand a chance, and he was desperately trying to avoid the humiliation of public defeat. On August 9, the terms were announced for a twenty-four-game match between Lasker and Capablanca in Havana. There were still details to be worked out, and Lasker threatened to withdraw in a dispute over traveling expenses. But these disputes were smoothed out, and the match started on March 16, 1921.

With the frame of mind he was in, Lasker was lost before the first Pawn was pushed. At that, the invincible Cuban could make only slow headway against the canny veteran. After nine games he had won only one; the rest were drawn. *The New York Times* sighed for the good old days of Morphy. "For these magnificos," said the *Times,* referring to Lasker and Capablanca, "it is something between humiliating and disgraceful that in nine games there should have been only a single decision." But at the end of the fourteenth game the score stood 4–0 in Capablanca's favor. Lasker's age was telling on him. At that point he resigned the match, giving illness as the reason. But he also gallantly said that in any event he could not have beaten Capablanca. A short time after the match he told a friend that Capablanca was unique. "Never had I met a player who could preserve for so long the delicate balance of a position and continue very gradually and by almost imperceptible degrees to increase a trifling, scarcely more than a theoretical, advantage until it became real and eventually decisive." Capablanca, who could not stomach Lasker any more than Lasker could tolerate him, was honest enough to rate Lasker at his true worth. As late as 1937 he said that Lasker was too old for a match, but for a single game he was still the most dangerous player in the world.

Lasker continued to play after he lost his title. He won a tournament in 1923. At the great tournament in New York in 1924—in which Capablanca, Alekhine, Réti, Nimzovich, Spielmann, Maróczy, the very best players then alive, participated—Lasker at the age of fifty-six took first place. He was getting old and looking it; he already had lost his teeth, he was gray, he looked shrunken. Many a veteran attending the tournament must have thought of the Lasker of 1894. The *Times* described the veteran of 1924: "Short, stocky, grizzled hair and moustache, aquiline nose, now and then a haze of tobacco smoke about him, the doctor, especially when he holds his left knee in his hands, looks like a sort of chess god, such is the inhuman calmness of the man." Lasker still was a commanding presence.

The following year he came in second at the big Moscow tournament. But the next time he hit the headlines, in 1927, it was under unpleasant circumstances. In January, 1927, he was invited to play in a New York tournament. Lasker curtly refused. He wrote a sizzling letter to the organizing chairman, Dr. Norbert L. Lederer, charging that in the 1924 New York tournament he had not received a fair share of the gate receipts and, worse, that he had been given a clock that had robbed him of at least fifteen minutes during the game. Lasker was unwise enough to make his letter public. A regrettable and most undignified yelling match followed. Lederer, clearly a man of spirit, answered by saying that Lasker had forgotten to stop his clock after one of his moves. Then the aroused Lederer filed some countercharges of his own. He in effect accused Lasker of being a cheat, saying that the doctor purposely smoked cheap, long, black cigars and puffed the smoke into his opponents' face. Why is it, Lederer rhetorically asked, that when Lasker was away from the chessboard he smoked nothing but the best Havana cigars? To support this, Lederer waved a clipping from a newspaper story: "As soon as the ex-champion lighted up one of his five-cent cigars other persons in the room hastily presented him with expensive cigars. These Dr. Lasker put away for his leisure, while he continued to puff energetically at the acrid black ones."

Said the appalled Dr. Lederer: "He indulges in virtual gas attacks on his opponents."

And there was yet more. Another trick of Lasker's, said Lederer, was to offer an illegal draw. If there is a triple repetition of moves, the rules call for a draw if the player on the move requests it. Lasker refined this rule to a fine art, said Lederer indignantly. He would offer a draw after a *double* repetition:

> He used that device in 1924 on the late D. Janowski, an extremely nervous player, who at the time was winning the game. . . . Janowski was so upset that he went all to pieces and Lasker took the game. In another game, with G. Maróczy, Lasker made a practice of jumping to his feet when Maróczy was deep in thought and haranguing the crowd for silence. He did that four or five times in succession, and Maróczy, much disturbed, finally protested.

Then Capablanca got into the act. Capablanca was disturbed by Lasker's insinuations that he was not a perfect sportsman. So Capablanca backed Lederer, and issued a statement to the press on February 3, 1927:

> Twice since 1921 I have found it necessary to defend myself against unwarranted attacks on the part of Dr. Lasker, and as a result have refused to talk to him for a number of years at a time. . . . It seems that Dr. Lasker tries to find an alibi every time he loses a game to me. In Havana it was a heat unheard of even in that climate, to say nothing of the food and even the sun, although we played at night. In New York his alibi was the clock. I have no doubt that if we played elsewhere he would find the climate too cold for him. One would imagine that since Dr. Lasker lost

the chess championship he is bent on obtaining some other championship. At the rate he is going, if he is not the alibi champion already, he very soon will be.

Lasker, on March 24, had the last word. His statement to the press called Dr. Lederer a tool of Capablanca's. Lasker scoffed at the charges made against him. "In conclusion," he wrote, "I beg to say that Mr. Lederer is by nature a partisan hero-worshipper, emotional, praiseworthy to that extent, but without sufficient impediments, irrational, incapable of constructive policy, and as an organizer and an impartial judge an utter failure.

Returning to Berlin, Lasker undoubtedly hoped to take it easy for the rest of his life. He announced his retirement early in 1931. But the Nazis came into power. Lasker and his wife fled to England and their property was confiscated. Once again he was penniless, and once again he had to turn to chess. He entered a few tournaments, not doing very well, though he did make a miraculous effort at Moscow 1935, winning a series of games before his age caught up. It was then that he decided to remain in Russia as director of a chess academy. Those were the years of the Stalin purges, and Lasker's protector was picked up one day and executed. Lasker immediately went back to England. His last tournament was Nottingham 1936. He ended up in sixth place. But that position does not tell the real story. Botvinnik and Capablanca, who tied for first, had ten points. Lasker had eight and a half. To give an idea of the might of this tournament, other players included Alekhine, Fine, Euwe, Reshevsky, Tartakower, and Bogolyubov, all at the peak of their career. The sixty-seven-year-old Lasker held his own against the best of the new generation.

His last years were spent in New York, where he taught chess, gave exhibitions, and did a little writing. But most of his income was derived from bridge. Lasker was a bridge player on a professional level; it was not generally known that he had been the leader of the German team at the Bridge Olympics. On January 11, 1941, he died. "The superman of the chess world," Fine said, and there were none to disagree with him.

10 ♛

Antiphlogistine, Madjesoomalops

During Lasker's long career, players came and went, but no player with the one exception of Capablanca came up so fast and with such explosive impact as Harry Nelson Pillsbury, "The Hero of Hastings." He was a legend in his day, this tall, good-looking, easygoing, chain-cigar-smoking American from Somerville, Massachusetts. Harry Nelson Pillsbury: he of the imperturbable chess game and the freak memory. In a brief career of ten years, this successor of Paul Morphy shed brilliant light on the world of international chess. Then, like Morphy, a mental disintegration set in. But Pillsbury's mental illness had physical rather than Freudian causes.

He learned the moves at sixteen, showed amazing talent, came to New York, settled in at the Brooklyn Chess Club, became the strongest American player at the age of nineteen, and at twenty decided to become a chess professional. Word of his strength got around, and even though he had no experience at all in international play he was invited to England to participate in the Hastings Tournament of 1895. What a lineup that tournament had! The new world's champion, Lasker, and the ex-champion, Steinitz, were among the players. Adolph Albin, the Rumanian-born master who was in the United States at the moment, also came from New York to participate. Albin was a famous theoretician of the day. England was represented by Bird, Gunsberg, and the dreaded Blackburne. Bardeleben of Germany was there, and Janowski from Paris, and the thirty-year-old Jac-

Harry Nelson Pillsbury, "The Hero of Hastings." Lasker blamed his early death on "overexertion of the memory cells."

ques Mieses from Leipzig, who was beginning to make a great name for himself. (Mieses had one of the longest chess careers in history. He started his tournament career at the age of twenty-three and was playing sixty years later. In 1948, at the age of eighty-three—he still had six years to live—he played an eighty-four-year-old Dutch master named van Foreest. Mieses won. "Youth has triumphed," he chortled. A nice man.) Karl Schlechter, the drawing master, and Siegbert Tarrasch, the teacher of chess to all Germany, came to try their skill. The young Richard Teichmann, who went on to a long and honorable career, was in his first major tournament. From Russia came the flashy Mikhail Tchigorin, one of the favorites to win. There was also a scattering of lesser players. Hastings 1895 probably had the strongest group of masters ever assembled for one tournament up to that time.

Among this Caïssaic constellation Pillsbury moved, as an unknown, with appropriate modesty. But as he started to topple the giants, the British press rushed to interview him. He made a good impression. Journalists said he looked like Lincoln, with his prominent nose, hollowed cheekbones, and piercing eyes. "Mr. Pillsbury," ran one description, "is decidedly pleasant and unassuming in manner, and a perfect type of American, and a tremendous smoker. He is remarkably self-composed and sits at the chess table in comfortable style and with a self-confident look on his face." His profile was described as "cameo-like, nobly cut," and his bearing "dignified and of gentle elegance." At the board he was said to have "an absolute strong calmness in his face; not a single muscle moves, only now and then he will blink a bit faster."

Pillsbury started out by losing to Tchigorin. Then he rebounded to beat the great Tarrasch—not only outmaneuvering him, but mating him on the fifty-second move:

	WHITE: PILLSBURY	BLACK: TARRASCH
1.	P-Q4	P-Q4
2.	P-QB4	P-K3
3.	N-QB3	N-KB3
4.	B-N5	B-K2
5.	N-B3	QN-Q2
6.	R-B1	O-O
7.	P-K3	P-QN3
8.	PxP	PxP
9.	B-Q3	B-N2

10.	O-O	P-B4
11.	R-K1	P-B5
12.	B-N1	P-QR3
13.	N-K5	P-N4
14.	P-B4	R-K1
15.	Q-B3	N-B1
16.	N-K2	N-K5
17.	BxB	RxB
18.	BxN	PxB
19.	Q-N3	P-B3
20.	N-N4	K-R1
21.	P-B5	Q-Q2
22.	R-B1	R-Q1
23.	R-B4	Q-Q3
24.	Q-R4	R(1)-K1
25.	N-B3	B-Q4
26.	N-B2	Q-B3
27.	R-B1	P-N5
28.	N-K2	Q-R5
29.	N-N4	N-Q2
30.	R(4)-B2	K-N1
31.	N-B1	P-B6
32.	P-QN3	Q-B3
33.	P-KR3	P-QR4
34.	N-R2	P-R5
35.	P-N4	PxP
36.	PxP	R-R1
37.	P-N5	R-R6
38.	N-N4	BxP
39.	R-KN2	K-R1
40.	PxP	PxP
41.	NxB	RxN
42.	N-R6	R-N2
43.	RxR	KxR
44.	Q-N3ch	KxN
45.	K-R1	Q-Q4
46.	R-KN1	QxBP
47.	Q-R4ch	Q-R4

48.	Q-B4ch	Q-N4
49.	RxQ	PxR
50.	Q-Q6ch	K-R4
51.	QxN	P-B7
52.	QxP mate	

This pretty win showed Pillsbury's fighting spirit. He had not been discouraged by his loss to Tchigorin, and he had not changed his style. In short order Albin fell to him, and Mieses, and—this electrified everybody—Steinitz. Remorselessly Pillsbury mowed them down—Emanuel Schiffers (one of the Russian players), James Mason, Janowski, and Teichmann. Finally Lasker snapped the string (Tarrasch thought that Pillsbury had a won position in this game but that he had thrown it away "by careless play"). Then a draw with Blackburne and Walbrodt, and wins against Bird, Burn, and Bardeleben (the Bardeleben win on a forfeit). At this point in the tournament there was a triple tie for first place. Lasker, Tchigorin, and Pillsbury each had thirteen and a half points.

In the meantime, it had not been all work for the contestants. Their British hosts tried to keep them entertained. All these entertainments were duly noted in the official book of the match, one of the more delightful browsing books in chess literature, full of charming little observations. On August 8 "the masters are taken to a special concert on the pier, and the enjoyment manifested proved the oft-made assertion that chess players are generally musicians. The masters had the option also of seats at the theatre to see *Charley's Aunt,* but *all* chose the music." Think of that. On August 15 the masters go to a reception, "and the gathering is of the most enjoyable character. The steps are draped with red cloth and lined with foliage plants, producing a very pretty effect." At this reception there was a musical program during which Miss May Mukle entertained the guests with two cello solos. (Miss Mukle was then fifteen years old. She later went on to a distinguished career.) On August 22 there was a banquet, the menu of which, "served with the usual excellence of the establishment," illustrates the staggering culinary intake of the Victorian Age:

Tortue Claire.
Saumon et Concombre, Sauce Mouselline.
Filets de Soles Frites.
Petites Bouchées de Homard.
Poulet Sauté à la Chasseur.
Aloyau de Boeuf.
D'Agneau Rôti, Sauce Menthe.
Légumes de Saison.
Caneton d'Aylesbury.
Pouding St. Clair aux Abricots.
Compôte de fruits.   Gelée au Marasquin.
Tarte de Pommes.   Custard.
Bavarois au Chocolat.
Pouding Glacé Nesselrode.
Dessert.

All was jollity at the banquet:

The usual toasts were honored, and some capital speeches made. Of the competitors, Mr. Lasker in the course of his speech spoke in favor of tournaments, and told us that he had taken up his residence in England and considered it his second fatherland. Mr. Steinitz told us that our Tournament would create a new era in chess. Herr Tchigorin chiefly thanked the Committee for kindly treatment, and took the opportunity of announcing the coming St. Petersburg Tournament. Dr. Tarrasch said that the excuse of some for doing badly was a good one, viz., that the lovely town was too charming and attractive, and a number of enchanting causes rendered them too happy. Mr. Bird spoke of the Tournament as unique.

The tie was broken on August 28. Pillsbury lost to Schlechter, while Tchigorin drew and Lasker won. But next round Lasker lost to Tarrasch, while Pillsbury beat Samuel Tinsley. Now Tchigorin was in the lead. There were three rounds to go. Pillsbury had no trouble winning from the weak Benjamin Vergani of Italy, and he then had a stroke of luck: Tchigorin was upset in only sixteen moves by Janowski, and Lasker lost to Blackburne. Thus, at the last round, Pillsbury was half a point ahead. Could he hold it? There was no problem. Gunsberg put up a good fight

but was outplayed. In this final game, Pillsbury showed the assembled masters something about end-game technique. Lasker,
who analyzed it for the program book, was highly impressed by
Pillsbury's thirty-eighth move, where he sacrificed a Pawn to push
his other Pawns through. A "remarkable combination," Lasker
wrote. Gunsberg tipped his King; Pillsbury was the winner of
the game and of the tournament, and "the cheers ring for him
in true British style." First prize was 150 pounds. Tchigorin,
Lasker, Steinitz, and Tarrasch were the runners-up. Vergani,
who came in last, got a consolation prize of two pounds. Hastings 1895 then disbanded. But everybody was talking about Pillsbury. There was amazement then that an unknown should take
first prize in so powerful a field, In later years theories were to be
advanced. The Spring, 1964, issue of the *Baker Street Journal*
had a learned article "proving" that the great Sherlock Holmes
impersonated Pillsbury at the tournament. But this theory is not
generally accepted in chess circles.

It was, of course, clear to the players at Hastings that Pillsbury had not won by a fluke. His style was imaginative, fertile,
and daring, and it was obvious that a new great player had unexpectedly appeared. If he could do this at his international
debut at the age of twenty-three, what would he not be capable
of when he grew up?

The American press received the news of Hastings with
ecstasy. A new Morphy had arrived. Americans promptly started
calling Pillsbury the world's chess champion. Had he not come
out ahead of Lasker and Steinitz? Pillsbury was amused and tried
to play down the acclaim. When he arrived home, on September
25, 1895, he told reporters that he had not expected to win the
tournament, though he thought that he would have a good chance
of finishing among the top three. "I don't know whether I would
win another important tournament," he said, "but I don't see
why I should not duplicate my success, for I now have valuable
experience and practice." About his loss in the first round: "I
was a little nervous when I was scheduled to play with Tchigorin
in my first game. I considered it hard luck, but during the
progress of the game this feeling wore off and changed to morti-
fication when I had to resign the game. I still feel sore on that
point. I boiled with rage but it stimulated me greatly for the

The great tournament at Vienna 1898. Every great player of the world at the time except Lasker can be seen here. Seated, left to right: Tarrasch, Blackburne, Pillsbury, Steinitz, Tchigorin, Janowski, Schiffers, Lipke. Standing, left to right: Schwartz, Schlechter, Fähndrich, Caro, Maróczy, Showalter, Marco, Alapin, Halprin, Baird, Burn. Pillsbury and Tarrasch tied for first place.

subsequent battles." Tchigorin, he said, was the strongest living match player. He calmly dismissed the others. "I should not feel at all troubled if I had to meet either Steinitz, Lasker or Tarrasch in a set match. I figure my chess is as good as theirs." Pillsbury, gentleman though he was, had the ego of any great chess player. What a pity that he and Lasker never met in a match.

Pillsbury never repeated his great triumph at Hastings, though he was always among the leaders in any tournament in which he participated. In 1895 he came in third at St. Petersburg, behind Lasker and Steinitz. It was there that he contracted the syphilis that was responsible for his early death. In 1896, Pillsbury tied for third at Nuremberg and was clear third at Budapest; in 1898, second at Vienna; in 1899, second at London; in 1900, tied for first at Munich and came in second in Paris. After that his health deteriorated badly, and he did not come in among the leaders at Cambridge Springs 1904.

He had a remarkable aptitude for blindfold chess and other memory freaks, and his exhibitions were famous in their day. Pillsbury would play up to twenty-two blindfold games at a time while also playing a hand of whist. Before his chess exhibition he would do memory tricks. Fifty numbered pieces of paper, each with a five-word sentence, would be given to him. He would read them and drop them into a hat. Then somebody would draw them out, one at a time, announce the number of the slip, and Pillsbury would rattle off the appropriate sentence. At the end, he would recite each sentence backward. Or a list of thirty words would be submitted to him, and he would memorize them instantly. Sometimes he would do this trick of word memorization *during* his combination of blindfold chess and card playing. In London a pair of professors decided to stump him and came up with the following list:

Antiphlogistine; periosteum; takadiastase; plasmon; threl-keld; streptococcus; staphylococcus; mirococcus; plasmodium; Mississippi; Freiheit; Philadelphia; Cincinnati; athletics; no war; Etchenerg; American; Russian; philosophy; Piet Potgleter's Rost; Salamagundi; Oomisillecootsi; Bangmamvate; Schlechter's Neck; Manzinyama; theosophy; catechism; Madjesoomalops.

Pillsbury glanced at it, returned the list, recited the words, and then repeated them backward. The following day he repeated the feat to show that he had *really* memorized the list.

To make a few extra dollars Pillsbury took anything in chess that came along. One of his jobs was to operate Ajeeb, the mechanical chess player. The eighteenth and nineteenth centuries saw three famous chess-playing automatons, the most famous of which was The Turk, originally built in 1769 by Wolfgang von Kempelen. This ingenious toy was a life-sized figure dressed as a Turk, and it operated amid a great hocus-pocus of cogs, gears, and other machinery. The Turk passed into the hands of Johann Maelzel, friend of Beethoven and inventor of the metronome. Maelzel brought it to the United States in 1826, and it ended up in the Chinese Museum in Philadelphia, where it was destroyed by fire in 1854. A chess player was of course hidden in it. Edgar Allen Poe figured that out in 1836 in his famous essay: "There is a man, *Schlumberger* . . . about the medium size, and has a remarkable stoop in the shoulders. Whether he professes to play chess or not, we are not informed. It is quite certain, however, that he is never to be seen during the exhibition of the Chess-Player, although frequently visible just before and just after the exhibition. . . ." Mephisto, another chess automaton, was shown in England in 1876. Gunsberg was hidden in it for a while, during which period Mephisto never lost a game. Ajeeb, which Pillsbury operated from 1898 to 1904, was originally built in England. This automaton ended up in Coney Island and was destroyed by fire in 1929.

Pillsbury was genuinely admired as a human being as well as one of the chess geniuses of his day. And he was at his peak for only five years, from 1895 to 1900. He had it in him to be the world's champion; during those years only Lasker was of equivalent stature. But those were also the years during which Lasker, concentrating on his doctorate, was relatively inactive in chess. Pillsbury always had bad luck. The chess world watched his physical and mental deterioration with dismay, and when he died, on June 18, 1906, genuine sorrow was expressed. Lasker, in an appreciation of Pillsbury written for *The New York Times,* blamed it all on Pillsbury's blindfold exhibitions; "He died from an illness contracted through overexertion of his memory cells" (a disease hitherto unknown in medical annals). In his magazine, in the issue of July, 1906, Lasker mourned over "that youthful, great and lovable man. . . . Those who knew Pillsbury in the days of his early youth will never forget the striking, almost beautiful face, which he bore in those days." Lasker went on to say that Pillsbury's success as a chess player came from "the newness of his analytical researches, a fine sense of combination, a sound position-judgment and an unlimited capacity for active study during the game." But Pillsbury, according to Lasker's diagnosis, was forced to overextend himself physically and mentally to earn his daily bread, and that gave Lasker a chance to get started on his favorite topic, the lack of money in chess. Had Pillsbury been able to earn a decent income, he would not have killed himself by the mental strain of blindfold play and memory exhibitions. "The victor of Hastings, the pathfinder in the thickest of chess theory, gifted with pleasant and lovable traits, a source of pleasure and joy and a teacher for thousands, he should not have been suffered to be without the comforts that make work easy and keep health intact. Instead he had to work hard, he had to spend the valuable matter of his brain on many 'entertainments' lasting six to ten hours in order to earn a barely sufficient livelihood."

11

The New Wave

Nearly all the players who dominated chess during the first two or three decades of the twentieth century were born within fifteen years of each other. Consider: Frank Marshall in 1877; Ossip Bernstein, Oldrich Duras, and Akiba Rubinstein in 1882; Rudolf Spielmann in 1883 (some sources give 1884); Eugene Znosko-Borovsky in 1884; Milan Vidmar in 1885; Aron Nimzovich in 1886; Saviely Tartakower in 1887; José Raúl Capablanca in 1888; Yefim Bogolyubov and Richard Réti in 1889; Alexander Alekhine in 1892. For years they were the foundation of any international tournament; none could be called complete without the roly-poly Spielmann unleashing his combinational thunders against the wily Tartakower; or without Capablanca and Alekhine grimly jousting each other and hating each other; or without Nimzovich, eccentric in manner and play, trying his newfangled theories against the romantic, debonair Marshall. From city to city they went, like the members of an opera company on tour, playing Hastings this month, Baden-Baden the next, Munich after that. And these players were as egocentric, temperamental, and bizarre a group as the members of any opera company; they regarded anybody else in the troupe as Mme Adelina Patti regarded Mme Etelka Gerster: definitely unsound; overblown reputation; what does the public see in *her*; what *can* the public see in her?

Of these prima-donna chess virtuosos, one of the greatest and perhaps the most tragic was Akiba Rubinstein, who came from the Polish ghetto, enjoyed some ten years of all but unbeatable chess, and then slowly, slowly, slipped into oblivion, a catatonic, living in his own mad world. A less likely candidate for grandmastership could hardly be imagined. For the first years of his life he spoke only Yiddish and Hebrew; he had been brought up in his native city of Stawiski to be a rabbi. At the age of sixteen he discovered chess and soon was strong enough to beat anybody in his vicinity. Any thoughts of the rabbinate were dropped, and he soon started international play. Rubinstein was a quiet man, not very bright, not very interesting, but when he started to appear on the circuit he had people talking to themselves, and the chess world suddenly realized that an overpowering genius had appeared. In 1903 he played in his first important tournament, at Kiev, and finished fifth. Four years later he was among the leading masters. In 1907 at Ostend he shared first with Bernstein. The same year he took an undisputed first at Carlsbad, ahead of Nimzovich, Schlechter, Vidmar, Tartakower, Janowski, and Tchigorin. In 1909 at St. Petersburg he shared first with Lasker. In 1912 he swept the field, taking first place in four consecutive tournaments. By 1914 he had appeared in twenty-two important tournaments, winning eight outright, tying for first four times and coming in second or tying for second six times.

Chess with him was an *idée fixe*. He worked full-time at the game and thought of nothing else. Rubinstein was as dedicated and compulsive as any player who ever lived or was to live. He once told an interviewer that he studied theory for six hours a day, three hundred days a year. Another sixty days were spent playing in tournaments. The remaining five days he rested. His grasp of chess was all-encompassing, and he could attack with the best of them. But it was his end game that was especially famous. The end game is absolute chess, pure chess, pure technique and imagination, the chamber music of chess. Major pieces have been traded off and now the object is to push the Pawns through. Rubinstein had no peer in the end game, and his opponents trembled when they came to the end game in a position that would appear to be an automatic draw. Somehow Rubinstein found continuations unseen by anybody else; his ingenuity was breathtaking. He sat over the board like a rabbi over the Torah, close to his God, seeming to draw strength from supernatural sources.

Akiba Rubinstein, child of the ghetto. For about fifteen years he was all but unbeatable. Then he slowly went mad.

His peers accepted him for the great master he was, and successive generations have raved about his superhuman intuition. "Rubinstein," says Euwe in his *Development of Chess Style,* "probably has more model games than any other player—flawless end games and also fantastic attacks studded with all manner of sacrifices." One such attacking game is Rotlevi-Rubinstein at Lodz 1908. It is called "Rubinstein's Immortal Game" because of its amazing Queen sacrifice:

	WHITE: G. ROTLEVI	BLACK: RUBINSTEIN
1.	P-Q4	P-Q4
2.	N-KB3	P-K3
3.	P-K3	P-QB4
4.	P-B4	N-QB3
5.	N-B3	N-B3
6.	PxBP	BxP
7.	P-QR3	P-QR3
8.	P-QN4	B-Q3
9.	B-N2	O-O
10.	Q-Q2	Q-K2
11.	B-Q3	PxP
12.	BxP	P-QN4
13.	B-Q3	R-Q1
14.	Q-K2	B-N2
15.	O-O	N-K4
16.	NxN	BxN
17.	P-B4	B-B2
18.	P-K4	QR-B1
19.	P-K5	B-N3ch
20.	K-R1	N-N5
21.	B-K4	Q-R5
22.	P-N3	RxN
23.	PxQ	R-Q7
24.	QxR	BxBch
25.	Q-N2	R-R6
	Resigns	

Games like this, Richard Réti says, are all the more amazing because Rubinstein suffered from nerves that would exhaust him and make him prone to blunder. "The fact that he could obtain such results in spite of this handicap speaks much for his truly great abilities. For Rubinstein has also created the most perfect games of the epoch since Steinitz." Rubinstein was "the keystone of this generation . . . the greatest artist among chess players. His games create the impression of a great structure from which not one stone could be shifted. . . . a priest in his art." Reuben Fine echoes Réti's estimate: "Better chess cannot be played by mortal man."

In his quiet way, Rubinstein was perfectly aware of his ability, and was proud of it. He even had a puckish sense of humor that once in a great while would surface. One charming story —one of the very few involving Rubinstein—has come out of the Carlsbad 1907 tournament. Rubinstein was in first place, closely followed by Maróczy. In the twentieth round, Rubinstein met Heinrich Wolf. The German player had the White pieces, and he offered Rubinstein a draw—the so-called "grandmaster draw" —on the tenth move. In a grandmaster draw two players, feeling lazy, or tired, or for some reason unwilling to go through the effort of playing the game, willl make a few perfunctory moves and end quickly by tacit consent. All Rubinstein needed was the draw to ensure first place, but he refused. He played on, had Wolf in a vise, and then offered a draw to Wolf, who gratefully and immediately accepted. Why? Everybody wondered. Why? Rubinstein had an easy win. And why had he refused Wolf's offer of a draw in the first place? He was asked. "With Wolf," Rubinstein said, "I make a draw when *I* want to, not when *he* wants to."

But even during his great years Rubinstein was having mental problems, and they began to interfere with his play after 1910. At best his behavior was peculiar. During a game he would study his position and, after making a move, rush away and hide in a corner while his opponent was in turn studying the board. Rubinstein did this because of natural politeness and deference to his opponent; he did not wish to disturb him while he was on the move. But it was noticed that while Rubinstein was away from the board he would cover his mouth with his hands and have conversations with himself. He would never shake hands with people; they were trying to contaminate him with germs. He never ate in public, only in his room.

Then there was the sad business with the fly. After San Sebastian 1911, Mieses met Rubinstein on a train to Munich. Rubinstein told Mieses that he was going to see a famous doctor because of the fly. A fly was settling on his head and disturbing him during play. Constantly it kept buzzing. And every night, Rubinstein earnestly continued, there was a knocking on his door and on the walls, so that he could get no sleep.

With all this, Rubinstein continued to play winning chess, and a championship match between him and Lasker was being worked out in 1914 when the war came. But already poor Rubinstein was on his way down. At St. Petersburg 1914, he was not among the prize winners for the first time since his youth. After 1918 Rubinstein was completely erratic. He did some playing and once in a while could pull himself together and get good results; but more often his play was feeble and he would make elementary blunders. Silent previously, he was now entirely uncommunicative. At Bad Kissingen 1928, one of Rubinstein's last tournaments, Tartakower mentioned, halfway through, that Rubinstein had uttered his tenth word in two weeks. After 1932 the rest was silence. Rubinstein lived in Brussels and was catatonic toward the end. An appeal for funds to help him was made by the *British Chess Magazine* in 1933, and some money was raised. Rubinstein was threatened with actual starvation. At his death in 1961 he had not played chess for about thirty years.

On the opposite side of the pole was the flamboyant, crowd-pleasing Frank Marshall of the United States. After Morphy's two great years in 1858 and 1859, there were about three decades of quietude on the American chess scene. Some promising talent was developed, but there is a difference between being a promising talent and being an international star. The Civil War may have been responsible; goodness knows how many geniuses in how many fields may have been destroyed. In *Lasker's Chess Magazine* of December, 1905, there is a tantalizing reference to "J. A. Leonard, who died during the Civil War. He was a young lad, receiving the odds of a Queen from the leading players of New York, and a week later defeated them all on even terms, and won several tournaments and matches with an ease and confidence that was truly astonishing." And so there went a potential Pillsbury. James Mason, the Irish-born master whose family emigrated to the United States when he was a child, developed into a strong player, but alcoholism kept him from the heights. Later he returned to England. Mason had the habit of beating the greatest masters and of being beaten by weak ones. As the *Chess-Monthly* said, "Mason must be judged by what he could do, not by what he has done." Another émigré was Scotland's George Henry Mackenzie, a dependable and talented player. There was Jackson Whipps Showalter, "The Kentucky Lion," who was strong enough to beat Janowski in two matches. These were all good players with respectable international records. But then came Pillsbury, to restore the United States almost to the pinnacle to which it had been raised by Morphy. And after Pillsbury came Frank Marshall.

Marshall had a long life—1877 to 1944—and there are still many around who remember the great old man. He habitually wore flowing ties that made him look like a Shakespearean actor; a cigar was always glowing in his mouth; a twinkle was always in his eye. Marshall, tall, courtly, dignified, delighted in simultaneous exhibitions and at one time held the world's record by taking on 155 players (that was in 1922; he won 126, lost 8, and drew 21). It was Marshall who had played one of the most sensational moves in chess history against Lewitzky at Breslau 1912. It used to be said that when Marshall made the famous twenty-third move, the chessboard was showered with gold pieces. It should have been, but the story is apocryphal. Chess audiences do not *have* pieces of gold to throw away. But nevertheless that move is legendary:

	WHITE: LEWITZKY	BLACK: MARSHALL
1.	P-Q4	P-K3
2.	P-K4	P-Q4
3.	N-QB3	P-QB4
4.	N-B3	N-QB3
5.	KPxP	KPxP
6.	B-K2	N-B3
7.	O-O	B-K2
8.	B-KN5	O-O
9.	PxP	B-K3
10.	N-Q4	BxP

11.	NxB	PxN
12.	B-N4	Q-Q3
13.	B-R3	QR-K1
14.	Q-Q2	B-N5
15.	BxN	RxB
16.	QR-Q1	Q-B4
17.	Q-K2	BxN
18.	PxB	QxP
19.	RxP	N-Q5
20.	Q-R5	R(1)-KB1
21.	R-K5	R-R3
22.	Q-N5	RxB
23.	R-QB5	Q-KN6
	Resigns	

If White takes the Queen with either Pawn, mate follows almost immediately. White's best move is QxQ, but after 24. N-K7ch, 25. K-R1, NxQch, 26. K-N1, NxR, 27. PxR, White is a piece down. So Lewitzky resigned.

Marshall was born in New York. His family moved to Canada when he was a child. He discovered the game before he was ten years old. "Chess began to absorb my whole life," he later wrote. "My head was full of it, from morning to night—and in my dreams as well." From the age of ten he played at least one game of chess every day in his life; and, as a full-time professional, he appeared in every tournament he could enter, every match he could promote. When not playing in tournaments he was teaching, or giving simultaneous exhibitions, or running his famous chess club in Greenwich Village. He could lose, and lose badly, as he did to Lasker and Capablanca, but back he always bounced, eternally optimistic, glorying in the battle of chess and the clash of opposed personalities. He was, first and last, an attacking player, a combination player, a master in the style of Anderssen and Blackburne but with a better positional sense than either of those two. Marshall had a *feeling* for chess. "It's just like card sense or an ear for music," he explained. "Some have it, some don't." He knew his style, he understood its limitations—and he would have it no other way. "From the first I was an attacking player, forever on the offensive. This often got me into trouble.

... As a chess player I suppose I am a little like Jack Dempsey as a fighter. Dempsey used to start slugging at the opening gong and never gave an opponent a chance to get started." When Marshall encountered another attacking player it was indeed a slugfest, with Marshall generally knocking out his opponent. But that would not work against such complete players as Capablanca, and Marshall admitted that he always had trouble with defensive players.

It was at the age of sixteen that he knew he was going to become a chess professional. He went overseas in 1899, and in 1900 came in third at his first important tournament, in Paris, beating Pillsbury and Lasker in single games. That was promising, and Marshall made London his headquarters. It was easy to get to the big tournaments from London. From 1901 to 1903 his record was spotty. Time after time he lost first place because of his determination to win every game. "When will I learn that a draw counts more than a loss?" In 1904 he started to show major results: first at Cambridge Springs 1904 ahead of Lasker; first at Scheveningen 1905; at Nuremberg 1906; and at Düsseldorf 1908. Players marveled at his ability to retrieve games apparently lost, and the term "Marshall swindle" entered the chess vocabulary. He married and returned to New York. For many years—from 1906 to 1936—he was the United States chess champion and the spiritual father of American chess. Although he stopped his international tournament play in the 1920's, his influence remained widely felt; any young player coming up in the United States was helped one way or another by Frank Marshall.

Capablanca summed up Marshall's position as a chess player in a *New York Times* article written in 1927. Marshall, he said, never rose to the championship because of impulsive attacks and inaccuracies in combinations. But nevertheless Marshall was a player to be reckoned with:

> A hard worker with original ideas, Marshall has contributed many a startling move to the technique of the openings. For years in different openings he has played variation after variation not accepted as correct by most of the leading experts of the time. Some of these experts looked upon certain of those variations with absolute contempt; yet time after time, through these variations,

Marshall could bring about brilliant and startling defeats of his opponents. . . . By temperament an attacking player, he is capable when called upon of putting up a very stubborn defense. In the endings, contrary to many people's idea, Marshall is an A1 performer.

Central Europe was represented at the turn of the century by such players as Milan Vidmar and Oldrich Duras. Vidmar was the first player of importance to come out of Yugoslavia; he was born in Ljubljana in 1885 and developed into a steady competitor: never a world-beater but not a man to be trifled with. Alekhine wrote of Vidmar rather condescendingly: "All told, perhaps, he is no lion in the realm of chess, but he is highly dangerous to those who permit themselves to be intimidated [deceived?] by his apparent harmlessness." Duras from Prague continued the tradition of Maróczy and the young genius Rudolf Charousek (1873–1900), who died at the age of twenty-seven from tuberculosis. Charousek, born near Prague but later resident in Budapest, was of potential championship caliber, and Lasker himself predicted that one day he would be defending his title against the young Bohemian. But the Keatsian life of the unfortunate Charousek put an end to that. Duras flourished during a ten-year period from 1903 to 1914, when he usually came out very high in tournaments. After 1914 he played little chess, though he lived until 1957.

Then there was Rudolf Spielmann (1833–1942) from Vienna, nicknamed "The Last Knight of the King's Gambit" because of his predilection for that attacking game. Spielmann was the Frank Marshall of Austria. When it came to attack he deferred to nobody; and it was predictable that when he came to write a book it should be named *The Art of Sacrifice in Chess*. He was in private life a mild little man who took out all his aggressions over the chessboard. This led to unequal tournament results. There were times when he was unstoppable, as at Semmering 1926, when he took first place ahead of Alekhine, Vidmar, and Nimzovich. And he captured many other important tournaments during the course of his career. Toward the end of his life he had to flee to Sweden; otherwise he would have ended up in a Nazi gas chamber. He died neglected and forgotten.

In his day he was a feared player, but he seldom posed a threat to Capablanca or Alekhine. Attacking players like Spielmann and Marshall never do very well against the completely rounded master. As Alekhine wrote, Spielmann was too great a gambler: "It is well known that this sensitive artist is capable of top-notch performances, but also that when he is not in form he can disappoint most grievously." Alekhine alluded to Spielmann's great win at Semmering, as opposed to his poor showing at Bad Kissingen 1928. "He has to conquer errors of a sporting nature as well as such as have to do with chess. As an artist he is impelled by an impetuous passion for combinations, which, although they have earned him a number of brilliancy prizes, have also lost him many an important point in tournament scores." Alekhine also suggested that Spielmann could be too easygoing —"a slightly exaggerated good-naturedness which at times could not be distinguished from indifference." To the fierce, competitive Alekhine, who concentrated on every move the way Toscanini or Szell concentrated on every note, that attitude was sinful. Szell was once told that he conducted as though every note was a matter of life or death. "But don't you see?" he said, "It *is*. It *is*." Alekhine had the same attitude about every move he made in chess, and tended to despise players without his kind of dedication.

From Russia suddenly came a powerful group that culminated in Alekhine. It became so strong that the Russians were to "own" international chess; a Russian held the championship from 1927, when Alekhine conquered Capablanca, until 1972, when Fischer took the title from Spassky (with the exception of the two-year period when Max Euwe held the championship). Tchigorin was the first Russian player to come storming out, and it was he who sparked the Russian chess renaissance. After him came, in chronological order, Tartakower, Bernstein, Znosko-Borovsky, all born in the 1880's, and Alekhine, born in 1892.

Some of these, it is true, were Russians only by virtue of having been born on Russian or Russian-owned soil. Tartakower, for instance, was born in Rostov-on-Don of Austro-Polish parents and left Russia in 1899. His parents were murdered in a pogrom. Tartakower studied in Switzerland, took a law degree in Vienna, and eventually became an Austrian citizen, serving with distinction as an infantry lieutenant during World War I. After the war he concentrated on chess, becoming a professional and taking up residence in Paris (he became a French citizen in 1924). An inveterate gambler (like Janowski, he invariably lost his prize money at the roulette tables), a poet, philosopher, screen-writer, Tartakower was something of a loner, and he had no real friends. Not that he went out trying to make friends. He was bitter and sarcastic and would not let anybody get close to him. During World War II he served under de Gaulle. He died in Paris in 1956, alone and penniless.

A strong player and a prolific writer, Tartakower was very important in the development of modern chess, for he was both player and theorist on the highest level. He won many tournaments, but never had the ambition or dedication that would have put him into world championship competition. Yet he compiled an impressive tournament record: firsts at Nuremberg 1906 and Vienna 1923; Hastings 1926, 1927, and 1945; Ghent 1926; Paris 1929, 1940, and 1947; Liege 1930; Nice 1930; Lodz 1935. As a chess stylist he straddled the romantic school of Anderssen and the hypermodern of Breyer and Réti. Indeed, he was the first to call Réti and his school "hypermoderns." Tartakower himself was of no school. He played for the beauty of it; he was, it was said, more interested in a beautiful move than in a winning move. And he was a hard man to beat. He loved to revive all kinds of forgotten openings and variations—which, of course, he had thoroughly studied in advance, and which caught his opponents by surprise. He also had a wry wit, and the world of chess delightedly seized upon his observations. Tartakowerisms, they were called:

> The blunders are all there, waiting to be made.
> The winner of a game is the one who has made the next-to-last blunder.
> Sacrifices only prove that somebody has blundered.
> It is always better to sacrifice your opponent's men.
> Moral victories do not count.
> A threat is more powerful than its execution.
> An isolated Pawn spreads gloom all over the chessboard.
> Tactics is knowing what to do when there is something to do; strategy is knowing what to do when there is nothing to do.

Top left: Frank Marshall (right) *playing a skittles game with Alexander Alekhine. Marshall was one of the great romanticists and attacking players of history.*

Top right: Rudolf Spielmann, the sacrificial genius, "The Last Knight of the King's Gambit."

Bottom left: Aron Nimzovich, the hypermodern. His opponents accused him of being as confused as they were.

Bottom right: Saviely Tartakower, grandmaster and theorist, creator of "Tartakowerisms."

Ossip Bernstein and Eugene Znosko-Borovsky were two other players who left Russia and settled in Paris. Bernstein (1882–1962) took a law degree at Heidelberg in 1906, then returned to Russia and became a practicing attorney. After the Revolution he escaped to Paris, where he continued as a lawyer-businessman-chess player. From 1903 he was placing high in tournaments. Had Bernstein concentrated on chess he might have been one of the strongest players in the world. But there were long periods when he did not play at all, and it is a wonder that Bernstein came out as well as he did. Even as an elderly man he was dangerous, and as late as 1956, at the age of seventy-four, he was scoring 50 per cent in his tournaments. He even won a tournament in Montevideo in 1961, the year before his death. At one time he was considered world championship material. Which is more than can be said of Znosko-Borovsky (1884–1954), a good player but one who lacked the stamina for the long run. A Parisian after 1917, Znosko-Borovsky wrote several highly regarded chess books and also achieved some fame as a literary and drama critic.

Yefim Bogolyubov (1889–1952), like so many Russians, fled after the Revolution. But he was not one of the group to end up in Paris. Instead, he became a naturalized German. During the 1920's he was at his height and was generally considered the world's third strongest player, below Capablanca and Alekhine. If nothing else, though, his ego was on a par with theirs. Bogolyubov honestly believed he could win against anybody at all times. "When I play White I win because I have the first move," he once said. "When I play Black I win because I am Bogolyubov." Then the smart younger players started coming up, and Bogolyubov began to lose steadily against such hungry demons as Botvinnik, Fine, Keres, and the others. "The young people have read my book," he explained. "Now I have no chance." Fat, easygoing, inclined to laziness, Bogolyubov was interested in only two things: chess and beer. He was the cause of great merriment at Nottingham 1936. Bogolyubov knew only one word of English. At dinner a waiter in his hotel came up and asked him for his room number. "Beer," Bogolyubov said.

From next door to Russia came Nimzovich of Riga. Nimzovich (or Niemzowitsch, as his name was invariably spelled in the 1920's) has been called "The Father of Modern Chess." He took from Tartakower, refined Tartakower's ideas, and was a strong influence on the hypermodern group of the 1920's. Nimzovich was the Steinitz of his day. His opponents could not figure out what he was trying to do and complained bitterly about his strange, crabbed, often illogical-appearing moves and cramped positions. Even so great a player as Capablanca, who did pay tribute to the "extraordinary powers" and originality of Nimzovich, wondered what was going on in his mind. Not only were Nimzovich's opponents confused, said Capablanca, but Nimzovich himself was as confused as they were. "He plays such bizarre openings and such complicated games that very often he is just as much puzzled as his opponent, if not more so."

This bizarre kind of play worked for Nimzovich, who won six (and twice tied for first) of the twenty-four major tournaments in which he participated. Like Lasker, Nimzovich always felt confident of outplaying his opponent.

He was born in 1886 and learned the game at the age of eight. In 1904 he went to Berlin, where he was supposed to attend the University. Instead, he played chess incessantly at the Kaiserhof. Then he started his international career, taking up residence in Copenhagen. His prewar record was only fair, and not until the 1920's did he hit his stride. His greatest success came at Carlsbad 1929, where he came in first ahead of Capablanca, Tartakower, and Bogolyubov. He was not popular with his colleagues; he was surly, arrogant, conceited, almost paranoiac. People were out to poison him. Noise bothered him. Spectators bothered him. Playing conditions bothered him. *Everything* bothered him. Not unnaturally, he was in constant controversy with other players. They objected to his antics and he objected right back. At one tournament the entire body of players registered a protest against Nimzovich. How could they concentrate while he was doing calisthenics on the stage, doing knee bends, and standing on his head? He did all this because he had been told by a physician that exercise was good for him.

Possibly he could have become world's champion if not for his pathological nervousness. Certainly he had the talent. He examined chess orthodoxy and called it faulty, accusing Tarrasch of routine dogmatism. Nimzovich had a different and new set of ideas: first restrict, then blockade, finally destroy. He worked out a kind of chess, fully explained in his book *My System,* that threw overboard the Tarrasch concept of a Pawn center. The center, Nimzovich preached, could be controlled *without* Pawns. The opponent had to be kept from expanding and developing. Thus arose the theory of the blockade, a concept that was to be refined still further by Réti and Breyer. Nimzovich died in 1935, leaving to posterity some of the most puzzling and yet most subtle games on record. A representative example of his play would be his game against Salwe at Carlsbad 1911. Nimzovich himself nominated it as the first hypermodern game in history, "the first in which my new philosophy of the center was exhibited." The idea of this game centers around a dour, stubborn struggle for domination of White's K5 square. Note how Nimzovich eventually succeeds in blockading the center with BxN instead of blockading with his Pawns. The result is a constricted game for Black. This, in 1911, is altogether modern chess:

	WHITE: NIMZOVICH	BLACK: SALWE
1.	P-K4	P-K3
2.	P-Q4	P-Q4
3.	P-K5	P-QB4
4.	P-QB3	N-QB3
5.	N-B3	Q-N3
6.	B-Q3	B-Q2
7.	PxP	BxP
8.	O-O	P-B3
9.	P-QN4	B-K2
10.	B-KB4	PxP
11.	NxP	NxN
12.	BxN	N-B3
13.	N-Q2	O-O
14.	N-B3	B-Q3
15.	Q-K2	QR-B1
16.	B-Q4	Q-B2
17.	N-K5	B-K1
18.	QR-K1	BxN
19.	BxB	Q-B3
20.	B-Q4	B-Q2

21.	Q-B2	R-KB2
22.	R-K3	P-QN3
23.	R-N3	K-R1
24.	BxRP	P-K4
25.	B-N6	R-K2
26.	R-K1	Q-Q3
27.	B-K3	P-Q5
28.	B-N5	RxP
29.	RxR	PxR
30.	QxP	K-N1
31.	P-QR3	K-B1
32.	B-R4	B-K1
33.	B-B5	Q-Q5
34.	QxQ	PxQ
35.	RxR	KxR
36.	B-Q3	K-Q3
37.	BxN	PxB
38.	K-B1	B-B3
39.	P-KR4	Resigns

12 ♛

The Chess Machine

When José Raúl Capablanca defeated Lasker in 1921 to become the chess champion of the world, there were various emotions expressed by his colleagues, the press, and the public, but among those emotions the element of surprise was missing. For so many years Capablanca had been invincible that the result of the match was confidently anticipated by everybody. In the 1970's much was written about "Fischer-fear," but the concept had been used long before in relation to the great Cuban player. Capablanca was wrapped in a mantle of invincibility; he had the aura; and even the best players in the world had a dreadful feeling of inferiority and inadequacy when they sat before him. It was magic. Without seeming to do anything wrong, they would somehow drift into lost positions. The games of all other players showed tension, struggle, work. Capablanca's games were smooth, effortless, simple-looking. How did he do it? But the results spoke for themselves. In Capablanca's first nine years of international play, from 1909 to 1918, he played 155 games, winning 100, drawing 46, losing only 9. In the next twenty years he won 191 and lost 24. From 1914 to 1924 he played 126 tournament and match games and lost only 4. At the New York 1924 tournament he lost to Réti. So unexpected was that loss, so unbeatable had Capablanca been, that *The New York Times* commemorated Capablanca's loss in a headline: CAPABLANCA LOSES/1ST GAME SINCE 1914. (The *Times* for once was inaccurate, for Capablanca had lost a game to Chajes in New York in 1916.) In his entire career

Capablanca in 1927, the year he lost his title to Alekhine. Nobody had expected him to lose. Alekhine never gave him a chance for a return match.

of some seven hundred games, Capablanca lost only thirty-five. No wonder he was called "The Chess Machine." And he publicized chess more than any other player who ever lived prior to the emergence of Bobby Fischer. People who knew nothing at all about chess followed his exploits breathlessly. His very name was an international trademark; he was to chess what Paderewski was to the piano and Einstein to theoretical physics: a symbol, known to everybody.

Perhaps there is a relationship between a child prodigy and having a classic style. In music the greatest of the prodigies—Mozart, Mendelssohn, Saint-Saëns—turned out to be classicists, perfect technicians to whom everything came effortlessly. Their music was clear and emotionally uncluttered. In chess, three of the four supreme prodigies were also classicists. The exception was Reshevsky, who favored close, complicated positions. But the other three—Morphy, Capablanca, and Fischer—represent open positions with long lines and clear developments. Simplicity rather than baroque complication is the hallmark of their style—that plus the total technique that comes as a result of growing up with, and being as one with, the materials of their art. The Mozarts of music and the Capablancas of chess do not even have to *think* when creating a masterpiece; much of it is done on an intuitive level. Capablanca, who during his lifetime said things that threw the chess world into a tizzy, once remarked, "To play chess requires no intelligence at all." This statement caused excitement, especially among the grandmasters of the day. Great chess players have always had pleasure in passing themselves off as giant intellects. Nonsense, said Capablanca. Chess was not scientific. Rather it was an artistic manifestation. Creating a chess game was like drawing a picture, except that two persons rather than one were engaged in the undertaking.

Certain it was that Capablanca's gifts had a Mozartean purity about them. His mind operated at a level of synthesis that took in everything over the board as naturally as breathing. He learned the moves at the age of four while watching his father; he seemed to absorb the essence of the game from a hidden source, and he never had to study. Many players say they do not study, but with Capablanca it was true. When he defeated Marshall in a match in 1909, with a lopsided score of 8 to 1 with fourteen draws, he had done a great deal of offhand playing at the New York chess clubs but had not studied theory at all. "The most amazing thing of all," Capablanca wrote about the Marshall match in his autobiography, with a certain complacency, "was the fact that I played without ever having opened a book to study the openings." He claimed that in his whole career he had studied only one chess book, a treatise on the end game given to him when he was a child. He did not have to study. "I knew at a glance what the position involves. What may happen. You guess. I know." There was nothing wrong with Capablanca's ego. But his good opinion of himself was echoed by his colleagues; indeed, *had* to be echoed by them. For Capablanca was not merely an idle braggart; he was demonstrably in a class by himself, and even his closest rivals were forced to admit it. "Neither before nor afterwards have I seen such flabbergasting quickness of chess comprehension," admitted Alexander Alekhine, who did know something about chess himself. And: "His speed of play was incredible. What others could not discover in a month he saw in a glance," said Reuben Fine.

Capablanca was born in Havana on November 19, 1888. His father, an officer in the Spanish army, was an enthusiastic chess player. Capablanca says that his father never taught him the moves. At the age of five the boy was already a strong player. At twelve he defeated J. Corzo, the champion of Cuba, in a match. This was the decisive game:

	WHITE: CORZO	BLACK: CAPABLANCA
1.	P-K4	P-K4
2.	N-QB3	N-QB3
3.	P-B4	PxP
4.	N-B3	P-KN4
5.	P-KR4	P-N5
6.	N-KN5	P-KR3
7.	NxP	KxN
8.	P-Q4	P-Q4
9.	PxP	Q-K2ch
10.	K-B2	P-N6ch
11.	K-N1	NxP
12.	QxN	Q-B4

13.	N-K2	Q-N3
14.	QxQ	RPxQ
15.	N-Q4	B-QB4
16.	P-B3	R-R5
17.	B-K2	BxNch
18.	PxB	RxQP
19.	P-N3	N-B3
20.	B-N2	R-Q7
21.	B-R5ch	NxB
22.	BxR	P-B6
23.	PxP	N-B5
24.	B-K5	R-N7ch
25.	K-B1	R-B7ch
26.	K-K1	N-Q6ch
	Resigns	

After finishing high school in Havana, Capablanca was sent to the United States. He entered Columbia University in 1906. He was supposed to study chemical engineering, but instead he spent most of his time at the Manhattan Chess Club, where nobody could hold him. "As one by one I mowed them down, my superiority became evident." Soon he dropped the pretense of becoming a chemical engineer and left school for good. Chess occupied all his time. He made a tour of the United States and then arranged for a match with Marshall, who did not especially want to meet the young Cuban. Who was he? A flashy club player at best. And Marshall must have known that he had little to gain and everything to lose in a match with Capablanca. Marshall, after all, was an internationally famous player who only two years previously (1907) had played Lasker for the world's championship. If he now conquered Capablanca, that was to be expected. If he was unable to beat Capablanca . . . Marshall, being Marshall, did not give much thought to that prospect. He sat down to teach the upstart a lesson.

Marshall shortly learned, as Blackburne, Anderssen, Janowski, and the other attacking players had learned before him, that attack was of no avail against a player with supreme technique. The well-rounded master will always beat the pure romantic. Capablanca exulted in his 8 to 1 victory. "I can safely say

that no player ever performed such a feat, as it was my first encounter against a master, and such a master, one of the first ten
in the whole world."

In 1911 Capablanca went overseas to San Sebastian. It was his
first international tournament, and it was a very strong one. All
the world's leading players except Lasker were there. Some objected to Capablanca's admission; he was not strong enough; he
had no reputation; San Sebastian was not for flashy amateurs.
Ossip Bernstein was the one who objected the loudest. Capablanca met him in the first round, won handily, and got a brilliancy prize for the game. "Before this game the strongest of the
masters looked upon me as an easy prey to their wiles; but after
it the feeling changed to something more akin to awe than anything else." Capablanca had no false illusions about his skill. In
this tournament he was especially proud of his win against
Janowski. In his notes to the game, he wrote: "I should add that
the end game coming is perhaps the finest of its kind ever played
over the board, and that for some unknown reason it has not been
properly appreciated. It is a masterpiece." Capablanca won the
tournament, losing only one game, to Rubinstein. It was the
greatest entry into international chess since Pillsbury startled the
world at Hastings 1895.

Tours followed. In 1913 the Cuban Government gave Capablanca a position in the foreign ministry. It was really an honorary
position. Capablanca never worked much as a diplomat. But the
job removed all financial pressure from him, and both sides were
happy: Capablanca because he could devote himself undisturbed
to chess, and the Cuban Government because Capablanca was
the best good will ambassador the country had ever had. Wherever Capablanca was playing, the Cuban Government transferred
him to a post in that particular city. It could do no less for its
living legend. And Capablanca was a most attractive legend.
Easygoing, full of Latin charm, he was five feet, eight inches tall,
clean-shaven, with an olive complexion and a brilliant smile. He
was always in perfect health, was an enthusiastic tennis player, an
avid card player (bridge especially), a good billiards player, and
in general a happy extrovert. He was spoiled and had to have his
way; the same might be said of every major chess player in history. He was also a ladies' man. His first marriage ended in di-

vorce, after which there were the ladies of three continents to console him. Late in life he remarried, and it was a happy union. He was a night owl. "During the years in which I saw a great deal of him," Edward Lasker has written, "I do not remember his ever breakfasting before I had my lunch." *The New York Times* gives a good description of Capablanca in 1921, after he had won the championship from Lasker:

> In appearance the new champion is utterly unlike the popular conception of a chess player. The beard, the spectacles, the furrowed brow, the rounded shoulders, the clouds of smoke, the careless attire—all these are absent. The new champion looks more like a successful business man than a chess player. When not studying the board he seems younger than he is . . . and he is nearly always in high spirits, full of fun, a real wit in all the humors of the chess room.
>
> Furthermore he is good-looking, smooth-shaven, of medium height, with a well-proportioned body of patrician mold, the head and brow being of particularly fine cast. He dresses with care, has excellent manners, and converses in fluent English, including an apt use of idioms. Also, unlike the traditional chess master, he is by no means absorbed in the game. Everything interests him. Except when playing or preparing for play, he forgets chess and enjoys life as any healthy, lively minded young man of 32 should who can afford it.

During his European tours Capablanca met them all, winning tournaments and defeating the best that the world had to offer. At St. Petersburg 1914 there was a temporary setback. He came in second—for him, dreadful. Capablanca blamed it on "exhaustion" and "poor physical condition." Yet from that tournament came a game that Capablanca selected for Marshall's *Chess Masterpieces* as his very best "from the artistic point of view." Capablanca was playing the Black pieces against Bernstein. Marshall annotated the game and was ecstatic over Capablanca's twenty-third move: "It must have been at this juncture that Mr. Capablanca worked out the beautiful combination which led to one of the most artistic and dramatic conclusions ever seen in master play." At the end, White has the choice of losing his Rook or being mated, so he resigns:

WHITE: BERNSTEIN   BLACK: CAPABLANCA

1.	P-Q4	P-Q4
2.	P-QB4	P-K3
3.	N-QB3	N-KB3
4.	N-B3	B-K2
5.	B-N5	O-O
6.	P-K3	QN-Q2
7.	R-B1	P-QN3
8.	PxP	PxP
9.	Q-R4	B-N2
10.	B-QR6	BxB
11.	QxB	P-B4
12.	BxN	NxB
13.	PxP	PxP
14.	O-O	Q-N3
15.	Q-K2	P-B5
16.	KR-Q1	KR-Q1
17.	N-Q4	B-N5
18.	P-QN3	QR-B1
19.	PxP	PxP
20.	R-B2	BxN
21.	RxB	N-Q4
22.	R-B2	P-B6
23.	KR-QB1	R-B4
24.	N-N3	R-B3
25.	N-Q4	R-B2
26.	N-N5	R-B4
27.	NxBP	NxN
28.	RxN	RxR
29.	RxR	Q-N7
	Resigns	

During the war years Capablanca spent most of his time in the United States, touring, giving simultaneous exhibitions, and appearing in what few tournaments there were. An interesting thing happened at a tournament in New York in 1918. Marshall, who had been smarting ever since his drubbing in 1909, had something up his sleeve for Capablanca. He had analyzed one of the games that he had lost, had found a brand-new continuation

that would give him (or so he thought) a won position, had secretly tested it through the years, and had reserved it for Capablanca. In 1918 he served up this prepared variation to Capablanca with a smug smile. (Prepared variations are common in
master play. Pillsbury, for instance, had been beaten by Lasker at
St. Petersburg 1895. Pillsbury then spent much time analyzing
that game and worked out a new idea in the opening, saving it
for use against Lasker. He wanted revenge. Finally, at Cambridge
Springs 1904, he had a chance to use his new move against Lasker,
who could not solve it over the board and lost the game.) Marshall
waited almost ten years to spring his new move on Capablanca.
One look, and Capablanca knew it was a prepared variation. But
noblesse oblige. He accepted Marshall's challenge. As Capablanca
tells the story:

> I thought for a while before playing this, knowing that I would
> be subjected to a terrific attack, all the lines of which would of
> necessity be familiar to my adversary. The lust for battle, however,
> had been aroused within me. I felt that my judgment and skill
> were being challenged by a player who had every reason to fear
> both (as shown by the records of our previous encounters), but
> who wanted to take advantage of the element of surprise and of
> the fact of my being unfamiliar with a thing to which he had de-
> voted many a night of toil and hard work. I considered the posi-
> tion and then decided that I was honor bound, so to speak, to take
> the Pawn. . . .

Capablanca, relying on his instinct, solved Marshall's prepared variation over the board and went on to win the game.

It was ironical that Capablanca, after chasing Lasker since
1911, after finally achieving his goal of becoming the chess champion of the world, should immediately adopt Lasker tactics and sit
on his title. Not until six years later did he meet his first opponent, Alekhine. There was restlessness in chess circles during
those six years, and a growing feeling that something should
be done about the situation. But who was empowered to act?
There was no governing body, and the newly created Fédération
Internationale des Échecs had no teeth as yet. Rubinstein challenged Capablanca after the Lasker match but was unable to
raise his share of the purse. In London, 1922, a group of grand-

José Raúl Capablanca, "The Chess Machine," in Havana, 1921, during his match with Lasker. At that time Capablanca was considered invincible.

masters got together to work up a set of rules for future championship play. These London Rules stipulated that a champion must play within a year of receiving a challenge from a bona fide player. But nothing came of that. Nobody could *force* the champion to play. Alekhine challenged Capablanca in 1924, and nothing came of it. In 1925 the chess community felt that the world chess championship was too important to be left to the champion. There were demands that Capablanca defend against Alekhine, against Bogolyubov, against *somebody*. Finally, in December, 1926, Alekhine's backers in Buenos Aires put up $10,000 guaranteed by the Argentine Chess Club. Capablanca, at long last, accepted. He probably had no worries. Alekhine had yet to win a single tournament or match game from him. Before the start of the match Capablanca wrote an estimate of himself for *The New York Times*. It was an honest piece of self-analysis and had some curiously negative things to say. Could it be that Capablanca was getting old? Was this a hint that something unusual was going to happen? Capablanca contrasted the player of youth with the player of maturity:

> It might be interesting to compare the past with the present. At San Sebastián in 1911, our first international encounter, we did not have much confidence of carrying the chief prize, but we had plenty of ambition, and having been favored by the goddess of chance, we succeeded in winning the honor.
>
> Today we have plenty of confidence, the confidence which only years of continuous success can give, but most of our ambition is gone, and the fickle lady has not been kind to us of late.
>
> Then we were practically ignorant of our opponents' qualities, but we had a tremendous capacity for work. Today we know our opponents thoroughly, but alas! our capacity for work is not the same.
>
> Then we were very nervous and easily upset. Today we are cool and collected and nothing short of an earthquake can ruffle us. We have more experience but less power.

In this article Capablanca also presented a picture of the challenger as he saw him. Alekhine, he said, was the scion of a noble Russian family, over six feet tall, light-haired, blue-eyed, altogether a commanding figure. He was highly cultured and

Capablanca and Lasker, the two old antagonists, face each other at the tournament in Moscow 1925.

spoke over half a dozen languages fluently. "He has what is probably the most marvellous chess memory that ever existed. It is said that he knows by heart every game played in any tournament by either a first-class club player or a master during the last twenty-five or thirty years. He certainly knows by heart all the games played by any of the first-class masters."

But Capablanca was not alarmed. For, he wrote, Alekhine "has not the proper temperament for match play. We think that he has not the proper combative spirit. Furthermore, he is extremely nervous, qualities both of which should work to his detriment in a long and protracted struggle against a cool and resourceful opponent." How Capablanca misjudged his man! If there was *one* thing Alekhine had, it was determination. No more combative player ever existed. In view of what happened during the match, Capablanca's estimate of Alekhine has its ironical aspects indeed.

Naturally, Capablanca was the heavy favorite. Earlier in the year he had played a tournament in New York in which he had come in first, ahead of Alekhine, Marshall, Spielmann, Nimzovich, and Vidmar, without losing a game. Thus he should have been in perfect shape for the Alekhine match, which started in Buenos Aires on September 17, 1927. The London Rules of 1922 were used: the winner would be the first to take six games. Draws did not count. A time limit of forty moves in two and a half hours was imposed (this time control was the one to be followed in nearly all subsequent grandmaster matches and tournaments).

The Capablanca-Alekhine match turned out to be a long, murderously exhausting struggle, featured by draw after draw. Capablanca suddenly found himself fighting for his life. Alekhine had studied all his games and had come to the conclusion that Capablanca was not invincible. There were weak spots unexplored by previous players. Perhaps, too, Alekhine was banking on Capablanca's overconfidence. For the first time in his career Capablanca found himself up against an opponent he could not dent. After the first twenty games, the score was 3 to 2 in Alekhine's favor, with fifteen draws. At this rate the match threatened to stretch over into 1935; the irresistible force had met the immovable object, and the two mighty forces were canceling each other out. Through October and November they battled, and the Argentine Chess Club had to put up additional funds. Who had expected a match of this duration? But it was Capablanca who cracked under the strain. Alekhine won the twenty-first game. Now he was leading, 4 to 2. Games twenty-two through twenty-eight were drawn. Capablanca was not giving an inch; and yet he was unable to make headway. Capablanca won the twenty-ninth game, making the score 4 to 3. Games thirty and thirty-one were drawn. On November 23, Alekhine won his fifth game, the thirty-second game of the match. A draw followed. On November 26, in the thirty-fourth game, Alekhine adjourned with the advantage of a Pawn. Capablanca fought all the way to a second adjournment. On November 28 there was still another adjournment after the eighty-first move. But at this point Capablanca was in a hopeless position. Alekhine knew that he would win the game and the match. He announced that if he won—not that there was any doubt about it—Capablanca would have the first chance to challenge. On November 29, Capablanca resigned without resuming play. The score was 6 to 3 with twenty-five draws, spread out over seventy-four days.

Capablanca said that Alekhine had won by not missing more than one or two chances while he, Capablanca, had missed no less than ten, "enough to win two matches." Chastened, he said that he had learned from the match that he was no longer able to enter a contest without preparation. "It is evident to us that in the future if we wish to succeed in any such enterprise we shall have to enter the arena fully prepared both physically and mentally and lead the kind of life that will keep us in the best condition, since we possess no longer, neither mentally nor physically, the great resisting power that formerly carried us through on so many occasions."

As for Alekhine, he was—or pretended to be—astonished. Most likely it was no pretense. Deep down, nobody expected to beat the Capablanca of 1927. Years later Alekhine was asked how he had won. "I must confess that even now I cannot answer that question," he said.

For the rest of his chess career Capablanca unsuccessfully chased after Alekhine, demanding a rematch. He never had a chance. Alekhine would play anybody in the world—except Capablanca. This came as no surprise to many grandmasters. Ossip Bernstein and others had predicted that there would never be a return match. But although Capablanca pursued Alekhine in vain, his career was far from over. In 1931 he defeated Euwe in a match, and in 1936 he took first places at Moscow and Nottingham, both powerhouse tournaments. Then deteriorating health made him slow down. He developed high blood pressure and retired from competition in 1939. On March 7, 1942, while watching a game at the Manhattan Chess Club, he had a stroke and died the following morning.

A good way to start an argument among chess players is to bring up the topic of the greatest natural chess player of all time. Some will say Morphy. Some will say Capablanca. Some will say Fischer. There are no other real candidates. Capablanca played so easily and fluently that he made chess appear to be the simplest of games. Indeed, he played so effortlessly that he tended to become bored. Only a bored player would have asserted, as Capablanca did in 1925, that chess had become too dry and mechanical, too bookish, too subject to analysis. He suggested adding two extra squares and two new pieces to the board, an idea that was greeted with something less than enthusiasm in chess circles. Those were the days, after all, when Alekhine was showing the world how inexhaustibly fertile the game of Philidor, Morphy, Steinitz, and Lasker could be. But Capablanca closed his eyes to that kind of chess. His kind from the beginning avoided complications. That was because he found his style as a boy and never went through a maturing phase (like Mendelssohn and the E flat Octet at sixteen and the *Hebrides* Overture at seventeen). As the Swedish grandmaster, Gideon Stahlberg, once pointed out, Capablanca had inborn chess genius almost as a baby. As a player he was *born* mature, and there was to be little difference between early and late Capablanca. Chess was not the struggle, the Idea of struggle, to Capablanca that it had been to Steinitz and Lasker. There were those who accused Capablanca of perpetually taking the easy way out in his effort to avoid struggle— of avoiding battle, of playing superficially, relying on his immense technique to see him through, and settling for a grandmaster draw if the going threatened to get difficult.

During the Lasker-Capablanca match, the number of uneventful draws aroused much comment; and through his entire career Capablanca was criticized for the inordinate number of lackadaisical draws to his (dis)credit. In 1922 chess circles were up in arms at the London Tournament, at which Capablanca and Rubinstein agreed to a thirteen-move grandmaster draw. Neither felt like playing that day, and the sponsors of the tournament, not to mention the paying public, made it clear that the two great players were in effect cheating. But what to do about it? One suggestion was that the strongest players meet in the earliest rounds. Thus they would not arrange or (perish the thought) prearrange draws when the half point had a real bearing on their tournament standing. Another suggestion was that draws count one-third instead of one-half of a point. Anything to stop this deplorable conduct. *The New York Times* condemned the behavior of Capablanca and Rubinstein, and also charged Alekhine with accepting a grandmaster draw in the same tournament. "Although these players," said the *Times*, "knew perfectly well that the games between Capablanca and the two others were looked forward to by chess followers all over the world, they deliberately refused to play those games. They went through a few perfunctory moves and then announced a draw. Neither the champion, who could have added to his prestige, nor his rivals, who might have gained new fame, tried to win. All were afraid to risk a loss. They preferred to make sure of their standing in the tournament at the time."

That and that alone is the only shadow on Capablanca's radiant chess career. This flawless technician, who made a science of chess, who (in the words of Dr. Euwe) "banished the romantic and the experimental" by his superprecise play—this genius only too often failed to extend himself to his full powers. Capablanca "is not sparing in offers to agree to a draw," wryly noted Dr. Euwe. Perhaps it was that he could not accept the possibility, no matter how remote, of losing. The "invincible" Capablanca would have found it too great a blow to his ego. Otherwise he lives permanently on as the Mozart of chess—pure, classic, elegant, subtle, refined, yet capable of demonic force in his great moments: the master of masters, the complete technician, the creator of many beautiful games unflawed in their logic and inevitability.

13 ♛

Outrageous, Unprecedented, Monomaniacal

Just as matter is opposed to antimatter, so there had to be an Alexander Alekhine in opposition to a José Raúl Capablanca. Where Capablanca's games were of unsurpassed clarity, striving for simplicity and classic balance, so Alekhine's games were of immense complexity, characterized by a striving for complications. Alekhine's style was bewildering, baroque—and successful. In his tournaments he took first prize thirty-five times, tied for first twelve times, and was second five times. At San Remo 1930, in a tournament that contained most of the world's best players, he swept the field 14 to 1 without losing a game. Few could solve the problems he threw at them over the board. "His playing was fantastically complicated, more so than any player before or since," Bobby Fischer has written. ". . . He played gigantic conceptions, full of outrageous and unprecedented ideas." If Capablanca was the Mozart of chess, Alekhine was the Wagner. He was so resourceful, so much a master of all phases of chess, his orchestrations were so rich and sonorous, his harmonies so chromatic and verging on the dissonant, that hardly anybody of the day could follow him. The saying arose that Alekhine had to be beaten three times in any single game—once in the opening, once in the middle game, once in the end game. Edward Lasker calls him the greatest *inventive* genius the game has ever had. Euwe calls him the greatest attacking player of all time. He could shake combinations out of his sleeve and suddenly explode a position that ap-

Alexander Alekhine—amoral, alcoholic, and one of the greatest, most inventive minds in the history of chess.

peared to be static. Always his restless mind was experimenting, testing, inventing. Always he worked on chess; with Rubinstein before him and Fischer to come, he was one of the all-time mono-maniacs. After the London tournament of 1922, he and Capablanca were taken to the music hall by a chess patron. Capablanca never took his eyes off the girls on the stage. Alekhine never took his eyes away from a pocket chess set. The "greatest" chess player who ever lived? The argument is futile; there is no greatest anything. But Alekhine belongs among the select four or five in chess history, with Morphy, Lasker, Capablanca, and Fischer.

The man was a chess genius. During and after his lifetime the chess world paid full homage to his extraordinary ability. But few would care to say much in his favor as a human being. Not that many knew him very well. Alekhine, like so many chess geniuses, was a loner with no close friends. Socially he was a monster. For many years an alcoholic, he would drink brandy by the tumblerful, and once while drunk he urinated on the floor during a match. A virulent racist, he wrote anti-Semitic articles in the *Deutsche Zeitung in der Niederlanden* for the Nazis during World War II. It infuriated him when his name was pronounced Al-OKCH-in. That was a Jewish pronunciation; the correct pronunciation was Al-YEKCH-in. Chess patrons learned never to invite Alekhine to their homes; he was known to steal money and attempt to seduce their wives. His ferocious will to win in *everything* made him even more unpopular with his colleagues. The story is told of a ping-pong game he played with Salo Flohr: just as Flohr was about to serve the winning point Alekhine grabbed the ball and yelled, "Stop the game! Adjourned!" Alekhine tried to pass it off as a joke, but everybody knew that he could not stand losing to Flohr. Reuben Fine has written about his first encounter with Alekhine:

> I recall when he visited New York in the early part of 1933, he came to the Marshall Chess Club, where I was the champion, and played a number of offhand games with me. This was in itself most unusual, as I was impressed by the throng of famous masters who kept themselves aloof from chess outside of tournament play. But not Alekhine. In these games I just about held my own with

him and at this he became so furious that he demanded that a skittles match be arranged for a small stake; he could not bear the thought that anyone might beat him, even in offhand games. In other games his will to win was just as great and soul-consuming. When he lost at ping-pong he would crush the ball in anger. . . . A great genius but a sick man.

This strange man was married four times. His last three wives were considerably older—at least twenty-five years older, Edward Lasker believes. "Besides Bacchus, Oedipus must have been among his ancestry." He could be as superstitious as a Russian peasant, and during his second match with Euwe he wore a jersey with a black cat embroidered on it. That would bring him luck. Alekhine had a thing about cats. He always had a Siamese around, and often would bring it to tournaments, where it would stroll through the congress rooms. Even among chess players Alekhine's ego was colossal; that was one reason why he had no friends. The world could contain only him. After a while he was not even interested in women, partly because of his heavy drinking, and partly because his consuming passion for chess blocked out every other activity.

It was a passion that led him to create many of the most brilliant games in the literature. He was a nervous tiger who stalked his prey with involuntary physical twitchings and psychic lust. Always he was in motion while playing a game, chain-smoking, pacing back and forth, twisting a lock of his hair. A game with Alekhine was seldom cut and dried; he aimed for a disruption of balance, throwing the openings out of "book" and plunging directly into unknown territory. Nobody could figure out how his games darted into such peculiar conformations. "I can see the combinations as well as Alekhine," said the baffled Spielmann, "but I cannot get to the same positions." Alekhine envisaged chess as the creation of a perfect, inevitable structure. While playing he could get infuriated at a player whose vision was not on a level with his own. For then the game was flawed, imperfect, dishonest even, and not through any fault of his own. This was an artistic sin not to be borne; it prevented Alekhine from realizing the product of his brain and of his vision. "Right here," he once wrote, "enters that moment where the art of chess may be called the most tragic of all the arts, because the chess artist, in a measure, is dependent on an element that is totally outside the scope of his power: that element is the hostile co-workers who through carelessness constantly threaten to wreck a flawless mental edifice. The chess player who tries to demonstrate the 'how' of a game will view the single point scored a poor offset for the failure to gratify his artistic yearnings." Thus Beethoven raged at a violinist who dared come between him and his vision.

The game that Alekhine considered one of his two most brilliant was played against Réti at Baden-Baden 1925. Réti had White, and used his hypermodern opening, P-KN3. The game developed into an example of the incredible complications Alekhine could get into. On his twenty-sixth move he found a startling Rook sacrifice. But White cannot accept it, for if he takes the Rook, QxPch followed by NxP wins for Black. Alekhine relentlessly increases the pressure and White finally is forced to resign because he must lose a piece:

	WHITE: RÉTI	BLACK: ALEKHINE
1.	P-KN3	P-K4
2.	N-KB3	P-K5
3.	N-Q4	P-Q4
4.	P-Q3	PxP
5.	QxP	N-KB3
6.	B-N2	B-N5ch
7.	B-Q2	BxBch
8.	NxB	O-O
9.	P-QB4	N-R3
10.	PxP	N-QN5
11.	Q-B4	QNxQP
12.	N(2)-N3	P-B3
13.	O-O	R-K1
14.	KR-Q1	B-N5
15.	R-Q2	Q-B1
16.	N-QB5	B-R6
17.	B-B3	B-N5
18.	B-N2	B-R6

19.	B-B3	B-N5
20.	B-R1	P-KR4
21.	P-N4	P-R3
22.	R-QB1	P-R5
23.	P-R4	PxP
24.	RPxP	Q-B2
25.	P-N5	RPxP
26.	PxP	R-K6
27.	N-B3	PxP
28.	QxP	N-B6
29.	QxP	QxQ
30.	NxQ	NxPch
31.	K-R2	N-K5
32.	R-B4	NxBP
33.	B-N2	B-K3
34.	R(4)-B2	N-N5ch
35.	K-R3	N-K4ch
36.	K-R2	RxN
37.	RxN	N-N5ch
38.	K-R3	N-K6ch
39.	K-R2	NxR
40.	BxR	N-Q5
	Resigns	

Born in Moscow on November 1, 1892, Alexander Alekhine was the son of a nobleman. His mother was the daughter of a rich industrialist, and it was she who taught him the moves. At fifteen he was playing in tournaments. He also studied at the Imperial Law School in St. Petersburg. In his first international tournament, Hamburg 1910, he came out in a tie for seventh. Alekhine did not make the cometlike appearance of a Pillsbury or Capablanca; he matured more slowly. He took first place at Stockholm 1912, however; he tied Nimzovich for the Russian championship in 1914; and that same year came in fourth below Lasker and Capablanca and Tarrasch at the spectacular St. Petersburg Tournament.

There are varying stories about his war experiences. Alekhine never bothered to clear them up. Some sources state that Alekhine served with the Russian Red Cross, was decorated for bravery, was captured by the Austrians and spent most of the war years in a prison camp. Another version, which appeared in a biographical account of Alekhine in *The New York Times* of December 8, 1937, states that he was in Mannheim when the war broke out, and that he was interned at Triberg, along with Bogolyubov and other enemy aliens. There he spent the war with nothing to do but play chess and sharpen his game. Still another version has him escaping from Triberg, joining the Russian army, and being wounded on the Austrian front. There are other romantic Alekhine stories of the period. According to one account, he was imprisoned on his return to Russia after the war and sentenced to death as a White Russian. The intercession of an important Bolshevik admirer saved him.

In 1920 he won the Russian championship. The following year he took up residence in Paris and got a doctorate in law from the Sorbonne in 1925, the same year he became a French citizen. Alekhine never practiced law. He was too busy playing chess, and from 1921 he became the terror of the circuit. Player after player fell before him; tournament after tournament was captured by him. A match with Capablanca was inevitable; they were the two greatest players alive at the time. Capablanca, of course, was considered invulnerable in 1927. Alekhine showed that he was not.

But after Alekhine became the world's champion, he too followed precedent by not being anxious to defend his title very often or against the strongest opposition. And he ran the other way when Capablanca's name was mentioned. After their title match in 1927 they did not play each other until nine years had passed.

They finally faced each other at Nottingham 1936. Capablanca won the game and also shared first prize with Botvinnik for the tournament. How Alekhine and Capablanca hated one another! They were not on speaking terms and would have spirited quarrels if they happened to be thrown together. Alekhine spent a considerable part of his literary output trying to "prove" that Capablanca was not the player he was reputed to be. And he spent an equal amount of time trying to outdo Capablanca in everything. If Capablanca could play 200 players simultaneously, which he did in New York in 1931 (fifty tables, each with a team of four players), Alekhine could go that one better, as he did in Paris in 1932, when he took on 300 at the Hotel Claridge, repeating the feat later in the year at the 7th Regiment Armory in New York. And Alekhine excelled in at least one aspect of the game that never interested Capablanca—blindfold chess. In Paris, on February 1, 1925, Alekhine established a world's record of twenty-eight boards, winning twenty-two, losing three, and drawing three. At Chicago 1933, he broke his own world record by playing thirty-two simultaneous blindfold games. The exhibition took twelve hours. Alekhine won nineteen, lost four, drew nine. When it was all over he made a characteristic comment: "I would have no fear in tackling thirty-five, maybe up to forty . . . and would not set the limit even there."

Constantly he was sniping at Capablanca. In a *New York Times* article on August 1, 1929, he discussed modern chess and broke it into two groups. The Capablanca-Maróczy-Vidmar-Euwe group was one. These kinds of players, Alekhine scornfully said, do not look on chess as an art. They are interested only in winning. The "what" of chess is more important to them than the "how"; and "only in rare instances, when their creative instinct masters their sporting will, do they become interested in the 'quality.' " The chief villain of this school was Capablanca, a "pseudo-scientist" whining that the game has become sterile and played out. How different are the players of the other group! Look at Breyer, Réti, Bogolyubov, Nimzovich, Sämisch, and Colle. (Breyer and Réti headed the hypermodern school of the 1920's. Friedrich Sämisch was a German player and theoretician. Edgar Colle was a promising Belgian who died at the age of thirty-four in 1932.) These masters, unlike Capablanca, have demonstrated that "there remains plenty of scope for the development of the imagination, temperament, and will power. To their achievements the game of chess, since the war, owes its unexpected advance." And, writing as an observer at Carlsbad 1929, Alekhine managed to insert some snide and even contemptuous remarks about Capablanca: "It is true that the Cuban has succeeded [in winning the tournament]—but not without some lucky accidents

—to carry through his obvious intention to draw games against dangerous opponents and 'swallow all the small fish' by means of his superior technique." And elsewhere: "Capablanca has not been confronted with the absolute necessity of demonstrating some big idea or of creating something positive." He wins merely by sitting back and waiting for his opponents to make mistakes.

These remarks bear the stigmata of envy and even fear. The fact remains that Alekhine never gave Capablanca a chance to play for the title. It was not for want of Capablanca's trying; his chase after Alekhine was unremitting. Alekhine kept dangling vague or, in some cases, specific, promises; then he would promptly renege. Capablanca's cries of lamentation were loud, his tears evoked a sympathetic response from everybody, his efforts were herculean—but no match. In January, 1928, he asked the National Chess Federation of the United States to intercede in his behalf. Alekhine promised to meet Capablanca for a match in the United States in 1929. But he demanded the same conditions as in the Buenos Aires match. Capablanca wanted a sixteen-game match. That gave Alekhine an excuse for dropping the negotiations. On February 26, 1929, Capablanca told the Associated Press that a match with Alekhine had "definitely" been worked out. There was, to be sure, a championship match later that year—but it was Alekhine versus Bogolyubov in a thirty-game series. On December 4, 1929, newspapers reported that Alekhine had accepted Capablanca's challenge for a match in 1930. On June 17, 1930, the story broke that an Alekhine-Capablanca match would start on February 15, 1931. But, Alekhine ominously said, he did not want to play in Cuba because, as a native of a northern country, he would be at a disadvantage in the hot climate. There was no match. And so the game of hide-and-go-seek continued year after year. It got to the point where Capablanca formally claimed the title by default, but nobody listened to him.

During those years Alekhine kept a sort of franchise on the title by playing Bogolyubov twice. He knew full well that the burly "Bogo" would give him no trouble. The first Alekhine-Bogolyubov match was held between September 6 and November 12, 1929, in four European cities. Alekhine won, 11 to 5 with

*Alexander Alekhine (left) and Yefim Bogolyubov during their title match
in 1929. Unidentified standing man is probably the referee. Bogolyubov
never had a chance. That is why Alekhine selected him as his opponent.*

nine draws. At the end of this match Alekhine made a speech saying that he would now be prepared to defend his title against Capablanca or Nimzovich. Of the two he preferred Nimzovich. In an article assessing the match with Bogolyubov, Alekhine wrote that the playing was on "an immeasurably higher level" than a match with Capablanca would have been. Bogolyubov at least had imagination, while Capablanca was merely a technician with a "negative" style. But at the Alekhine-Bogolyubov rematch in 1934 there was a plethora of dull games and draws. Alekhine beat Bogolyubov 8 to 3 with fifteen draws. At the end of the match Alekhine promptly announced a title match with Machgielis (later shortened to Max) Euwe of Holland, to be held in 1935. He also announced that Capablanca would be next in line—provided that Capablanca would agree to the same conditions as in the 1927 match.

To the infinite surprise of the chess world, Alekhine proceeded to lose the match and his title to Euwe. It was known that Euwe was a strong player—but *that* strong? Euwe, born on May 20, 1901, near Amsterdam, was a prodigy who learned the moves at four, won a tournament at ten, and was Dutch champion at twenty. He also studied mathematics at the same time and received his doctorate in 1923. After that he took up teaching. Euwe always was a part-time chess player, and when he won the championship he described himself as an amateur. Urbane, courteous, civilized, a thorough sportsman, Euwe as a chess player represented the scientific school. A profound student of opening theory, the author of many chess books and articles, Euwe was a player who believed in the immutability of logic in chess and in life. He was very precise in his play. "Does the general public, do even our friends the critics, realize that Euwe has virtually never made an unsound combination?" Thus Alekhine, no less, in the Manchester *Guardian*. The debonair Euwe asked Hans Kmoch to analyze him and his play in his (Euwe's) own book, *Meet the Masters*:

> Euwe will go down in chess history as the apostle of method. He is a Doctor of Mathematics, a qualified actuary, licensed to teach book-keeping, an accomplished boxer, swimmer and aviator. He

has written more books than any three other living masters put together. How does he do it? By ordering his whole existence like a railway time-table, dividing it neatly into water-tight compartments, applying to his life the same sort of disinterested logical analysis that another teacher of mathematics might reserve for his theories alone. . . . He cannot fall back on instinct because he has supplanted instinct by reason. He probes into a position as methodically as ever; given unlimited time, he could work out the theorem; but, alas, his clock is ticking against him and he blunders —he has committed more blunders in good positions than any other chess master who ever lived.

The Alekhine-Euwe match, for a purse of $10,000, started in Zandvoort on October 3, 1935. According to the terms, the winner had to score fifteen and a half points in the thirty games of the series, draws counting half a point. Alekhine took an early lead of 6 to 3, but Euwe managed to pull abreast. On December 13 the score was 15 to 14 in favor of Euwe (nine wins, eight losses, thirteen draws). On December 15 Euwe won the championship. The twenty-sixth game, promptly christened "The Pearl of Zandvoort," in effect drove the final nail into Alekhine's coffin:

	WHITE: EUWE	BLACK: ALEKHINE
1.	P-Q4	P-K3
2.	P-QB4	P-KB4
3.	P-KN3	B-N5ch
4.	B-Q2	B-K2
5.	B-N2	N-KB3
6.	N-QB3	O-O
7.	N-B3	N-K5
8.	O-O	P-QN3
9.	Q-B2	B-N2
10.	N-K5	NxN
11.	BxN	BxB
12.	KxB	Q-B1
13.	P-Q5	P-Q3
14.	N-Q3	P-K4
15.	K-R1	P-B3

16.	Q-N3	K-R1
17.	P-B4	P-K5
18.	N-N4	P-B4
19.	N-B2	N-Q2
20.	N-K3	B-B3
21.	NxP	BxB
22.	NxQP	Q-N1
23.	NxP	B-B3
24.	N-Q2	P-KN4
25.	P-K4	PxP
26.	PxP	B-Q5
27.	P-K5	Q-K1
28.	P-K6	R-KN1
29.	N-B3	Q-N3
30.	R-KN1	BxR
31.	RxB	Q-B3
32.	N-N5	R-N2
33.	PxN	RxP
34.	Q-K3	R-K2
35.	N-K6	R-KB1
36.	Q-K5	QxQ
37.	PxQ	R-B4
38.	R-K1	P-KR3
39.	N-Q8	R-B7
40.	P-K6	R-Q7
41.	N-B6	R-K1
42.	P-K7	P-N4
43.	N-Q8	K-N2
44.	N-N7	K-B3
45.	R-K6ch	K-N4
46.	N-Q6	RxKP
47.	N-K4ch	Resigns

It was a close match. The final score was 15 1/2 to 14 1/2, Euwe immediately offered Alekhine a rematch. Alekhine accepted, blaming his loss on a combination of factors:

I was absolutely stale after about eighteen months of uninterrupted chess work. . . . The result was that I arrived for the opening of the match really sick of chess; and to force myself to think of chess I had recourse to various stimulants, such as tobacco in excess and, above all, alcohol. These stimulants might have done little harm in a short contest (and, indeed, I played fairly well in the first few games), but proved absolutely fatal in the long run. In these circumstances, defeat became inevitable.

Alekhine, really shocked, was not going to make that mistake again. He stopped smoking and drinking and concentrated on regaining his title. He spent much time carefully analyzing every game Euwe played in the 1935 to 1937 period, read all Euwe's articles and commentaries, and worked on new lines of play, saving them for Euwe. When they met once again in 1937, Euwe (who had been lionized by his countrymen and was perhaps overconfident) was outplayed, and Alekhine became the first deposed champion in history to regain his title. The final score was 11 to 6, with thirteen draws. Euwe took the loss like the good sport he was, and he also became the first player in history *not* to explain his defeat by ill health or natural cataclysm. He came right out and said that the match had turned up weaknesses in his play. "Nevertheless, if my tournament results justify my doing so, I may make an attempt to recapture the title four or five years from now. For the time being such an idea is out of the question, for my opponent is indisputably my better." But that was not to be. There was little international play during World War II, and Euwe refused to participate in local tournaments sponsored by the Nazis. After the war, Euwe resumed playing. He had a good result at Groningen 1946, coming in second to Botvinnik and ahead of Smyslov, Najdorf, and Szabó. But he was in last place in the 1948 tournament to find a successor to the late Alekhine. After that, Euwe played no serious chess. In 1972, as president of FIDE, he had the unpleasant task of dealing with Bobby Fischer in Reykjavík.

As champion again, Alekhine was free to pick his opponent. He started talking about a match with the sensational newcomer, Salo Flohr of Czechoslovakia. But the chess world decided to make up his mind for him, knowing full well that Alekhine would never meet a player who was a strong threat to his title. A tournament

Max Euwe (left), *who defeated Alekhine in 1935 and lost in 1937. Euwe represented the new scientific school. Here he is playing the American star Reuben Fine in Holland 1936.*

was organized in 1938 by the Dutch Broadcasting Company—the Algemeene Vereeniging voor Radio Omroep. The initials of that company—AVRO—gave the tournament its name. Alekhine played in it, as did Capablanca, Euwe, and the best players of the new generation, including Fine, Keres, Botvinnik, Reshevsky, and Flohr. This was a formidable field. Surely the next world champion was among these players. But Alekhine, in a speech to the assembled dignitaries and players before the match started, squashed the idea of AVRO's being set up to find his challenger. According to a report in the *Chess Review* of December, 1938, Alekhine

> stated that all sorts of rumors were being circulated to the effect that the winner of this tournament would have preference over all others in arranging a match with him for the world championship. These rumors presumably originated because of his contract with the AVRO, in which he agrees to play the winner under conditions to be formulated later. He stated that he retained, however, the right to first play for the world title with others, and that the AVRO contract clause *had not created new rights or preferences*. He placed himself on record as believing that a tournament, no matter how strong the players, cannot be a preponderant factor in deciding the question of the world championship. The practical side of the matter is that political conditions in Czechoslovakia have made the proposed match with Flohr impossible, and that he feels free at present to accept a challenge *from any recognized master*. . . . As to conditions other than financial, Alekhine said that it is his right to refuse to play in any country where public opinion is against him. . . .

Fine and Keres tied for first place, and Keres was declared the winner by a tie-breaking system. Alekhine was in third place, Capablanca in sixth. It was the first tournament Capablanca had ever played in where he was not among the leaders.

On October 25, 1939, Alekhine announced arrangements with the Argentine Chess Federation for a title match with—Capablanca! It was scheduled to begin on April 14, 1940. "All signs point to a satisfactory conclusion of the negotiations," said the report. But a short time later, on December 7, the negotiations collapsed. "Insufficient financial backing," reported the United Press. The last word on these negotiations for a possible Alekhine-Capablanca match came on December 31, 1939. "The long drawn-out negotiations . . . have so far come to naught and . . . have been discontinued for the time being." There was one final flurry. Alekhine, it was stated in *The New York Times* of May 2, 1941, would like to come to the United States for a return match with Capablanca in Havana. Alekhine started the negotiations from Lisbon. But Capablanca died in 1942.

Alekhine was in Lisbon, penniless and alcoholic, as a refugee from both sides of the warring combatants. Nobody knows the entire story, but as much as can be pieced together, Alekhine was in Buenos Aires at the outbreak of hostilities, as captain of the French team in the Chess Olympiad. He returned to Paris and joined the French army as an interpreter. His story is that he fled to Lisbon after the fall of France, but his wife remained behind. The Nazis put pressure on him. If he played in a tournament in Munich, his wife would be allowed to join him. That, at least, was Alekhine's position. He spent much of the war in Poland and Czechoslovakia, and anti-Semitic articles were published under his name. After the war Alekhine denied having written them. He explained his chess appearances in Germany and other occupied countries by saying: "That was not only our means of subsistence but also the price of my wife's liberty. . . . My conscience is clear." He was, however, a little inconsistent. Later he admitted having written the chess articles but claimed that the Nazis had inserted the racist material. There seems to be little doubt that Alekhine was a collaborationist. Certainly the entire chess world believed so, and he was roundly condemned.

But he was still the world's champion, and contenders had to approach *him*. Russia offered Botvinnik as a challenger, and Alekhine was interested. He was in desperate need of funds. Only fifteen days before his death he called upon a magazine writer to collaborate with him on an article. "I am completely out of money and have to make some to buy my cigarettes." He died on March 24, 1946. According to a Reuters dispatch, the autopsy showed that he had choked to death on a piece of meat. "He was dining alone in his hotel bedroom at the Estoril at the time. The meat was three inches long and unchewed." (Years later there was a story that Alekhine did not choke to death; the doctor in attendance was said to have told chess players that the real cause of death was a cerebral hemorrhage caused by excessive drinking. But that is hearsay, and nobody has actually disproved the autopsy report.) The Portugal Chess Federation paid the funeral expenses. Services were delayed at the request of the French consul, who tried unsuccessfully to trace Alekhine's wife, believed to be in Paris. He went to his grave as he had lived— alone, without a close friend to mourn his passing. But his works were not forgotten, and ten years later the International Chess Federation had his remains brought back to Paris and interred in the Montparnasse Cemetery. Above the grave is a statue of Alekhine in white marble, sitting before a chessboard.

14 ♔

Hypermodernismus

Shortly after World War I, a group of players came into prominence whose ideas were to cause a considerable revision in chess thinking. Richard Réti (1889–1929) and Julius Breyer (1894 –1921) headed the school. Both died young—Breyer at twenty-seven and Réti at forty—but their influence helped shape chess as it is played today. They were part of the *Zeitgeist* that was agitating all Europe in the immediate postwar period. In music there was the dissonance of Bartók and Prokofiev and the puzzling dode-caphony of Schoenberg. In art there was the Cubist revolution and the growing trend away from naturalism. In mathematics there were Einsteinian relativity and the quantum theory, both of which departed from the physical "naturalism" of Euclid and Newton. Dogma was being questioned everywhere, and there was no reason why chess should have been excepted. And so there were the newfangled, unheard-of manipulations of a Réti. Conservatives in all fields were aghast. What was music developing into? Sheer cacophony. What was chess developing into? Anarchy, ugliness. Réti and Breyer were the Caïssical cacophonists.

Réti and Breyer asked much the same kind of questions other artists in other fields were asking. Musicians were wanting to know what was so sacred about traditional harmony, with its triads, tonics, and dominants. Chess players similarly were wanting to know what was so sacred about 1. P-K4 or 1. P-Q4. Those were the orthodox moves for opening a chess game. The center had to be seized. Dr. Tarrasch had said so. Then the pieces had to

come out, first the Knights, then the Bishops. The opening sequence of moves was assembled like the elements of an orthodox
sonata, and the harmony of the chess game was organized in such
a manner as to avoid dissonance. Then came *hypermodernismus*.
All of a sudden there was dissonance on the chessboard. An entirely new *concept* was being preached, and chess players everywhere took time out to become familiar with the new theories.
For chess is the most pragmatic of the arts. If a concept works, it
is immediately incorporated into the existent body of knowledge
and put to practical use. If it does not work, it is discarded.

The hypermoderns agreed that it was necessary to control
the center. But, they insisted, it could be done otherwise than by
1. P-K4 or 1. P-Q4. They carried the Nimzovitch idea one degree
further. Do *not* create a Pawn center that can only be attacked.
The exuberant Breyer announced that if White's first move was
P-K4, then "White's game is in its last throes." The New Idea in
chess postulated that the important thing is the *solidity* of the
center rather than its breadth. The advance of the center Pawns
can be deferred with advantage, provided that the opponent is not
allowed to build up an impregnable center. Instead of physical
occupation, White looked for *control* of the center.

This was achieved by such devices as the fianchetto of the
Bishop, where it sits on KN2 or QN2, bearing down the long di-
agonal and menacing the opponent's center. Thus the first move
in a game would be N-KB3, followed by P-KN3 and B-N2. Instead
of bringing pieces out, the hypermoderns kept the pieces in. This
necessitated an entirely different kind of maneuvering, and
players were as puzzled as old-fashioned pianists, brought up on
Mozart and Chopin, trying to make their fingers coordinate to a
Bartók or Prokofiev concerto. The whole *feel* was different; the
new chess required a different kind of *reflex*. Even the new conformations on the board looked different. Positions were bizarre;
nothing like this had ever been seen before. "We, the young players, are not interested in the rules but in the exceptions." That
was the credo of *hypermodernismus*. They delighted in the outré.
There were the Bishops at a distance, exerting a long-term men-
ace on the center, unmolested by hostile Pawns. With this concept of "hidden energy" the player would hold back, not striking
until ready, letting the opponent overextend himself. A whole

new repertory of openings had to be developed. Analysts and theoreticians were being kept very busy during the 1920's.

A representative example of Réti's hypermodern chess would be his game against Gruber at Vienna 1923. Réti rubbed his hands after Black's sixth move. "Whereas the older masters considered it an advantage to place the Pawn in the center, I take the view that the King Pawn is now the sore spot in Black's game." So Réti takes dead aim at it. His twentieth move is a surprise. No matter what happens, Black must lose a piece:

	WHITE: RÉTI	BLACK: F. GRUBER
1.	N-KB3	N-KB3
2.	P-B4	P-Q3
3.	P-KN3	B-B4
4.	B-N2	P-B3
5.	P-N3	Q-B1
6.	P-KR3	P-K4
7.	B-N2	N-R3
8.	N-B3	P-R3
9.	P-Q3	B-K2
10.	Q-Q2	N-B2
11.	N-Q1	O-O
12.	N-K3	B-R2
13.	O-O	N-Q2
14.	N-R2	N-K3
15.	P-B4	PxP
16.	PxP	P-KB4
17.	K-R1	N-B3
18.	R-KN1	N-R4
19.	B-KB3	N(4)xP
20.	N-Q5	NxN
21.	PxN	B-N4
22.	PxN	QxP
23.	Q-B3	B-B3
24.	Q-Q2	K-R1
25.	R-N2	R-B2
26.	QR-KN1	B-K4
27.	P-Q4	B-B3
28.	P-Q5	Resigns

Richard Réti, the Caïssical cacophonist. His new theories completely altered chess theory.

Réti himself insisted that the hypermoderns were not trying to "change" the concept of chess. Just as Arnold Schoenberg was insisting, at much the same time, that his music was an extension of the great mainstream, so Réti kept insisting that the hypermoderns were merely exploring new ideas in the hope of uncovering a further extension of Steinitzian principles. Breyer, who worked out the principles of the New Style with Réti, died too young to make much of an impression on grandmaster play, and he appeared in very few tournaments. But Réti, who died in his prime, did develop into a grandmaster-eater, and also the author of several provocative books about his theories.

Réti came out of Czechoslovakia—a big, heavy man who liked his food, "a good-natured black bear," as he was described. He was happy when he played chess. "Looking at the board, he almost always smiles at it, as a gourmet regards his favorite dish." Among his colleagues he was popular—up to a point. Old-timers remember him as tight and stingy, always the last to reach for the check, always concerned about money. His early tournament career was undistinguished, but starting in 1918, with a first at the Charousek Memorial Tournament, he began to make his presence felt. He won at Gothenberg 1920, tied for first at Teplitz-Schönau 1922, and handed Capablanca his first defeat in eight years at New York 1924. He also was a formidable blindfold player who at one time held the world's record of twenty-nine games (in 1925). His tournament record would have been better had he played as strongly against weak players as he did against the giants. For some reason he relaxed when faced with an "easy" game, and that cost him many a tournament point. Gideon Stahlberg's assessment is that Réti never achieved a success worthy of his gifts in over-the-board play. He was not a fighter and he lacked staying power. And, after 1925 or so, the Réti innovations were so heavily analyzed that his bizarre moves no longer came as a surprise. Yesterday's revolution had become today's platitude. Even weak players were soon able to cope with the hypermoderns.

Yet the hypermoderns had added a valuable new tool to chess. What appeared at its time to be so daring and unprecedented was, in reality, an extension of old principles, newly interpreted; but those principles opened up a completely new area. Today it is possible to view hypermodern theory as the analyst

R. N. Coles does, as "a stage between the old Classicism and the new Dynamism."

The new dynamism was represented by such players as Fine, Kashdan, Keres, and Botvinnik, all eclectics, all of whom seized upon the entire technique of chess, all of whom were of potential championship caliber (Botvinnik, of course, made it). Even some of the older players were able to absorb hypermodern theory into their repertory. Ernst Grünfeld (1893–1962), the Austrian grandmaster, was highly successful in the postwar period and captured several major tournaments between 1923 and 1934. He had a comprehensive knowledge of opening theory and seemed to have by heart every opening that had ever existed. Sweden's great player was Gideon Stahlberg (1908–1967), who remained in South America during World War II and, with Miguel Najdorf, dominated chess there. In 1948 he returned to Sweden, where he resumed playing international chess and compiled a distinguished record. At the point of writing he still holds the world's record for simultaneous play—400 players over a thirty-six hour period, in 1937. Stahlberg won 379.

Najdorf, born in Poland in 1910, was also in Buenos Aires at the outbreak of war. He remained there, becoming an Argentinian citizen. His style was exuberant, with a tendency toward reckless attack and, withal, great tenacity in defense. No wonder he has always been a crowd-pleaser. In the 1940's he was considered among the world's half-dozen strongest players, and he put in a claim for the world's championship. There were others, however, who had either a prior or a more legitimate claim, and Najdorf was not invited by FIDÉ to compete in the tournament to decide the championship.

For a while there was much excitement about Salo Flohr (1908-   ). There was a period when he seemed unbeatable. Born in Russian Poland, he lost his parents during World War I and was sent to Czechoslovakia, where he became a professional chess player. In 1929 he came in second at Rohitsch-Sauerbrunn and then took first at three Hastings tournaments, from 1931 to 1934. The following year he tied for first at Moscow. Alekhine, Botvinnik, every grandmaster in the world fell to him at one time or another, and in 1937 he was selected by FIDÉ as official challenger to Alekhine. During World War II, Flohr went to Russia and became a Soviet citizen. After the war he was, for some reason, a different player. His style suddenly turned cautious, and he became a drawing master. One reason may have been the ideological pressure that every Soviet player feels; they then become careful and do not take many chances. Psychologist Reuben Fine advances another reason: "Flohr was a hero in Czechoslovakia, where chess was extremely popular. There were Flohr cigars, Flohr collars, Flohr pastries. With this support endangered, Flohr found it impossible to concentrate on his own growth as a chess master. His childhood had left psychical scars which he was unable to eradicate. And so he chose, unconsciously perhaps, the method most suited to keep him near the top to make him feel safe; nothing else mattered."

After Flohr there was the brilliant Paul Keres, born in Estonia in 1916. For many years he was consistently the number two player of the world. "The face of a cherub and the chess-playing mind of a young demon" said William Winter of the young Keres. In his youth Keres was a frightening adversary—a superb technician, a ruthless attacking player, a combinational genius almost on a level with Alekhine. There is something tragic about this handsome, polite, extraordinarily talented man who *should* have been the world's champion but who, through a combination of bad luck and nerves, never quite made it to the very top. Yet he was the most dazzling player to have appeared since the days of the young Capablanca. He started playing chess at four, was the champion of Estonia while he was still in his teens, and started playing international chess in 1935. In his first international tournament, at Warsaw, he lost to Alekhine in the second round. Nevertheless, he came away with the feeling that he could meet the best grandmasters on even terms—which he did. He tied for first with Alekhine at Nauheim in the following year, then took top prizes in two tournaments, and topped those with first prize at the powerful and important Semmering 1937. After his victory at AVRO in 1938, he was designated as a challenger for Alekhine's title—except that Alekhine did everything to avoid meeting so powerful a player on the full crest of his momentum. Had not Alekhine imposed all kind of roadblocks, there would have been a title match between him and Keres in 1938. Alekhine ended up evading Keres, as he had

Paul Keres from Estonia. Brilliant, resourceful, probably the world's best player for some years—and never the champion.

evaded so many other strong contenders. Then the war came, Alekhine died, and that was that. The overwhelming consensus was that the aging Alekhine would never have been able to handle the fiery young grandmaster from Estonia.

In 1948, FIDÉ drew up a tournament that would give the world a new chess champion. Keres, Botvinnik, Euwe, Fine, Reshevsky, and Smyslov, considered the six best players alive, were invited to participate. Fine dropped out; he was not in practice, and his studies and professional life in New York did not give him time for adequate preparation. When the tournament started in The Hague, Botvinnik took immediate charge. Keres became frantic and lost his head. "Instead of resigning myself to the hopeless nature of the struggle for the world championship title," he wrote, "I concentrated my efforts on trying to overhaul Botvinnik in a desperately forced style of play. The consequences of such thoughtless tactics soon manifested themselves. I lost in succession to Smyslov, Reshevsky and Botvinnik. . . ." Thus ended Keres's dream for the time being. Botvinnik won the tournament and was proclaimed champion.

But Keres still pursued his goal. In the 1950–1952 period he took first place in four major tournaments. At the Candidates' Tournament of 1953 he missed out by trying for second with Reshevsky and Bronstein. At the Interzonal in 1955, at Gothenberg, he came in second, which allowed him to proceed to the Candidates' Tournament in Amsterdam, 1956. Ten grandmasters participated, and Keres came in second to Smyslov. In 1959 Keres started his quest again. This time Mikhail Tal edged him out. And in the Candidates' Tournament at Curaçao 1962, again Keres found himself in second place. In 1965 he was once more in second place, being edged out by Spassky. In all, Keres took second in five Candidates' Tournaments. Always he had his fingertips on his Grail and never quite succeeded in pulling it to him. Keres continued tournament play and continued to be dangerous to any living player, but he no longer had the stamina for the long, three-year obstacle course to the championship. Strictly speaking, there is no luck in chess (or, as Capablanca once observed, out of his vast experience and wisdom, "The good player is always lucky"). But practically speaking, Keres was the unluckiest player who ever lived. One tiny shift in his fortunes, one won game instead of a draw, and more than once he would have been playing for the championship instead of Bronstein, Smyslov, or Spassky.

In America, the two strongest players were Reuben Fine and Samuel Reshevsky. There were other fine ones, of course. Isaac Kashdan, born in 1905, worked up an imposing streak of international victories in the 1930's, but after that he was eclipsed by Fine and Reshevsky, and retired into chess journalism and administration. Kashdan was phenomenally gifted, and was spoken of as a possible contender against Alekhine. Other strong players of the period included Arthur Dake, Arnold Denker, and Israel A. Horowitz. But Fine and Reshevsky towered over the field.

Samuel Reshevsky, born in 1911, first came into prominence as the most remarkable of all child prodigies. He was easily on the level of a Morphy or a Capablanca. Unlike them, he was constantly being exhibited to the public. Morphy and Capablanca never had to go through the touring child-prodigy phase, but Reshevsky was put on show like the young Mozart, Hofmann, or Menuhin. This is no way to develop into a well-adjusted human being. There are thousands of pictures of the young Sammy Reshevsky, child prodigy, dressed in a sailor suit, his head barely above the table, gravely playing chess with teams of bearded elders. At the age of eight (he had learned the moves at four by watching his father) he already was at master strength. He also was a good blindfold player. Fortunately his career as a trained monkey was cut short. After 1921 he retired —at the age of ten. His parents wisely put him in school, and he went through the normal educational courses, graduating from the University of Chicago in 1933.

Two years before that, however, he resumed playing, winning the Western Association Tournament in 1931. That was in the nature of an experiment: could the former prodigy still play chess? Apparently he could. After receiving his degree he had a choice to make. Should it be the world of chess or the world of business? "Now Sammy is at the crossroads," editorialized the *Chess Review* in 1933. "If he continues in chess, he has every prospect of repeating his triumphs as a child wonder. But as a young man looking for a place in the business world, he would have very little time for serious chess. The time is at hand when

The nine-year-old Samuel Reshevsky in 1920. He is here engaged in playing the entire West Point team.

he must choose. The chess world is keenly interested in his decision, as it must be in following the career of its most famous prodigy."

Reshevsky opted for chess. Unlike the other prodigies, he did not exhibit a natural, classic style. His games were gnarled, complicated, and, many thought, uninteresting. Reshevsky played for minute positional advantages and was prepared to outsit his opponent for one hundred moves if need be. Another way he differed from the other great prodigies was in the slowness of his play. Morphy, Capablanca, and Fischer were noted for their rapid play. Reshevsky turned out to be the slowest of the great players, constantly in time trouble. His game with Alekhine at AVRO 1938 was typical. At the end of the eighth move, Reshevsky had taken fifty-eight minutes and Alekhine only *two*. That suicidal deliberateness made almost every Reshevsky game a cliffhanger; everybody wondered if he would beat the clock or lose on time. In the Alekhine game at AVRO, there was a typically *furioso* final. The *Chess Review* has described it:

> As usual, Reshevsky is in time trouble. He has to make *20 moves in 8 minutes . . . 16 moves in 6 minutes.* His opponent, Alekhine, becomes very nervous, gets up and paces restlessly back and forth. Reshevsky, on the contrary, is quiet. He even takes one minute of precious time to tell Alekhine to calm himself. *12 moves to make in 2 minutes.* Everyone, players as well as spectators, is jittery, except Reshevsky, who, with lightning rapidity, completes his fortieth move on the last second of his allotted time.

After his great victory at Margate 1935, when Reshevsky came in first ahead of Capablanca, there was no doubt that he was one of the strongest living players. He continued to win or come in close to the top in successive tournaments, and he also captured the United States championship with monotonous regularity. In his way he was a killer. The tiny man with the bald head (in recent years Reshevsky has been using a hairpiece) would sit patiently and immobile over the board, squeezing out win after win by sheer determination, eager to annihilate his opponent. Reshevsky never was a specialist in the openings, and he probably had less book knowledge than any of the other leading players; but he was a magnificent strategist and technician who would seize upon a minuscule advantage and worry it until his opponent bled to death. His will to win often carried him through. "Others get tired, or excited, or rattled, or lose interest, or lose hope; Reshevsky never," says his archrival, Reuben Fine. For some reason Fine could never beat Reshevsky for the United States Championship, though for some years he was his equal in strength and most likely his superior. Reshevsky had his number. But Reshevsky, like Keres, never made it to the top. One reason may have been that he was a better match than tournament player. After his victory over Najdorf in a match held in 1952, *The New York Times* in an editorial called Reshevsky the "chess champion of the free world," and suggested a match with Botvinnik for the title: "one type of Soviet-American conflict that all people would welcome." Needless to say, the Soviets passed over the suggestion in silence.

Reuben Fine, born in 1914, had a greater natural gift than Reshevsky—indeed, he was one of the most brilliant natural players in history. But he retired early from chess, and remains one of the great might-have-beens in chess history. Fine was playing very powerfully at the age of ten, and developed into a player with a pellucid style and an unerring instinct for position. In 1935 he won first prize at Hastings, returned to the United States, and then went back for an extended stay in Europe. In 1936 he took first prize at Zandvoort ahead of Euwe, Keres, Tartakower, and Bogolyubov—a remarkable achievement. His greatest triumph came at AVRO 1938, when he tied for first with Keres (only to be placed second by a tie-breaking system). That was the virtual end of Fine's chess career. During World War II he was busy in Washington; then he turned to psychology, earned a doctorate, entered practice, and was too busy to return to chess. He did continue to write books and articles, but his short career as an active player was over. Had he decided to devote himself to the game, there is no telling what he was capable of; his play had extraordinary finesse.

Two other interesting players of the decades after World War I must be mentioned—Vera Menchik and Mir Malik Sultan Khan.

Menchik (1906–1944), born in Moscow, was the first woman player in history ever invited to play in top international tournaments. The daughter of an English mother and a Czech father, she left Russia in 1921 and settled in England. From 1927 until her death she was women's world champion. The "Vera Menchik Club" started in 1929, at Carlsbad. She had been invited there to play in a tournament that contained such worthies as Capablanca, Nimzovich, Tartakower, and Euwe. Albert Becker, the Viennese master, poked fun at her presence and said that anybody who lost to her should be forced to join the Vera Menchik Club. He became the first member. Although she seldom came out very high in her tournaments, she did beat such giants as Reshevsky and Euwe in individual games. And, living in England as she did, she was frequently meeting such strong British players as Sir George Thomas, C. H. O'D. Alexander, Frederick Yates, and William Winter, and getting her share of victories against them. No less than Alekhine was impressed. "It is certain," he wrote, "that she is an absolute exception to her sex. She is so highly talented for chess that with further work and experience in tournaments she will surely succeed in developing from her present stage of an average player into a highly classed international champion. . . . It is the chess world's duty to grant her every possibility for development." Her greatest tournament success was at Ramsgate 1929, where she ended up in a tie for second, half a point behind Capablanca. It was the first tournament at which she had played against men. She also won a match against Mieses. In 1937 she married an Englishman, R. H. Stevenson. He died in 1943. She followed him a year later; she was killed, with her mother and sister, in an air raid on London.

Sultan Khan (1905–1966) was the most unusual chess player on the international circuit during the 1920's and early 1930's. He was an unlettered, illiterate genius who came out of India, showed a breathtaking aptitude for the game, then disappeared into obscurity. The only parallel would be the case of the Indian mathematician, Srinivasa Ramanujan, who out of nowhere in 1913 sent a letter to the great G. H. Hardy in England. The letter contained 120 theorems, and Hardy was overwhelmed. Even he could not follow the depth, complexity, and subtlety of Ramanujan's thought. A single look at the theorems, wrote Hardy, was enough "to show that they could only be written down by a mathematician of the highest class. They must be true because if they are not true, no one would have had the imagination to invent them." Ramanujan was brought to Cambridge, and then arose the problem of what to do with him: "What was to be done in the way of teaching him modern mathematics? The limitations of his knowledge were as startling as its profundity. Here was a man who could work out modular equations, and theories of complex multiplication, to orders unheard of . . . and had indeed but the vaguest idea of what a function of a complex variable was. . . . All his results, new or old, right or wrong, had been arrived at by a process of mingled argument, intuition, and induction, of which he was entirely unable to give a coherent account."

The parallel between Ramanujan and Sultan Khan is close. It would appear that Sultan Khan's mind worked on an equivalent level, but only in chess. Born in the Punjab, he was playing chess at nine. Soon he had no competition in his own country. In 1928 he was brought to England as, in effect, a slave by a diplomat named Col. Sir Nawab Umar Hayat Khan. Within a year Sultan Khan was the chess champion of England, and this despite the fact that he could not read English and had to learn many of the rules on his arrival. The chess he had played in India, for example, did not allow the Pawn to be moved two squares on the opening move. Yet Sultan Khan, when he started playing international tournaments, placed high and was able to topple such players as the mighty Capablanca. What would happen, grandmasters were asking, if Sultan Khan really decided to study instead of doing everything by instinct?

But he had only about four years in European chess. His owner, who used him as a servant (when Col. Sir Nawab Umar Hayat Khan entertained the American chess team at his home one evening in 1933 the table waiter was Sultan Khan, to the embarrassment of all except the illustrious Colonel), took him back to India in 1933, and that was the last anybody heard of Mir Malik Sultan Khan.

15

Wind from the East

The death of Alexander Alekhine left the chess championship of the world open for the first time since Steinitz had claimed it in 1866. But this time there was no longer going to be the kind of *laissez faire* that had been the prerogatives of champions of the past. FIDÉ, with the concurrence of all member nations, stepped firmly into the battlefield, waving the banner of Cäissa and then planting it firmly on the ground while conditions were dictated. There would be a tournament to which the best six players in the world would be invited, and the winner would be proclaimed champion of the world. Furthermore, and most important of all, future negotiations for the title would be out of the champion's hands. FIDÉ would take care of that. And so in 1948, five great players had their tilt in The Hague and in Moscow during April and May, and it was Mikhail Botvinnik of the Soviet Union who emerged over Smyslov, Reshevsky, Keres, and Euwe (Fine, it will be remembered, was not able to participate).

For the next twenty-four years Russia was to dominate international chess. Every world's champion was from the Soviet Union, and the winners of international tournaments generally were Russians. Indeed, if Alekhine is to be considered a Russian —for his French citizenship was really a *mariage de convenance* —the Russian hegemony goes back to 1927. Alekhine was his own man, but starting with Botvinnik the players represented The System. It was The System that had put them into such a commanding position. Had other countries geared themselves for a comparable effort, Botvinnik and Co. would have had more serious competition. But it was the Soviet Union alone that had put the might of its collective effort into a Soviet school of chess, nursing its talent, providing material comfort.

In pre-Revolutionary days, of course, chess in Russia operated like chess anywhere in the world. Chess players made it on their own or did not make it at all. The first strong player in the history of Russian chess was Alexander Petroff (1794–1867), who in 1824 came out with the first chess treatise ever published in his country. Petroff was more a theoretician than a player, and he did not enjoy much success in over-the-board play against the world's masters. Staunton, for one, beat him badly in London. But Petroff's importance as a chess propagandist in his own country cannot be overestimated. He even got the aristocrats of the court interested in chess, and that meant something close to official sanction for the game. An engineer, Petroff gave up his position as a professor of mechanics at St. Petersburg University to concentrate on chess. He and Carl Jaenisch (1813–1872) collaborated to produce some valuable work on the openings. Jaenisch was another one of those who found chess more important than the career for which he had been trained. He gave up his army career to devote himself to the game, and in 1842–1843 wrote a major book on the openings. Semyon Alapin (1856–1923) and Mikhail Tchigorin (1850–1908) were the first two Russian players to make a dent in international match and tournament play. Alapin was a good, steady player, but it was Tchigorin who turned out to be the Pushkin of Russian chess— the first authentically important player, the first really to put Russian chess on the map, the inspiration of future generations.

Tchigorin was a big, bearded, convivial man with a lust for chess. He came to it rather late, not learning the moves until he was sixteen, and not starting real work until he was twenty-three. His training ground was the Café Dominika in St. Petersburg. It was there that Tchigorin's strong, original play caught the attention of the experienced tournament master Simon Winawer, who visited St. Petersburg in 1875. Thanks to Winawer's advice and encouragement, Tchigorin threw everything he had

Mikhail Ivanovich Tchigorin, the founder of Russian chess. This photograph was taken in 1908, the last year of his life. Russian chess ideologists regard him the way political ideologists regard Lenin.

into chess. In 1881 he started his international career with a tie
for third at Berlin. His travels took him everywhere, and he was
quite familiar with the New World. In New York 1889, at the
American Chess Congress, he tied for first. In 1895 he was second
to Pillsbury at Hastings. There is a short description of Tchigorin
in the Hastings program book: "In difficult positions Tchigorin
gets very excited and at times seems quite fierce, sitting at the
board with his black hair brushed back, splendid bright eyes
and flushed face looking as if he could see right through the table.
When calm, however, he is decidedly handsome, and calculated
to beget confidence."

There were his two losses to Steinitz in matches for the
world championship; and matches with Gunsberg and Tarrasch, which he drew; and constant bouts of alcoholism; and
the editing of a Russian chess magazine; and a column for a
newspaper. Tchigorin, in his life as well as in his play, was a
romantic, but a most resourceful one, and his games have con-
sistent life and sparkle. In the 1920's he was to be deified by
Soviet chess ideologists as the founder of the Russian school,
the great experimenter, the archetype of the Soviet chess hero.

During those years, from 1925 to 1960, it was impossible to
read any chess story coming out of the Soviet Union that did not
have its required homage to Lenin, Stalin—and Tchigorin, "the
founder of our Soviet school." Chess after the Revolution of
1917 had become a political instrument of the State, and Tchigorin was the symbol. Chess, it was decreed, was more than a
game or sport; rather, it was a sociocultural manifestation like
drama, literature, art, music. As such, it had to reflect Soviet
ideals. Chess officially became a political instrument of the State
in 1924, at the third All-Union Congress. It was announced that
"Chess is a powerful weapon of intellectual culture." This was
the slogan under which Soviet chess was to develop. Chess did
become a weapon used to strengthen the growth of intellectual
culture among the industrial and peasant masses, bringing them
closer to a conscious participation in the political struggle of the
proletariat. An apparatus was set up, and chess was attached to
the Supreme Council for Physical Culture. The Communist
Party set to work to create a mass chess movement. Textbooks

were provided and the best players and teachers—such men as Grigori Levenfish, Fyodor Dus-Khotimirsky, Alexander Ilyin-Zhenevsky, Sergei Belavenets, and Ilya Rabinovich—were sent to the remotest points to give lectures, exhibitions, and classroom instruction. Chess clubs were set up, and the movement was given wide publicity.

Soviet chess was equated with the indomitable spirit of Soviet Man. Soviet chess was proclaimed confident and aggressive, as opposed to the kind of mean-spirited chess played by the bourgeois, decadent, capitalist, imperialist, formalist West. "The Soviet style is the Stakhanovite movement—struggle and victory!" cried L. Spokoiny in 1936. Western chess was dogmatic, Soviet chess creative. The entire thesis is set forth in Grandmaster Alexander Kotov's *The Soviet School of Chess* (1958). He first pays tribute to Petroff and Jaenisch, immediately immersing himself in an ideological hot bath. The Frenchman Philidor, he wrote, set chess off on the wrong track, for Philidor's viewpoint "could only limit the scope of creative chess, introducing as it did an element of fatalistic predetermination into studies of the theory of openings." But the Russian Petroff set this straight in his vigorous refutation of "attempts to impoverish creative progress." Kotov goes on to rate Jaenisch much higher than Western experts do. Kotov also praises the "gifted" nineteenth-century masters I. S. Shumov, S. S. Urusov, and V. M. Mikhailov, and pays special tribute to Emanuel Schiffers, "Russia's chess teacher." And Tchigorin! Old Tchigorin was the real genius of his day. "Steinitz and Lasker failed to understand the essence of creative thinking in chess, which they tried to subordinate to abstract and unrealistic principles." It was Tchigorin who laid bare "the vulnerable aspects of the Steinitz and Tarrasch theories" and provided a new understanding of chess. "His views on the essence of the game have survived the passage of time and today guide the creative thinking of chess players."

Passing hastily over Tchigorin's losses to Steinitz (indeed, he does not mention them at all), Kotov discusses Alekhine ("Russia's greatest player") and then the development of the Soviet school. "The traits of the Soviet man in general—his spirit of inventiveness, his resourcefulness, his dislike of resting on his laurels, his bold solution of theoretical problems and exacting, critical attitude toward himself—exercised their influence on the Soviet school." Russian players fight dogma. They never look for a draw and are always in there fighting to win. Two things explain that kind of drive: "the influence of the traits of the Soviet man of the socialist era, an ardent patriot and tireless seeker of the new; and second, a deep approach to chess, a struggle against scholastic conceptions of the essence of the game." Finally comes an analysis of every important Russian player up to 1958, with liberal illustration by means of games. The games are fascinating. Ideology aside, the Russian school had developed a group of chess-playing tigers. These were, consistently, the best players in the world.

In 1959 the Soviet Chess Foundation came into existence, and chess came under the wing of the Union of Soviet Sports Societies, which was responsible for developing the great reservoir of chess talent discovered by the Federation. The official publication of the Soviet Chess Federation was *Shakhmaty v SSSR*. "Our task," *Shakhmaty* told its readers in 1961, "is daily to educate chess players towards Communist consciousness, love of labor and discipline, and loyalty to the good of society, and to teach them to live and work in a Communist manner." The official organs of the party appproved this approach; and the victories of Soviet chess were held up as a demonstration of the validity of the system. When Botvinnik became champion, the party crowed. "Botvinnik's brilliant victory," cried *Pravda,* "is a victory of our socialist culture, an integral part of which is chess."

Looking for precedents, the cultural commissars deified Alekhine as well as Tchigorin. That was strange. Alekhine was a White Russian, an expatriate, as amoral as Richard Wagner or Jack the Ripper, a tool of the Nazis, an anti-Semite. But the ideologists never let facts interfere with their propaganda. Alekhine was reinstated and upheld as a major factor in the development of Soviet chess. Previously Alekhine had been attacked as "a bourgeois professional," but that was forgotten in the process of his rehabilitation. The official party line was that Alekhine at the time of his death had been preparing to return repentantly to Russia. In 1956 an annual Alekhine Memorial

Tournament was established in Moscow; and in 1958 Soviet chess publications were calling Alekhine the supreme Russian player. *Shakhmaty* made it official: "The name of Alekhine, whose play was formed in the traditions of the Russian school of chess, is near and dear to Soviet players. Alekhine created exemplary models of the art of chess, which clearly respect Tchigorin's play and Tchigorin's views on chess, and link this style of play and these views with the strongest ties to the Soviet chess movement."

The post-Stalin era did see a thaw. There was a relaxation of tension with the West and, more important to the Soviet intellectual, a relaxation of ideological tension. Chess propagandists timidly began to suggest that perhaps there were other players of the past besides Tchigorin and Alekhine worth admiring. Perhaps *some* good had come out of Western chess. It was broadmindedly admitted that Lasker, Capablanca, Nimzovich, Réti, and Euwe had made valuable contributions to chess playing and writing. Alexander Kotov, the chief spokesman for party orthodoxy, could write, in 1964: "I will be frank. Perhaps we are fascinated above all by Tchigorin and Alekhine because they are nearer to our hearts. But we also study systematically the heritage of such prominent chess geniuses as Emanuel Lasker, José Raúl Capablanca and others."

Another aspect of the party line was that the Russian grandmasters are amateurs. They are not money-grubbing professionals like Western players. All Russian chess players receive a full education; that is part of the Soviet system. They graduate with a specialty and go on to careers in other fields. The Soviets were constantly pointing this out. Was not Botvinnik an electrical engineer with a good deal of original work in his field? Was not Bondarevsky the shop manager of a steel plant? Was not Geller an economist? Was not Taimanov a concert pianist? Were not Spassky, Tal, Bronstein, Keres, and Petrosian journalists? But international chess circles knew better. With one or two exceptions—Botvinnik *really* was a scientist who worked at it—the Soviet grandmasters did nothing but chess. Journalists? Of course—they were *chess* journalists, one and all, which gave them an excuse for constant analysis and other work in chess. Tal in

1961 blew the pretense. "We are," he flatly told a journalist, "professionals of course, competing in tournaments, working on chess theory, visiting small towns for simultaneous displays."

A talented chess player in the Soviet Union need never worry. Russian chess players have it better, in many respects, than their equivalents anywhere else. They are spotted when young and, in effect, become wards of the State. They are supplied with chess teachers and chess manuals; they can and do play hours and hours a day from childhood. If they are good enough to rise through The System and reach grandmaster status, they receive many benefits—a salary at the top Soviet level, additional money for prizes and writing, a car, a dacha, an apartment. Chess is the national sport in Russia, where there are some three million registered players (as against some 65,000 in the United States), and there the great players are heroes on the level of cosmonauts. When Botvinnik, as the chess champion of the world, would attend a performance at the Bolshoi Theater, the audience would see him entering the auditorium and rise in homage.

But for all this the Soviet players have to pay a price.

The cases of Botvinnik and Shostakovich are instructive. Both were children of the 1917 Revolution and both grew up in the Stalin era. Both were geniuses in their field—the first Soviet chess player and the first Soviet composer to reach the international heights (Prokofiev, who did return to the Soviet Union in the late 1930's, is considered more a cosmopolite than a Soviet composer). Botvinnik and Shostakovich were symbols of Russian supremacy and, as such, they were compelled to reflect Soviet idology. Shostakovich, for instance, had to explain not only his music but all music in terms of the dialectical materialism of the 1930's. In his biography of Tchaikovsky, Shostakovich—although he certainly knew better—represented the famous composer as a friend of the masses, interested in writing proletarian music. Botvinnik also was prepared, in his equivalent way, to hew to the party line and explain his success in terms of Soviet ideology and the Soviet Man. After his tie for first at Nottingham 1936 he cabled Stalin: "Dearly beloved teacher and leader . . . I am infinitely happy to be able to report that a representative of Soviet chess has shared first place in the tournament with ex-champion of the world Capablanca. Inspired by your great slogan, 'catch up and surpass,' I am glad that I have been able to realize it."

Meanwhile, the Soviet press assured its readers that Botvinnik's victories were an inevitable result of The System. When Botvinnik won the championship, a front-page article in *Pravda* said, among other things, that Botvinnik was not merely playing chess; he was defending the honor of his country. (What a terrifying burden for a chess player to have to carry!) Soviet chess players, like Soviet representatives of the other arts, had to pay lip service to this principle if they expected to get anywhere. "When we compete in international tournaments," said Botvinnik in 1949, "and defend the honor of our country, we recognize our duty before the Soviet people, before the Bolshevik party, and the great cause of Lenin and Stalin." In 1949 Botvinnik wrote an article, "The Russian and Soviet School of Chess," and it is just as silly in its ideology as were Shostakovich's observations on Russian music of the past. This is not said in condemnation. Western chess players and artists in general did not have Josef Stalin looking over their shoulders. Soviet chess players *had* to take the line that Botvinnik had taken. If they did not echo these remarks, they could find themselves in trouble. There was another element of pressure: players who did not do well in international tournaments could find some of their privileges taken away. The Russians do not like to lose to the West, especially in chess, which for so many years had been their monopoly. Punishment can follow; players who make a poor showing can be accused of laziness, lack of cooperation, cult of personality and everything but direct sabotage. There is no hesitation in punishing even the elite of the chess players, just as there had been no hesitation in punishing the elite of composers (the Zhdanov Decree of 1948 came heavily down on Shostakovich and Prokofiev for writing "formalistic" music that did not reflect the ideals of the Russian people). "Leading Soviet players," said an article in *Shakhmaty* in 1961, "are well known for their modesty and openness. Unfortunately this cannot be said of Grandmaster E. Geller . . . a disdainful attitude towards his comrades and an unwillingness to consider their opinions. Brag-

Mikhail Botvinnik in 1949, the year after he became champion. He was a child of the 1917 Revolution and a symbol of Russian supremacy.

garts and boasters are not popular with us." After Spassky lost to Fischer in 1972, there was a shakeup in the Soviet Chess Federation and disciplinary measures were taken against some of the leading players.

For the Soviet players this makes a hard task even harder. It is enough of a problem to sit across a board facing a grim Fischer, Larsen, Reshevsky, or Gligorić. On top of that, every Soviet player in any important international tournament has on his back the realization that he is representing not only himself but also a System, a Culture, a society that is supposed to be superior to the society represented by his opponent. Small wonder that so many Russian chess players tend to play it safe, settling for a sure draw rather than gambling for a problematic win. Not many will take a chance, and the preponderance of draws among Russian players in international tournaments is unusually high.

Yet with all that, the Soviet school for many years was supreme in the world—not because their men were brainier than players anywhere else, not because of the superiority of their political system, but merely because the Soviet system caught the talent early along and gave it every opportunity to develop. In capitalistic societies players had to make a living, and there were surprisingly few full-time chess professionals. Who in the West had the luxury of spending *all* their time at chess, without anything to distract them? Soviet players could, and the system came to its glory in 1948 when Botvinnik became the first Soviet chess champion of the world.

16

Calculation, Order, Science

It was pragmatic chess that Botvinnik played, as befits an electrical engineer who had written a doctoral thesis later expanded into a book with the title of *The Theory and Prospects of Application of Asynchronized Synchronous Machines.* Capablanca had been called The Chess Machine. Botvinnik was called The Machine in Human Form. He was, or at least gave the impression of being, a cold, unsmiling, ultraserious man who did everything from thought rather than from feeling. It was as if he had programmed himself with one of his asynchronized synchronous machines. This robot in human form did everything precisely. When he prepared for a match he walked exactly two hours by the clock. Then a specific number of minutes was devoted to deep-breathing exercises. Then came the allotted time for study and analysis. Nothing was allowed to interrupt the routine. Everything in his chess, his scientific life, and his personal relationships was ordered and calculated.

He was the coming man of chess ever since he beat Capablanca in a simultaneous exhibition in 1925, at the age of fourteen. Capablanca predicted great things for the young Russian. Botvinnik at that time had been playing chess for only two years. He was born in St. Petersburg on August 17, 1911. His father was a dental technician, his mother a dentist. They separated when he was nine years old. Thus Botvinnik, like Spassky and Fischer, came from a broken family. Botvinnik learned the moves when he was twelve. "My brain was fresh, it could take in an unlimited

Botvinnik, the pragmatist, the man of routine, the representative of order and calculation.

amount of the information, the elementary knowledge, which is necessary to the perfection of a player's technique," he wrote in his *One Hundred Selected Games*. In 1926 he tied for second in the Leningrad championship; and, while waiting for entry into college, spent a year studying chess. In 1927 he tied for fifth in the USSR championship—not the kind of showing he would have liked to make. But he was confident. The turning point in his chess development, he says, came in 1930. It was then that he learned "the art of winning regularly against masters." For the next six years, however, he had to divide his time between chess and his electrical engineering studies. He was at the Leningrad Polytechnic Institute from 1927 to 1933, and he took his studies as seriously as he took everything else. Nevertheless, he found time to compete for the Soviet championship, and he won it in 1931 and 1933. At his first international tournament, Hastings 1934–35, he tied for fifth, but he redeemed himself later in the year at the Moscow International, tying for first with Flohr ahead of Capablanca, Lasker, and Spielmann.

That was his first big success. Many others followed. Botvinnik was second behind Capablanca at Moscow 1936; in a tie for first with Capablanca at Nottingham 1936. The chess world realized that Botvinnik was a player strongly on his way. "A first-class player with a perfect mastery of all phases of the game," said Euwe. Botvinnik had a good result at the famous AVRO Tournament of 1938, though he did not win it. Then the war came. Botvinnik did not see active service; he had more important work to do as a testing engineer on insulation problems at the high-tension laboratory at Molotov. With his electrical work on his mind, he did not do well in the 1940 USSR championship. Igor Bondarevsky and Andrei Lilienthal tied for first, while Botvinnik shared fifth with Isaac Boleslavsky. Perhaps nettled, Botvinnik concentrated on chess the following year, as much as his scientific work during the war would allow him, and he bounced back in 1941 to win the USSR championship, defeating not only Bondarevsky and Lilienthal but also Keres and the promising young newcomer, Vasily Smyslov. The Keres game was a crusher; seldom had the proud Estonian grandmaster been so maltreated:

	WHITE: KERES	BLACK: BOTVINNIK
1.	P-Q4	N-KB3
2.	P-QB4	P-K3
3.	N-QB3	B-N5
4.	Q-B2	P-Q4
5.	PxP	PxP
6.	B-N5	P-KR3
7.	B-R4	P-B4
8.	O-O-O	BxN
9.	QxB	P-KN4
10.	B-N3	PxP
11.	QxP	N-B3
12.	Q-QR4	B-B4
13.	P-K3	R-QB1
14.	B-Q3	Q-Q2
15.	K-N1	BxBch
16.	RxB	Q-B4
17.	P-K4	NxP
18.	K-R1	O-O
19.	R-Q1	P-N4
20.	QxNP	N-Q5
21.	Q-Q3	N-B7ch
22.	K-N1	N-N5
	Resigns	

Again in 1944 and 1945 Botvinnik won the USSR championship. There was no stopping him. In his first major tournament after the war he came in first ahead of Euwe, Smyslov, Najdorf, and László Szabó of Hungary at Groningen 1946. There were the negotiations for a title match with Alekhine, which of course came to naught after the champion's death at Estoril. There was a first at the Tchigorin Memorial in Moscow 1947. And then came the climax—the FIDÉ-sponsored tournament of 1948 in which, on May 8, he became the champion of the world. He was thirty-seven years old.

With his logical mind, it would follow that he liked clean-cut, logical positions. He once wrote that if acoustics was a science that informed the world about sounds, then music was an art that revealed the beauty of that world; and if logic was a science that revealed the laws of thought, then chess "in the form of artistic images" was an art that illuminated the logical side of thought. In the kind of play that can be reduced to a system, Botvinnik was invariably accurate. That kind of game he seldom lost, and he was generally successful in steering games in that direction. It was noted that in indeterminate positions he tended to feel insecure.

For the next three years after winning the championship, Botvinnik played hardly at all. Perhaps the Russians did not want to take the risk of having their star lose to a representative of decadent capitalistic chess. Or perhaps Botvinnik was anxious to resume work on his doctorate. He never had the chess monomania of an Alekhine or Fischer. "I can only play good chess when I have had a rest from it and my chess hunger has to be reawakened." So he went back to science, finished his thesis, wrote a book in 1949 (*Regulation of Excitation and Static Stability of the Synchronous Machine*), received his doctorate in 1951, and married a ballerina of the Bolshoi Theater—all just in time to meet David Bronstein for a title match.

Bronstein, born in 1924, was a bold, brilliant, innovative player somewhat in the style of the young Keres. For a while he was called "the genius of modern chess." He also was an ebullient young man, vivacious, in love with chess, in every way different from the sober, taciturn, pathologically suspicious Botvinnik. The champion, who was something of a recluse, seldom appeared in public or even at Moscow's Central Chess Club. Bronstein, however, also had his full share of curious mannerisms. Sometimes he seemed in a trance. In one game against Boleslavsky he looked at the board for *fifty minutes* before making his first move.

Botvinnik, who had not played in a tournament or match for three years, took six months off to prepare for his match with Bronstein. In one of his books Botvinnik gives a good idea of how he went about getting ready to defend his title. He starts work with a review of chess literature, making notes on interesting games as he goes along. He studies all his opponent's games, looking for opening lines to use. "In my view a player should not, and indeed can not, attempt to play all the openings known to theory.

For one competition, three or four opening systems for White and the same for Black are quite sufficient." Then there must be *secret* preparatory games with a close-mouthed partner. The opposition must not be tipped off to your plans. End-game studies must be part of the training. "Above all, before playing in competitions, a player must have regard for his health." Botvinnik suggests fifteen to twenty days of fresh air in the country. There must also be a complete five-day rest before the start of the match; otherwise the zest for battle could be lost. A chess player can be overtrained as much as a prizefighter. In his training Botvinnik thought of everything. He had a tendency to be bothered by tobacco smoke, and once he had a training match with Vyacheslav Ragozin. Ragozin's main job was to blow smoke in Botvinnik's face.

There was a period when nobody thought the Botvinnik-Bronstein match would ever get started. Botvinnik could be as difficult as Bobby Fischer was to be. He kept arguing over minor points. He wanted, for one thing, to make a new rule involving adjourned moves. In master play the game comes to an end after five hours. If there is still play in the position, the player on the move writes down his move, puts it into an envelope, and gives it to the referee. That is the "sealed move," and it is opened by the referee when play is resumed the next day or whenever. Botvinnik demanded that the sealed move be written *twice* and put into *two* envelopes. He requested this because a referee who was a friend of his opponent might be partisan enough or dishonest enough to change the move. The Soviet chess world was aghast at this peculiar degree of suspicion from the world champion. There was a month-long negotiation over this alone, and Bronstein finally gave in.

When the match finally did start, Botvinnik was in trouble. He did not play in his usual sharp manner; clearly he was out of practice. He managed to retain his championship on a draw. The final score was 5 to 5, with fourteen draws. (In world championship play, the titleholder has a half-point advantage; the challenger needs twelve and a half points in the twenty-four-game match to win.)

The 1951 match seemed to burn Bronstein out; he never was

the same player again. Nor was Botvinnik at his best after the match. He played in three tournaments during the next two years, and he came in fifth and third in the first two of them. Finally he pulled himself together for the USSR championship in 1953, where he tied for first with Taimanov and then won the playoff.

His next challenger was Vasily Smyslov, born in Moscow in 1921, who had started chess at the age of six, had tied for the USSR championship at seventeen, and was a grandmaster at nineteen. Trained at the House of Pioneers in Moscow, young Smyslov soon became one of the international stars, and he ran away with the Candidates' Tournament of 1953. But it had not been an entirely easy life for Smyslov. For ten years he had been chasing Botvinnik, trying in vain to beat him, to outdo him in the USSR championships. But always he just missed, and ever since 1941 was in the rank just under the champion, along with Keres and Bronstein. For a while he talked about giving up chess and becoming an opera singer (he had a good baritone voice) at the Bolshoi. He actually applied for a position there. "One gets the impression," Gligorić has written, "that he wanted to be an opera singer more than anything else, but his exceptional gifts transformed him into a chess champion." The tall, well-built, quiet Smyslov, says Gligorić, had no love for the patient memorization of variations and for the day-to-day analysis that modern competitive chess requires. Smyslov well knew that he had to fight himself. He was once asked who his most dangerous opponent was. "In chess, as in life, a man is his most dangerous opponent." Smyslov had to fight lassitude and the Dostoevskian gloom that often settles on Russian chess players. Defeats almost tore him apart. "There was a time," Kotov wrote, "when Smyslov lacked sufficient psychological stability; defeats had a demoralizing effect on him." But much as Smyslov had to fight self-doubt and despair, much as he was attracted to music, he nevertheless stuck to chess, and he became one of the redoubtable players of his day.

Smyslov was not so flashy a player as Bronstein, not so fertile in his ideas, but he was a more solid technician. His play was a model of all-around competence. Gideon Stahlberg, who acted as referee for the 1957 Botvinnik-Smyslov match, could pay

Vasily Smyslov, who defeated Botvinnik in 1957 to become the world champion. He lost the title in a rematch the following year. Many believed that he would have had a happier life as an opera singer.

no higher compliment than to suggest that "the clarity and logic of Smyslov's play is highly reminiscent of Capablanca. The new world champion has a more modern opening repertory than the famous Cuban, but he plays with the same amazing precision, is calm and collected in difficult positions, and is a big master of the end game. Like Capablanca, he solves simply what at first glance are difficult problems." Dr. Euwe said much the same thing: "His great strength really lies in his ability to make something out of nothing. He will maneuver patiently for hours without ever relaxing for one moment; he seems to be stealthily stalking his opponent. There is indeed something of the assassin about him, for all at once, when least expected, he will strike. Since moreover his end game technique is just about perfect, the smallest advantage in his hands is likely to lead to a win." One of Smyslov's most striking games came from the 1953 Candidates' Tournament. He was playing Black against Keres:

	WHITE: KERES	BLACK: SMYSLOV
1.	P-QB4	N-KB3
2.	N-QB3	P-K3
3.	N-B3	P-B4
4.	P-K3	B-K2
5.	P-QN3	O-O
6.	B-N2	P-QN3
7.	P-Q4	PxP
8.	PxP	P-Q4
9.	B-Q3	N-B3
10.	O-O	B-N2
11.	R-B1	R-B1
12.	R-K1	N-QN5
13.	B-B1	N-K5
14.	P-QR3	NxN
15.	RxN	N-B3
16.	N-K5	NxN
17.	RxN	B-B3
18.	R-R5	P-N3
19.	R(3)-R3	PxP
20.	RxP	P-B6
21.	Q-B1	QxP

22.	Q-R6	KR-Q1
23.	B-B1	B-N2
24.	Q-N5	Q-B3
25.	Q-N4	P-B7
26.	B-K2	R-Q5
27.	P-B4	R-Q8ch
28.	BxR	Q-Q5ch
	Resigns	

On move nineteen, Keres starts what at first glance appears to be an irresistible King-side attack. If Black accepts the Rook sacrifice, he is probably lost. But the complications are great—too great to be solved over the board during the pressure of an important game. So Smyslov spurns the Rook, finds a move that enables him to bring an extra piece into play, and goes on to smash Keres. The win helped Smyslov to take first place in the tournament. Keres tied for second, and his twenty-year quest for the world's championship received a severe setback with this game. Smyslov once defined chess as "an interesting sphere of creative ideas built up on the opposing thoughts of two chess players who, in the process of a tense struggle, are striving to create an artistic conception." This game is a concrete illustration of that definition.

To prepare for his match with Botvinnik, Smyslov went through the usual regimen, studying some 800 of the champion's games, getting himself into prime physical shape, and entering the 1954 match armed with prepared variations. He had every prospect of success; the champion was not getting any younger. But the wily Botvinnik again managed to squeak through with a draw (7 to 7, with ten draws). It was all the more a tribute to Botvinnik's tenacity in that he had played no chess at all in 1953. Yet he was capable of the kind of logical, remorseless play that characterized the twelfth game of the match:

WHITE: BOTVINNIK		BLACK: SMYSLOV
1.	P-Q4	P-Q4
2.	P-QB4	P-QB3
3.	N-KB3	N-B3
4.	N-B3	PxP

5.	P-QR4	B-B4
6.	P-K3	P-K3
7.	BxP	B-QN5
8.	O-O	QN-Q2
9.	N-R4	O-O
10.	P-B3	B-N3
11.	P-K4	P-K4
12.	NxB	RPxN
13.	B-K3	Q-K2
14.	Q-K2	PxP
15.	BxP	B-B4
16.	BxB	QxBch
17.	K-R1	P-KN4
18.	P-KN3	QR-Q1
19.	B-R2	KR-K1
20.	QR-Q1	N-B1
21.	RxR	RxR
22.	P-K5	N-Q4
23.	NxN	PxN
24.	Q-Q2	N-K3
25.	P-B4	PxP
26.	PxP	Q-B3
27.	P-B5	N-B4
28.	Q-N5	R-Q2
29.	R-KN1	P-B3
30.	PxP	N-K5
31.	P-B7ch	RxP
32.	Q-Q8ch	K-R2
33.	BxP	N-B7ch
34.	K-N2	Q-B3
35.	QxQ	RxQ
36.	KxN	RxPch
37.	B-B3	R-B5
38.	R-N4	Resigns

Smyslov had to go through the three-year cycle again, and he did so successfully, handily winning the Candidates' Tournament in Amsterdam 1956. He met Botvinnik once again for a title match in 1957, and this time he won, with a score of 12½ to 9½. But his triumph was short-lived. In those days the champion had a right to revenge the following year, and Botvinnik regained his title, 7 to 5 with eleven draws.

Botvinnik's behavior during the 1957 match was still another example of his peculiar nature. His suspicion amounted to paranoia. During training he was in complete seclusion. What was he doing? With whom was he working? Or was he working with anybody at all? Nobody knew. Botvinnik was not going to take any chances that information would leak out. In 1954, during his first match with Smyslov, he said (in his preface to the book of the match) that during training Smyslov had added something new: Smyslov had not only prepared against Botvinnik's *known* repertory of openings but also against his *unknown* repertory. That is, he knew in advance what new lines his opponent was going to introduce. The implication was clear: Botvinnik's second had obviously leaked the moves to Smyslov. This time Botvinnik had no second, nor did he have one in 1958 when he recaptured the title.

Then came the turn of Mikhail Tal, who came up as fast as Smyslov receded. Smyslov never again was in serious contention for the title after 1958, though of course he remained one of the world's best players. It was the young, dynamic Tal everybody was talking about—Tal, who had won the USSR championship at twenty-one, outplaying and outcombining such powerhouses as Keres, Bronstein, Petrosian, Tolush, and Taimanov. Tal the romantic. Dark, nervous, hungry Tal.

It was as if Anderssen and Zukertort had returned. Mikhail Tal, born in Riga on November 9, 1936, had learned chess at the Palace of Young Pioneers. Starting in 1957, an unknown, he had reeled off a spectacular series of successes, coming in first in five of his six tournaments. Short, slim, frail, with burning black eyes, he brought back romanticism in chess, sacrificing left and right with reckless (some said idiotic) abandon. Smyslov said that Tal's style was a mere "bag of tricks." But in about a year following Tal's entrance into international chess, not only the Russians but also players everywhere were discussing the phenomenon. Was it luck? That was hard to believe; one tournament win might be luck, but not five. Was it hypnotism? There were those who seriously thought so. Tal had the disconcerting habit of glaring at his opponents, and that unsettled them. The nervous, pacing (when not staring), chain-smoking Tal was a hard package to handle. Perhaps there really *was* something in that hypnotism theory? At one tournament the Hungarian Pal Benko (who later moved to the United States) put on a pair of dark glasses when playing against Tal. That was supposed to counteract the hypnotism. Tal, vastly amused, had somebody go out and get a pair of glasses for him too, a pair of sunglasses crazily exaggerated in shape. Benko protested to the referee and there was a howl of laughter. Benko looked foolish.

Like all natural players, Tal moved with amazing—almost contemptuous—speed. That, too, rattled his opponents. It is a psychological fact that a player is tempted to make fast moves against a very rapid player even though he himself has plenty of time on his clock. The result often is a glaring blunder, and it was surprising how many major players blundered against Tal. Everything came easy for the young Latvian. He took first place against the world's leading players at Riga, Moscow, Portoroz, Zurich, and Belgrade. His style was daring and devil-may-care. Over the board he posed so many problems that few could solve them. Later analysis may have shown that some of the Tal sacrifices were unsound, but that was scant consolation to those who had dropped whole points against him.

It was as though a fire was sweeping through the forest of chess. Up to Tal, chess had been increasingly scientific, bookish, technical, cautious. "In our time, only when Tal appeared did chess players see that there could be a different style," said Spassky admiringly. Spassky went on to describe Tal as not a very well-organized man. Rather, unlike the regimented Soviet players, Tal was a bohemian in life as well as in chess, "the kind of man you can imagine playing chess while strumming the guitar; a very sympathetic person." Yuri Averbakh, the Soviet grandmaster, described Tal as being like a wrestler on the mat, being pinned, who twisted and was suddenly on top of his opponent. Tal's ingenuity was startling. Gligorić tells of a

Mikhail Tal, the romanticist who at the age of twenty-three in 1960 became the youngest world chess champion in history. But he too was unable to contain the relentless Botvinnik, and he lost the rematch the following year.

typical game: "Our fourth meeting was at the Candidates' Tournament. I had found a saving combination which Tal overlooked. What did he do? He avoided the normal combination, for that would have given me a clear line of action. He took a risk and exchanged his Queen for two Rooks. He might even have lost, but he reckoned daringly on my extreme lack of time for thought. Quite right! I soon made a catastrophic blunder." Tal, wrote Gligorić, cannot play at his best if he thinks his opponent feels secure. His aim is to disconcert the opponent by outré moves and outlandish sacrifices. Tal *feels* when a sacrifice is right; he himself cannot analyze it. Perhaps it is sound, perhaps not. No matter. If the combination is not accurate, then the opponent's fatigue or lack of time will be enough compensation.

Typical of Tal's style is a game he played against Gideon

Barcza of Hungary in 1962 at the XV Olympiad in Bulgaria. The famous Tal sacrificial game starts at move thirteen. If Black accepts the offered Knight, immediate mate follows. If Black plays QxRP, then White has NxPch and Black soon loses. There are many possibilities. Black's best move may have been 13. P-KN3, which leads to wild complications. Instead, he played 13. P-R3, and was lost:

	WHITE: TAL	BLACK: BARCZA
1.	P-K4	P-K3
2.	P-Q4	P-Q4
3.	N-QB3	N-KB3
4.	B-N5	PxP
5.	NxP	QN-Q2
6.	NxNch	NxN
7.	N-B3	B-K2
8.	B-Q3	P-B4
9.	Q-K2	PxP
10.	O-O-O	P-QR3
11.	KR-K1	B-Q2
12.	NxP	Q-R4
13.	N-B5	P-R3
14.	NxPch	K-B1
15.	BxN	BxB
16.	B-B4	Q-N4ch
17.	K-N1	B-N4
18.	BxB	QxN
19.	B-R4	P-N4
20.	B-N3	BxP
21.	Q-K4	R-K1
22.	Q-N4ch	K-N1
23.	R-K3	K-R2
24.	R-N3	Q-K4
25.	P-KB4	Q-K7
26.	KxB	P-QR4
27.	R-Q7	Resigns

Tal won his right to a match with Botvinnik by sweeping the Interzonal at Portoroz in 1958, coming in ahead of Benko,

Petrosian, and Fischer; and then winning the Candidates' Tournament of 1959. It was at this Candidates' Tournament that Tal handed Bobby Fischer four defeats. Nothing like that had ever happened to the American. Later Fischer was to get revenge, but at the time there was no doubt who the better player was. And so, in 1960 there was the Botvinnik-Tal match—the methodical, accurate, veteran position player against the intuitive romanticist. The two men had never before played each other. Botvinnik took four months off to prepare, going through his usual timed-to-the-second-hand daily routine. Tal's way of preparation was to enter a tournament. Tal was—and is—the kind of compulsive chess player who will play day and night against any kind of opposition just for the pleasure of playing. When the match started, Botvinnik, who had drawn the Black pieces, threw aside his usual caution and went all out for a win. He lost the game in thirty-two moves and seemed demoralized after that. Perhaps he, too, had succumbed to the Tal mystique.

The match was fought according to Tal's imperative. For once Botvinnik did not seem to be able to get started. Tal was throwing things at him that he had never seen. "I know I made what appeared to be bad moves at times," said Tal, "but they served the purpose of making my opponent use up time figuring why I made such a move." At the twenty-first game, Tal needed only a draw to win the title. The tired, demoralized, discouraged Botvinnik looked up at the eighteenth move and quietly said, "Let's call it a draw, Mischa." The final score was 6 to 3, with thirteen draws. Tal, at twenty-three, had become the youngest world champion in history. After the match, everybody got into arguments over the question of whether Tal had won on his chess or on his psychology. Russian traditionalists were appalled. This was not chess. They called Tal's game too risky, reckless, "subject sometimes to just criticism and punishment. He should be more sober." But most chess lovers around the world were thrilled. This was the way a champion should play.

Their excitement did not last long. Botvinnik, as was his right, returned the following year for another match. Nobody expected him to win. But win he did, and it was the second time he recaptured his title. Tal played listlessly. Indeed, his play was inexplicable. Botvinnik won, 6 to 2 with thirteen draws.

He was fifty years old. Chess players are not supposed to be winning championships at that age. Immediately a round of speculation started. What had happened? Why was Tal's play so poor? Had he underestimated Botvinnik? As it turned out, there was a different reason. Tal was playing in ill health. He had developed kidney disease and was in weak physical condition. Tal never was the same player for many years after that; he lacked the stamina for long tournaments. Not until 1972 did he resume his winning habits. Up to that time Tal had to more or less watch from the sidelines while Botvinnik had it out with his final contender.

17 ♚

Draw, Draw, Draw, Draw…

With Tal out of the way, other eager pairs of eyes began to look at Botvinnik. And there were two players in the West who suddenly started to threaten the Russian monopoly. If Bobby Fischer of the United States and Bent Larsen of Denmark were in a tournament, the Russians were no longer automatically assured of sweeping it. It was Fischer especially who concerned the Russians. Nobody doubted that he had world championship potential; that had been evident from the time he was thirteen years old. On the other hand, he had personal problems that might keep him from achieving his full stature. Wait and see.

In the meantime, the two leading Soviet players, after Tal no longer was able to hold up his end, were Tigran Petrosian and Boris Spassky.

Petrosian, the older of the two, the cautious Armenian, was born in Tiflis on June 17, 1929. He started chess at eight, was champion of Georgia at sixteen, the USSR junior champion at seventeen, and the USSR champion at thirty. A Botvinnik-like technician without Botvinnik's will to win, Petrosian was not exactly the darling of the multitudes. Even at the beginning, his ultracautious, ultraconservative style was not to the liking of the chess ideologists, who found it hard to reconcile this kind of play with the received doctrine that Soviet chess was the image of the daring, indomitable Soviet Man. Kotov issued a warning: "Latterly, however, a tendency to avoid complications and try to win games by technical superiority has become apparent; colorless

"Iron Tigran"—the wily Tigran Petrosian, world champion from 1963 to 1969. He is considered the greatest drawing master since the days of Schlechter. But he is a very hard man to beat.

draws have appeared in his tournament play." As the years went on, Petrosian's style became, if anything, even more colorless. It was true that he was a very hard man to beat. Playing him was like trying to put handcuffs on an eel. There was nothing to grip. It was also very hard to become interested in Petrosian's unenterprising conception of the game. As a young man he played like an old one, and he often won by wearing down his opponents. Petrosian had antennae that could sense danger; he was like an alarmed centipede who would scuttle for the dark and lurk there, dangerous, ready to bite when threatened. But it was not going to be he who would initiate the attack. When Petrosian was playing another counterpuncher the results could be deadly dull; each would wait for the other to make the first move and, like as not, nothing ever did happen. In Petrosian's 1972 candidates' match with Korchnoi, monotonous draw followed monotonous draw with such regularity that even the Russian press complained. But that was Petrosian's style. He was, as Gligorić said, "very impressive in his incomparable ability to foresee danger on the board and to avoid any risk of defeat." Petrosian himself made no secret of it: "Obviously many people forget that nowadays in chess the struggle for points prevails over creative considerations. . . . It is naive to think that it is expedient (let alone possible) for a player striving for the top place in a tournament to play every game all out, putting all his creative effort into every encounter."

This was technical chess on almost an abstract level—a slow, laborious fight for control of key squares; a battle for the domination of space. All of this was accomplished by quiet moves, by skillful maneuvering; by lying back and waiting for a bored or frustrated opponent to make the first mistake. But it worked. In 1951 the dark-skinned, bushy-haired Petrosian began to make his presence felt. Invariably he scored high in his tournaments. At the 1952 Interzonal in Stockholm he did not lose a single game. The same thing happened at the Göteborg 1955 Interzonal— five wins and fifteen draws. There were, actually, entire years, as in 1962, when Petrosian did not lose a single tournament game. "Iron Tigran" he began to be called.

It cannot be said that his chess was very much admired, and some of his colleagues were brutally frank about it. Tal once described Petrosian to Spassky as a very careful player but a little bit cowardly; a very practical man; a real Armenian (whatever *that* may mean). More officially, Tal has described Petrosian's propensity for draws: "It seems to me that a large number of Petrosian's draws can be explained not by cautiousness or an unwillingness to take risks, but the desire to cut down to a minimum the concrete, active possibilities of his opponent and not allow him to exploit them. In paying such great attention to his opponent's potential opportunities he quite often underestimates his own. It is hard to judge whether this is a positive quality or, on the contrary, a fault; or perhaps it is just in this that the originality of Petrosian's style is most outlined." But this is doublethink. Tal's heart was not in it.

Year after year Petrosian went along this way, pointing at the world championship and slowly improving his chances of getting there. At the Stockholm Interzonal of 1962 he and all the other Russians must have had a terrible scare. Fischer ran away with it, gathering seventeen and a half points against the fifteen of his closest competitors, Petrosian and Geller. Now all Fischer had to do was win the Candidates' Tournament in Curaçao in 1962. If he played there as he had done at Stockholm, nobody would be able to come near him. Glumly the Russians prepared for the worst. At Curaçao were the players who had gained the first six positions at the Interzonal, along with Keres and Tal, who were seeded. This was the final standing at Curaçao:

Tigran Petrosian (USSR): 17½
Yefim Geller (USSR): 17
Paul Keres (USSR): 17
Robert J. Fischer (United States): 14
Victor Korchnoi (USSR): 13⅓
Pal Benko (United States): 12
Miroslav Filip (Czechoslovakia): 7
Mikhail Tal (USSR): 7

It was after this tournament that Fischer launched his famous charge of Russian cheating. Of the eight players, four were from the USSR and two more were from Soviet bloc countries. Fischer claimed that the Russians had agreed to prearranged draws or had actually thrown games to give certain players needed points; that they acted as a team against him. He cited as an example the twelve games among Petrosian, Geller, and Keres. All were drawn. These players, Fischer said, were not trying against each other. Statisticians examining those games noticed that their average number of moves was nineteen per game, as against 39.5 moves per game against other competitors. Whether or not Fischer's charges were true—some international players agreed, others pooh-poohed—the fact remains that FIDÉ soon made a ruling that no more than three players from any one country would be represented in an Interzonal Tournament (this rule no longer applies), and that the Candidates' Tournament would be replaced by a series of Candidates' Matches.

But that was for the future. It was Petrosian who won at Curaçao and earned the right to meet Botvinnik in 1963. Petrosian brushed up on his already all-encompassing theoretical knowledge and also spent two or three hours a day on the ski slopes. Physical endurance, he explained, was important; a long chess match of twenty-four games developed into an athletic event toward the end, and the player in better physical shape had a great advantage. Petrosian realized that he had a plus factor in Botvinnik's age; the champion was going to become physically and mentally exhausted long before Petrosian started to feel the effects. Petrosian also counted on Botvinnik's lack of familiarity with his play. They had not met each other many times in the past; only three times, as a matter of fact. Each game had ended in a draw.

Botvinnik, as was his habit, had played very little before the Petrosian match. Between the end of the Tal encounter in 1961 and his meeting with Petrosian, Botvinnik played in only four events—the European Team Championship in 1961; the 1961 Hastings Tournament, which he won; a tournament the following year in Stockholm, which he also won against not very strong competition; and the Chess Olympiad in Bulgaria, also in 1962, where he played first board for the Russian team, winning five, losing one and drawing six (one of the draws was against Fischer). Botvinnik came to the match faced with a new FIDÉ ruling. No longer was the champion entitled to a return match the following year if he lost the title. Instead, he would have to play in the Candidates' Matches and go through the last part of the three-year cycle. This ruling irritated Botvinnik no end.

The Botvinnik-Petrosian match was held in the Estrada Theater in Moscow—after the usual Botvinnikian demurrers. He and Petrosian argued interminably about the match conditions— the temperature of the hall, the referees, the conditions under which postponements could be made, everything. It even took long discussions to settle the location of the toilet. The suspicious Botvinnik did not bring a second along with him. Petrosian used Boleslavsky. A second in a chess match gives aid and comfort to his player, helps him analyze adjourned games, keeps him company, protects him from the outside world, buoys his confidence.

Petrosian lost the first game, drew even at the fifth, and then outsat his opponent, winning the title at the twenty-second game. The final score was 5 to 2, with fifteen draws. The last two games were perfunctory grandmaster draws, ten moves each. Botvinnik had given up. There was a feeling of disappointment about the performance of both players. Tal, for instance, had gone down in 1961 fighting to the very end, whereas Botvinnik was abjectly surrendering. "Certainly to play to win was a task," commented R. G. Wade in his book on the match. "But Petrosian with a life's ambition within his grasp might commit some indiscretion. There is nothing like emotions to upset the correct degree of application to any game." That was Wade's comment on the twenty-first game. At the twenty-second and last, Wade describes the actual surrender:

> The question was how long it would be before the two contestants agreed to a draw. The players were looking forward to it being all over. Petrosian had lost the best part of a stone [fourteen pounds] in weight. Botwinnik was looking tired and old. After nine moves Petrosian offered a draw but Botwinnik refused. Was it slight annoyance that Petrosian had taken the initiative in proposing? Petrosian moved and the minutes dragged past. The position was interesting. Was it this that fully occupied Botwinnik's thoughts? Or was he thinking back to that day in 1948 when he first became world champion? Botwinnik came to life and offered his hand. Draw. Petrosian was in fact world champion. His Armenian supporters invaded the stage, embraced him, kissed him and showered him with bouquets. In Armenia triplets were

named Tigran, Vartan (Petrosian's middle name is Vartanovich) and Petros. Botwinnik disappeared from the stage and slipped quietly away.

A typical example of Petrosian's boa-constrictor style of play is the fifth game of the match. Pieces are traded off, and at first the forces seem to be equal. Then Petrosian slowly crushes his opponent to death. Move by move he slowly gets his King into an active position and at the end is ready to pick off his opponent's King-side Pawns. Botvinnik therefore resigns:

	WHITE: PETROSIAN	BLACK: BOTVINNIK
1.	P-QB4	P-KN3
2.	P-Q4	N-KB3
3.	N-QB3	P-Q4
4.	N-B3	B-N2
5.	P-K3	O-O
6.	B-K2	PxP
7.	BxP	P-B4
8.	P-Q5	P-K3
9.	PxP	QxQch
10.	KxQ	BxP
11.	BxB	PxB
12.	K-K2	N-B3
13.	R-Q1	QR-Q1
14.	RxR	RxR
15.	N-KN5	R-K1
16.	KN-K4	NxN
17.	NxN	P-N3
18.	R-N1	N-N5
19.	B-Q2	N-Q4
20.	P-QR4	R-QB1
21.	P-QN3	B-B1
22.	R-QB1	B-K2
23.	P-QN4	P-B5
24.	P-N5	K-B2
25.	B-B3	B-R6
26.	R-B2	NxBch
27.	RxN	B-N5

28.	R-B2	K-K2
29.	N-Q2	P-B6
30.	N-K4	B-R4
31.	K-Q3	R-Q1ch
32.	K-B4	R-Q8
33.	NxP	R-KR8
34.	N-K4	RxP
35.	K-Q4	K-Q2
36.	P-N3	B-N5
37.	K-K5	R-R4ch
38.	K-B6	B-K2ch
39.	K-N7	P-K4
40.	R-B6	R-R8
41.	K-B7	R-R8
42.	R-K6	B-Q1
43.	R-Q6ch	K-B1
44.	K-K8	B-B2
45.	R-QB6	R-Q8
46.	N-N5	R-Q1ch
47.	K-B7	R-Q2ch
48.	K-N8	Resigns

Two years after the match, Botvinnik announced his retirement. He said that he would gladly have played Petrosian in a return match under the old rules. But since FIDÉ in its wisdom had seen fit to make the world championship match a three-year event, and since the deposed champion would have to go through the Candidates' Matches, he was bowing out. At the age of fifty-four it would be expecting too much of him to go through the mill.

And so the enigmatic Mikhail Botvinnik, the chess champion of the world from 1948 to 1963 (except for the one-year reigns of Smyslov and Tal), winner of the Stalin Prize in 1957, scientist, recluse, retired into private life, where he continued his work in electrotechnical theory and also started interesting himself in computer design, including the possibility of a chess-playing computer.

18 ♛

Poker Face, Inner Tears

During the six years that he held the title, Petrosian must of course have carefully studied his possible challengers around the world. There was always the threat of Bobby Fischer, but the American player had all but eliminated himself after Curaçao 1962 and his defiant declaration that he would no longer play in tournaments that included Russians. Reshevsky was too old. But maybe Henrique Mecking of Brazil would be the next Bobby Fischer. Much more of a problem would be Bent Larsen, with his fighting flair, his unorthodox style of play, his delight in obscure lines, his bizarre moves. Perhaps Svetozar Gligorić of Yugoslavia could stage a comeback, though he was getting a bit old. Within the Soviet bloc there were such fire-eaters as Lajos Portisch and Vlastimil Hort of Hungary, Borislav Ivkov of Yugoslavia, Ludek Pachman of Czechoslovakia or Wolfgang Uhlmann of East Germany. Within the Soviet Union itself were the always dangerous Smyslov; and Tal, who had been showing signs of reviving; and Geller, and Korchnoi, and Leonid Stein. And above all there was Boris Spassky.

But would Spassky have the determination to stick to it? There could be no questioning his brilliant gifts. There was some doubt about his psychological makeup. On the surface, Spassky was a rock. He seemed always to be calm, solid, unshakable. He had a poker face while playing. Win or lose, he never showed emotion—at the time. In 1964 Fischer told what it was like playing against him:

In a game I played with him several years ago, he lost a Pawn for no compensation. Then he played as if the Pawn he had lost meant nothing. While I was trying to figure out what was going on in his head, I blundered and lost the game. Spassky sits at the board with the same dead expression whether he's mating or being mated. He can blunder away a piece, and you are never sure whether it's a blunder or a fantastically deep sacrifice.

Underneath that strong, impassive exterior was a different man. Spassky throughout his career was beset with self-doubts, tormented by a feeling of inadequacy, actually physically sick when he lost a game. He worried about his losses and could not sleep; he would play the game over and over in his head, berating himself for making such stupid moves. Perhaps, many thought, Spassky was too sensitive to withstand the psychological pressures of constant tournament play. There was something of Dostoevsky in his makeup. He was handsome, urbane, cultured, well-mannered, highly intelligent. Everything seemed to be working in his favor. And yet there were those moments of uncontrollable despair. He had a strong ego, without which no chess player can go very far, but his was not the overpowering ego of a Steinitz, Alekhine, or Fischer. Rather, it was an inner-directed ego, and it could work against him as easily as it could work for him.

Born in Leningrad on January 30, 1937, Spassky was evacuated to Moscow during the war. His parents were divorced in 1944. Spassky took up chess at the age of five. Returning to Leningrad with his mother, he worked under the direction of Vladimir Zak at the Palace of Pioneers, and developed a passionate involvement with chess. There are many parallels between his career and Fischer's. Both were brought up by their mothers as a result of parental divorce. Both were born Jewish on the maternal side. Both were highly emotional about chess as children, crying when they lost a game. Both were supernaturally gifted. And both were prodigies, though Fischer as a teenager turned out better games. Spassky was good enough, however, to become a candidate master when he was twelve. At that time, he says, he played "like an old man, very positional and solid."

He went to the university, where he switched his major from mathematics to journalism (journalism was easier and also gave him more time for chess). He enjoyed sports and was a track-and-

Boris Spassky (standing) *and Yefim Geller in 1968, two of the candidates for Petrosian's title. Spassky won the finals and went on to become the world champion the following year.*

field man, able to jump more than his own height. Spassky is five feet, ten inches tall, and could clear five feet, eleven and three-quarter inches in the high jump. Between 1946 and 1950 Spassky worked on chess at least five hours a day. Yet he, with typical diffidence, described himself as lazy. "It is in my nature to be like a Russian bear. Someone who is very calm and lazy and finds it an effort to spend the time to stand up." He also doubted his own nature. "I believe in truth at the chessboard, but down deep I lack faith in myself." Chess aside, he enjoyed a normal growing-up period. Like all undergraduates, Spassky chased the girls, went out with his friends, attended concerts, and got through his studies with a minimum of effort. Spassky loves music and says that his favorite composers are Mozart, Scriabin, and Mussorgsky. His favorite author is—who else?— Dostoevsky.

His chess developed rapidly. Confidence returned; he over-came his tendency to be crushed when he lost a game. Now if he was beaten he felt "a great energy to fight again." But then there was a period when everything seemed to go wrong. He made an unhappy marriage, and there was a divorce in 1961. (Later he remarried.) He became unhappy with his trainer, Alexander Tolush; there was a personality clash between the two. During those years Spassky was beginning to compile an impressive record in Soviet chess—winner of the Leningrad Junior Championship in 1949; second in the Leningrad Championship of 1952; World's Junior Champion in 1955; third in the USSR Championship of 1955. Yet Spassky was dissatisfied. "I could do nothing right. I felt at the time I had talent, but I was very nervous." He actually felt that he was losing his grip. His account of an important game with Tal in 1958 is one of the best accounts ever written of the anxiety, nervous state, and psychological strain all chess players go through. The game was adjourned after forty-five moves, and both players were up all night analyzing the continuation. Spassky thought he had the edge:

> The game was adjourned and I had a good position; but I was very tired from analyzing and went to resume next morning unshaven. Before I played important games I usually tried to bathe, to put on a very good shirt and suit, and to look *comme il faut*. But on this occasion I had analyzed incessantly and came to the board looking very dishevelled and fatigued. Then I was like a stubborn mule. I remember that Tal offered me a draw, but I refused. Then I felt my strength ebb away, and I lost the thread of the game. My position deteriorated; I proposed a draw, but Tal refused. When I resigned there was a thunder of applause but I was in a daze and hardly understood what was happening. I was certain the world went down; I felt there was something terribly wrong. After the game I went on the street and cried like a child. I remember that in 1951 when I lost to Smyslov in his clock simultaneous was the last time I cried, and I promised myself never to cry again; but after losing to Tal I couldn't keep my word.

Spassky was not the only one who had doubts about Spassky. During this critical period he was not in high favor with the Soviet Chess Federation. It was felt that he was not putting forward his best efforts, and he was punished by being suspended from play abroad. Three times he was refused permission to participate in tournaments outside of the Soviet Union. Spassky, who never joined the Communist Party, may have been considered politically unreliable. The authorities were particularly unhappy when he lost to William Lombardy of the United States in 1960 at the world students' championship matches. They charged that he had not trained conscientiously enough, had not prepared properly. And yet, with all his personal troubles, he was capable of producing some sparkling chess. His win against Bronstein at the USSR Championship in Leningrad 1960 is an example of his sharp, precise play:

	WHITE: SPASSKY	BLACK: BRONSTEIN
1.	P-K4	P-K4
2.	P-KB4	PxP
3.	N-KB3	P-Q4
4.	PxP	B-Q3
5.	N-B3	N-K2
6.	P-Q4	O-O
7.	B-Q3	N-Q2
8.	O-O	P-KR3
9.	N-K4	NxP
10.	P-B4	N-K6
11.	BxN	PxB
12.	P-B5	B-K2
13.	B-B2	R-K1
14.	Q-Q3	P-K7
15.	N-Q6	N-B1
16.	NxBP	PxR = Qch
17.	RxQ	B-B4
18.	QxB	Q-Q2
19.	Q-B4	B-B3
20.	N(3)-K5	Q-K2
21.	B-N3	BxN
22.	NxBch	K-R2
23.	Q-K4ch	Resigns

Bronstein resigns because if K-R1, there follows 24. RxNch, and Black is in a mating net. The Pawn sacrifice on White's ninth move is typical of modern grandmaster play. Often a Pawn is surrendered for greater mobility of the pieces. But Spassky's offer of the Knight on the fifteenth move represents Spassky's style at its most enterprising and exuberant. (When Fischer encountered this game he was so struck by Spassky's conception that he prophesied Spassky's ascent to the title.)

Spassky is described as an all-around player, at home in all phases of the game. But where he excels, many believe, is in his adaptability; his eclectic style encompasses *all* styles. Gligorić says that Spassky's secret power is his "colossal ability to meet the different styles of each opponent. Only Alekhine, and perhaps Lasker, showed such ability before."

In 1961 Spassky took a new trainer, the veteran Igor Bondarevsky, and his playing perceptibly improved. A looser, freer quality was noted in his play. That year he won the USSR Championship. In 1964, Spassky was in top form. He tied for first with Smyslov and Larsen at the Amsterdam Interzonal, and then proceeded to beat Keres (6 to 4), Geller (5½ to 2½) and Tal (6½ to 3½) at the Candidates' Matches. In 1965 Spassky and Petrosian had it out for the world's championship. Spassky prepared by taking the physical as well as the intellectual side of his opponent under consideration:

> I am a little younger, seven years, and my advantage is in the fifth hour of play. I have to think how to organize the games in such a way that the climax of the fighting will come at the end of the session. Sometimes Petrosian plays rather passively in the opening, and then I have to find an effective plan which gives me a gradual middle game initiative. Botvinnik tried to win this way in the 1963 match, but he was a little too old for such an approach. Petrosian knows the openings much better than I do, so there I have to do a lot of work to maintain equal chances.

The theory was good, but something happened. Spassky lost. Petrosian outsat him, as he had outsat so many opponents, and the final score was 4 to 3 with seventeen draws—the highest number of draws in any championship match since Capablanca-Alekhine.

Spassky had to go through the Candidates' Matches again, in 1968. As Petrosian's opponent in 1966, however, he did not have to play at the Interzonal at Sousse, Tunisia, in 1967. That was the tournament Fischer quit at the halfway mark, although he was in first place at the time, having knocked out all the opposition with careless impartiality. At that point he was faced with four games in four consecutive days, because his schedule had jammed up. It had jammed up because Fischer, for religious reasons, will not play between sundowns on Friday and Saturday. He objected to the consecutive playoffs, claiming that the judges were taking advantage of him, subjecting him to cruel and inhuman punishment. He also pointed out, correctly, that he had entered the tournament with an assurance that such conditions would not prevail. But the judges would not change their ruling, and Fischer would not change his mind. So he went home; the point of principle was more important to him than the world championship. Petrosian in Moscow, keeping an eye on Sousse with a great deal of interest, must have heaved a huge sigh of relief. In the United States there was consternation. "Finally the United States produces its greatest chess genius and he turns out to be just a stubborn boy," said a saddened Hans Kmoch.

The qualifiers for the Candidates' Matches during 1968 were Larsen, Korchnoi, Portisch, Geller, Reshevsky, Gligorić, Tal, and Spassky. The eventual winner was Spassky, who in his matches beat Geller (5½ to 2½), Larsen (5½ to 2½), and Korchnoi (6½ to 3½). Now all Spassky had to do was beat Petrosian, and he did so in 1969 (6 to 4, with thirteen draws). Boris Spassky had achieved his goal. And who would his opponent be in 1972? Larsen or Korchnoi, most likely, said the experts. Not Bobby Fischer, who at Sousse had talked himself out of world championship competition once and for all.

19 ♛

The Ego Crusher

In the early 1950's the Manhattan Chess Club was located on the southwest corner of Central Park South and Sixth Avenue, and all the best young American players would consistently be there, slamming pieces around, playing rapid transit (chess at ten seconds a move) and blitz (instantaneous chess), indulging in horseplay, and infuriating the elder members of the club, who were constantly being distracted by the whoops and yells of the kids. At any given time one could see the Byrne brothers, Robert and Donald, and Larry Evans, and Arthur Bisguier, James Sherwin, Walter Shipman, William Lombardy, Attilio Di Camillo, Eliot Hearst. Some of these went on to become grandmasters, United States champions, writers on chess. But few became chess professionals. One had to go to college, marry, raise a family, and that could not be done on the income of a chess player. There was no future in chess. These boys could have challenged the Russian supremacy; they had the talent. But they did not have the atmosphere or the financial backing to devote themselves full time to chess.

Robert James Fischer, known to everybody as Bobby, started to haunt the Manhattan Chess Club in the middle 1950's, when he was about twelve years old. Even then hardly anybody could beat him. Playing against the best in the country, he more often than not demolished the opposition. The masters would gather around to watch him play fast chess. Skill at rapid chess is always a sign of innate talent, and it was clear that the boy was

258

Fischer in Argentina, 1971. At this time he already was a legend, as much for his brilliant chess as for his eccentricity. Not since Alekhine had there been such a will to win. "I like to see 'em squirm," he once explained.

unusual. Within a few years Bobby Fischer was in a class by himself. United States champion at fourteen; grandmaster at fifteen, the youngest in the history of the game; United States champion eight times; winner of tournament after tournament; and, finally, Chess Champion of the World after beating Boris Spassky in Reykjavik, 1972. And more: Bobby Fischer the eccentric, the rebel against authority, the culture hero of the American campus, the monomaniac, the *enfant terrible*, the money-hungry, ego-crushing titan of chess. And still more: Bobby Fischer who, in spite of himself, has done more to popularize chess than any other player who ever lived, whose tantrums and inexplicable actions have captured the imagination of the world, whose intransigence approaches sublimity. Bobby Fischer, who is so ineffably self-centered, spoiled, egoistic, stubborn, inconsiderate, that he is already a legend. His life has a kind of topsy-turvy grandeur unique not only in chess but in any field of human activity. Not even Richard Wagner, the all-time symbol of a self-centered genius who could arrange the world to suit himself, had this degree of monomania.

Bobby Fischer was a strange boy who grew up into a strange man. From the beginning he *always* believed he was right—right in chess, right in his attitude toward the people around him. When he could get his way, he was the voice of sweet reason. When he was crossed, he literally could go wild. Only one thing in life meant anything to him, but he had to pursue his goal in his own uncompromising way, making no concessions to anybody. That was as true when he was fifteen as it is today. Very few people have ever been able to advise him, very few people have ever been able to get close to him. Bobby Fischer moves through life as *he* sees fit. Yet he has managed to make everything come true for himself. Perhaps he has an instinct denied most other people; perhaps he is in such rapport with certain aspects of the *Zeitgeist* because he himself *is* the *Zeitgeist*. More than anybody else he seems to know what he represents in relation to the spirit of the time. Before the Spassky match he let it be known that he would not play unless the purse was at least $50,000. There was tolerant laughter. Everybody thought that Fischer was out of his mind. $50,000 for a *chess match?* Who on earth would be willing to put up that sum? But when it was all over, Fischer walked away with the winner's share of a purse of $250,000. It was, prizefight purses excepted, the largest single purse for a sporting event ever recorded. Spassky, when he had won the world championship, got $1400 as his prize money.

Born in Chicago on March 9, 1943, he settled with his mother and sister in Brooklyn after a restless traipse that took them to Oregon, Arizona, and California. His sister taught him the moves when he was six years old. They got a chess set and puzzled out from the directions what to put where. The boy loved games of all kinds. His mother remembered that as a baby he would "get those Japanese interlocking rings, and things like that, and take things apart I couldn't figure out at all." In school Bobby was a problem. Fresh from California, he had never worn a shirt—or, at least, he was never seen in one—and he rebelled against the necessity of dressing up. In the fourth grade, the Brooklyn Community-Woodward School gave him a scholarship. The boy's intelligence quotient has never been revealed, but school authorities said it was in the upper percentile. He was not a very good student, and he was a complete nonconformist. "We were able to adjust to him," an official of the school said. One thing noted by his teachers was his abnormal competitive urge in any kind of game. "He easily beat everybody," one of his teachers later remembered, "including the chess-playing members of the faculty. No matter what he played, whether it was baseball in the yard or tennis, he *had* to come out ahead of everybody. If he had been born next to a swimming pool he would have been a swimming champion. It just turned out to be chess."

Once Bobby became fascinated with chess there was no turning back. Nothing could interfere with his passion. The boy, of a poor family and without any friends, had an overwhelming urge to win, to dominate, and chess became his outlet. At eight he started going to the Brooklyn Chess Club. While most children his age were reading comic books and reluctantly doing homework, Bobby was memorizing games in *Shakhmaty* and *Chess Review*. He thought of nothing but chess, he studied nothing but chess, and his teachers at Erasmus Hall High School in Brooklyn wisely left him pretty much to his own resources. In his junior year Bobby left school for good because "the stuff they teach you in school I can't use one way or the other." He let it be known

Bobby Fischer at the age of thirteen. Already he could hold his own against the leading players. The following year he became United States champion.

that his future was set. "All I want to do, ever," he announced, "is play chess."

At thirteen, during the Rosenwald Tournament in New York, Bobby ripped off a staggering game against Donald Byrne. Hans Kmoch excitedly called it "the game of the century." And indeed it was an extraordinary conception from anybody, much more a boy entering his teens. There were sacrifices all over the place, but these were not wild attacks; everything was thought out and beautifully controlled. Not even Capablanca had shown this kind of ability at an equivalent age:

WHITE: D. BYRNE	BLACK: FISCHER
1. N-KB3	N-KB3
2. P-B4	P-KN3

3.	N-B3	B-N2
4.	P-Q4	O-O
5.	B-B4	P-Q4
6.	Q-N3	PxP
7.	QxBP	P-B3
8.	P-K4	QN-Q2
9.	R-Q1	N-N3
10.	Q-B5	B-N5
11.	B-KN5	N-R5
12.	Q-R3	NxN
13.	PxN	NxP
14.	BxP	Q-N3
15.	B-B4	NxQBP
16.	B-B5	KR-K1ch
17.	K-B1	B-K3
18.	BxQ	BxBch
19.	K-N1	N-K7ch
20.	K-B1	NxPch
21.	K-N1	N-K7ch
22.	K-B1	N-B6ch
23.	K-N1	PxB
24.	Q-N4	R-R5
25.	QxP	NxR
26.	P-KR3	RxP
27.	K-R2	NxP
28.	R-K1	RxR
29.	Q-Q8ch	B-B1
30.	NxR	B-Q4
31.	N-B3	N-K5
32.	Q-N8	P-QN4
33.	P-R4	P-R4
34.	N-K5	K-N2
35.	K-N1	B-B4ch
36.	K-B1	N-N6ch
37.	K-K1	B-N5ch
38.	K-Q1	B-N6ch
39.	K-B1	N-K7ch
40.	K-N1	N-B6ch
41.	K-B1	R-B7 mate

To this kind of flair and intuition, Fischer added an incredibly retentive memory and a comprehensive book knowledge. It is said that he has never forgotten a game he has played or an analysis he has read. As a boy he would walk around with his pockets stuffed with chess magazines; those and chess books constituted virtually his only reading. He was able to pick up exactly the amount of Russian, German, Serbo-Croatian, or Spanish needed to make sense out of chess publications in those languages. He was a sullen, moody, suspicious boy; he refused to wear anything but sports shirts, denims, and sneakers. Already he was an eccentric. Later he developed a taste for flashy clothing and handmade shoes, but in other aspects he changed very little as he grew up. He remained aloof from everybody. "Fischer wants to enter history alone," Grandmaster Najdorf observed. In Fischer's kind of total dedication to chess there was no room for girls, for friendships, for the social graces and the amenities of life. Once he was asked whom he sees socially. "Oh . . . chess players," he vaguely answered. In his life there are only two kinds of people: good players and lesser ones, referred to scornfully as "hacks." Fischer won't even talk about "fish" or "patzers," the mass of woodpushers who scarcely know the difference between a Nimzo-Indian and a Ruy Lopez. Whatever emotional life he had for most of his growing-up period was a kind of transference, possibly sexual in nature, over the chess board. As early as 1957, when he was fourteen, he said that he got a thrill out of watching his opponents suffer. "I like to see 'em squirm." Later, on a television talk show, he said that his great thrill in chess comes at the point where he realizes that his opponent is in a vise. He called this "crushing the opponent's ego." All are agreed that Fischer satisfies his emotional life by watching his opponents disintegrate. In the process his own ego is correspondingly built up.

Intensely close-mouthed about his personal life, he refuses to talk about his religion, his family, the way he amuses himself. His religion is fundamentalist. He is interested in the Worldwide Church of God, a group based in Pasadena that observes the Jewish sabbath and the Jewish holidays. Fischer will not play chess on Jewish holidays or between sundowns on Friday and Saturday. (That caused some amused speculation in Reykjavik, where in early July, the sun does not set until nearly midnight and it never gets dark. What, then, were the theological aspects of the sundown-to-sundown observances? Fischer solved it by choosing an arbitrary time and sticking to it.) For most of his life he has had no permanent address. He has been on his own from the age of sixteen or so; he and his mother are not on good terms. Usually Fischer lives in inexpensive hotel rooms, and he demands rooms that do *not* have a view. That would interfere with his concentration. In recent years he has been reading some publications outside of chess—the news magazines and *Playboy* especially. And he generally has a battery-operated radio at full volume in his room, blasting out the latest pop and rock. But mostly he continues to work at chess, studying openings, studying end games, working out new wrinkles, playing over games of opponents he will face, probing for weaknesses both technical and psychological. Dr. Euwe has gazed upon Fischer and marveled: "He studies chess day and night. In fact, I've never seen him do anything but chess."

Fischer does not apologize for his monomania. "Chess," he says, "demands total concentration. Yeah, and love for the game. The Russians have produced great players but not natural talents because they never had to struggle." Mention of the Russians somehow creeps into almost every Fischer conversation; he dislikes the Russian system, and it is said that his own political views are far right. "You can get good," Fischer has said, "only if you love the game. I'm not sure the Russians do. They are more interested in what they get out of it, and they don't develop character. It takes a certain amount of adversity to develop character. Everything has come too easy for the Russians. They get the red-carpet treatment." Fischer's dislike of the Russians is not only on abstract principles; a personal feeling also enters into it. He thinks they are out to "get" him. One reason he announced he would never again play in Russia, aside from the fact that the Russian players "cheated," was that "they" would annoy and harass him and prevent him from playing his best. "I won't play in Russia, period."

There is nobody Fischer would rather beat than a Russian, and it was the opportunity to do so that lured him out of retirement and set him on the path to the championship. His international record during the 1960's had been spectacular. First with Spassky at Mar del Plata 1960. First at Stockholm 1962.

Second to Spassky at the Piatigorsky Cup Tournament at Santa Monica 1966. Firsts at Monaco 1967 and Skopje 1967. (There were also a few failures, and an unfinished match with Reshevsky in 1961 that Fischer forfeited after a dispute with the organizers.) But after his argument at the Sousse Interzonal in 1967 he returned to California and did not play chess at all for some eighteen months. In March, 1970, there was a great tournament in Belgrade in which Russia challenged the world. Fischer was invited to play first board for the West and, to everybody's surprise, accepted. Whereupon Bent Larsen loudly complained. Larsen said that on the basis of his record *he* should have been invited to play first board for the West. He had a point. Larsen, after all, was considered the strongest player in the West, aside from Fischer, and his tournament record for 1969 and 1970 had been a series of brilliant successes, whereas Fischer had been inactive during that period.

If Fischer had surprised everybody by accepting the invitation, he utterly amazed everybody by backing down and accepting second board. That was very un-Bobbylike, but apparently he was anxious to return to international play. Also, as he later admitted, he thought he would have better chances against Petrosian than against Spassky, who was at the first board for the Russians. Fischer arrived in Belgrade just before the start of the tournament and astonished everybody (and perhaps himself) by winning the first two of his four games against Petrosian. *Nobody* wins two games in a row against Petrosian. Fischer was content to draw the next two games with the ex-champion, ending with a 3 to 1 score. In the meantime, Larsen drew with Spassky, lost to him, beat him, and everything depended on the final game. At this point Spassky became "ill," and the Russians replaced him with Leonid Stein. There were knowing nods. The Russians were not going to let Larsen get away with a possible plus score against the champion. Larsen, smoldering, beat Stein.

Stimulated by his plus score against Petrosian, Fischer entered the Zagreb Tournament two months later, and won it. After the Zagreb Tournament, Fischer was invited to play in a rapids tournament. Again there was general surprise when he accepted. Fischer in his maturity never had gone in for rapid or blindfold chess. He has stated that rapid chess, where a clock game has to be completed in *five* minutes, leads to sloppiness. "It kills your ideas," he explained. But he accepted the challenge, and the Russians were delighted. They figured on teaching Fischer a lesson and on bringing him down a peg or two. Petrosian and Tal were supposed to be the two best speed players in the world. But Fischer easily won that tournament too—won it going away. At this point it was inconceivable to the world of chess that the oncoming Interzonal could be held without Fischer. Clearly he was as good as any other player in the world, and most likely he was the best. A world's champion elimination match would be a mockery without the participation of Fischer. But there was one little thing: Fischer, strictly speaking, was not eligible. In bypassing the United States Championship play, he had not qualified as a FIDÉ contender.

So a special ruling was made, with the concurrence of the member nations. If one of the United States qualifiers dropped out, Fischer would be permitted to replace him. Pal Benko agreed, and Fischer took his place at the Interzonal at Palma de Majorca. He won it easily, with a superb score of 18½ to 4½ (fifteen wins, seven draws, one loss—to Larsen). Far behind in second place was Geller, 15 to 8.

Then Fischer started his series of Candidates' Matches. The rest is history. Fischer mauled the opposition in an unprecedented manner. In Vancouver he blanked Mark Taimanov, 6 to 0. Taimanov came to Vancouver with two seconds, both grandmasters. Fischer was alone. He thought that the sight of Taimanov and his seconds was the funniest thing he had ever seen. There Taimanov and his seconds would sit, six hands flying, pocket sets waving in the air, while variations were being spouted all over the place. And there sat Taimanov with a confused look on his face. Just before resuming play in one adjourned position, the seconds were giving Taimanov some last-minute advice. When poor Taimanov entered the playing room and sat down to confront Fischer, his head was so full of conflicting continuations that he became rattled, left a Rook *en prise* and immediately resigned. Sighed Taimanov, preparing to return to Russia, "I still have my music." (Taimanov is a Moscow Conservatory graduate and a fine concert pianist.)

In Denver, Fischer shut out Larsen, 6 to 0. Larsen blamed his defeat on the climate; it was too hot and he was not able to concentrate. Counting his last seven games at Palma de Majorca, Fischer now had a streak of nineteen consecutive victories in grandmaster play. This was unheard of in the history of chess. Even the Russians hailed the feat as a miracle, and Bobby became the most popular American in the Soviet Union, more so than even Van Cliburn. There was a great deal of consternation in Russian chess circles when Bobby's streak became known. Such great players as Spassky and Botvinnik had been telling the Soviet public for years that there was only a slight shade of difference among grandmasters. Botvinnik, when he was champion, had described himself merely as *primus inter pares.* If that was true, how to explain Fischer's insulting dominance over the best? Soberly the Russian press warned its chess fans that Petrosian, Bobby's next opponent, stood a good chance of losing the match, and that even the great Spassky would have a hard fight on his hands.

The Fischer-Petrosian Candidates' Match was held in Buenos Aires in October, 1971. It was prefaced by Fischer's usual temperamental haggling over playing conditions. In that respect Fischer always made Botvinnik look like an amateur. For years Fischer had been insisting on larger purses and better playing conditions. He would not play unless glare-free fluorescent lighting was installed. There had to be fresh air, good ventilation, and temperature control; and, above all, silence. Fischer's contract specified that the audience had to be a minimum of 40 feet from the playing area. (Many honestly believed that Fischer's ideal would be to eliminate the audience completely.) No photographers were allowed to operate during a game. When Fischer arrived at the scene of a match, he invariably found additional things to make him unhappy. Everybody's nerves, while dealing with Fischer and his conditions before and during a match, are shot—everybody's nerves, that is, except Fischer's.

Fischer won his first game against Petrosian, extending his winning streak to twenty. Then, at long last, he dropped a game. Three draws followed, and this was Petrosian territory. Bobby could be in trouble. Reports began to come out of Buenos Aires. Bobby was not feeling well. Bobby had a cold. Bobby was off form. It later was learned that Fischer actually did have a cold and was taking drugs for it. His pride would not allow him to postpone a game. Bobby's *opponents* are the ones who get sick and have to postpone, not Bobby Fischer. He was very quiet during the first week. Then he started to complain. He complained about his hotel room and changed it three times in three days. He complained about the food. He complained about the playing conditions. At that point the Americans in his small entourage knew that the old Bobby was back in action. He was healthy again. Watch out, Petrosian! Sure enough Fischer won the next four games and won the match, 6½ to 2½. Petrosian had been outplayed. But it is hard to play against Bobby Fischer in more ways than one; and a year or so later Petrosian, in a reminiscence about the Buenos Aires match, was indignant and at the same time wryly funny about it:

> It is impossible for two players to play under different conditions; it is difficult to fight when, before the first move, you must submit to the will of your opponent. Fischer wanted to play in Buenos Aires; I did not. When Fischer wanted to play, I had to play; when Fischer wants coffee, I drink coffee, etc. It sounds funny but it's not.

On his return to the United States after the Petrosian match, Fischer stated that he had never had any doubt about the outcome. "I played pretty good," he said. He conceded that Petrosian had not taken full advantage of his opportunities. "He had a good position in the first game and didn't press it." That was the game in which, uncharacteristically, Petrosian sprang a prepared variation and an attack on Fischer, catching him by surprise. But Petrosian, as if frightened by his temerity, soon drew back and Fischer went on to win. "He also had the advantage in the third game and maybe a win." Some experts kept insisting that Petrosian was off form, and that he should have had a plus score at the end of the sixth game. This kind of remark irritates Fischer, who is sick and tired of hearing that his opponents lose because they are not up to par. "People have been playing against me below strength for fifteen years," he says.

FIDÉ fixed the Spassky-Fischer match for the spring of 1972 and asked for bids from interested cities. It was at this time, with interest running high, that much attention was being paid to

Fischer's style, and many learned articles were written about it. What made him the player he was? The experts pontificated. "His game is sharp, cool and classical," said Larry Evans. "It is never unsound. It follows the truth. It also borders just this side of recklessness. Bobby hates defensive positions and is very strong at keeping the initiative. And there is no more accurate player alive. Against Bobby you can't make the slightest mistake. You're dead." William Lombardy characterized Fischer's game as machinelike, with "terrifically accurate positional play but never boring. . . . His opening repertory is encompassing. Certainly he's the greatest of all exponents on the Black side of a Sicilian or King's Indian. His end game is practically flawless. Bobby is the most complete player I've ever seen."

Another grandmaster, Robert Byrne, who later became the United States champion, talked about Fischer with rueful respect, for he had been on the wrong end of one of Fischer's great games. Byrne said that there was a lot of "idiot nonsense" written about Fischer:

> He's a classicist with a purely classic approach. Sure, he can win brilliantly, with sacrifices and everything, but every game is based on position. The frequent smashing attacks he gets are merely a result of his opponents' desperate attempts to avoid positional disadvantage. Bobby pursues the Idea of the game in its Platonic sense. All of us players have that ideal. But Bobby knows how to embody it. He has the ability to overcome the chaotic mess and the complexity of modern chess, the baroque scramble, and isolate a single theme, a single line of development, and carrying it through. How he does it is his secret. Nobody else can. Bobby's approach always is completely rational. Larsen, for instance, is a romantic who looks for the unusual move. Bobby will never do that. He may make the *unexpected* move but never the unusual or unharmonious one. He wins a classic theme over and over again—the superior Bishop versus the inferior Knight. Bobby scares them. I call it "Fischer-fear." I think that's what happened to Taimanov. He was terrified.

Fischer himself had a few words to say about his chess. He admitted to a comprehensive book knowledge. "There are no longer any surprises, any departures from book, any nineteenth-century gambits," he said. "The old gambits can't come back because players today know too much. Whatever position you've got it's been played before. There are only so many *types* of positions. There are concrete things happening, whether positional or tactical. Chess is not that hard a game. Everything has been worked out."

One of the peculiarities of Fischer's style up to the Spassky match was his invariable choice of a King's Pawn opening. The number of games in which he had *not* opened 1. P-K4 during his career could be counted on the fingers of a mutilated right hand. Fischer knows the King's Pawn openings better than any other player who ever lived. Opponents come to him well prepared; they know in advance what his first move will be. It makes no difference. As Gligorić says, it may seem naïve of Fischer "to enter always upon the same positions, like going with bared chest up against the guns of opponents well prepared to direct their fire. . . . Yet, out of these psychological and theoretical duels, it has almost always been Fischer who came out as victor from the queer fight. One position, one line, but innumerable hidden possibilities which Fischer alone has been able to disclose first." And always there was that clear, lyrical, effortless style. It comes as no surprise to learn that Fischer admires Capablanca. "I always understood what Capablanca was doing. Everything was logical. Then I became interested in Alekhine. Botvinnik also. I respect Botvinnik. He was a real thinker."

Ever since he was a boy, Fischer had loudly insisted that he was "the best." Botvinnik, Spassky—they were never in his class. Fischer went around saying that he could give Botvinnik Pawn and move and still beat him. Part of this was, of course, adolescent bravado. But after Fischer's extraordinary streak, culminating in his victory over Petrosian, who could argue with him? There was a growing feeling that Fischer was not only the greatest player of his time; he probably was the greatest player of all time. Certainly in the previous twelve months he had run wild over all the opposition. All, that is, except Spassky. The two had met five times, and Fischer had as yet to win a game; he had lost to Spassky three times and drawn twice. That made the forthcoming match all the more exciting. Perhaps Spassky, the Russian bear, the solid and reliable Spassky, was the only player who could hold the brilliant, temperamental Fischer. Perhaps Spassky would be the one player immune to Fischer-fear. Perhaps. It was pointed out that two years had passed since Spassky's victory over Fischer at the Olympiad at Siegen 1970, and that Fischer had made giant progress since then. Now Fischer was in full maturity, and also riding the momentum of his incredible spurt since March, 1970. The feeling was that Fischer should win, but that he would not have an easy time of it.

20 ♛

Alarums and Excursions

Reykjavik, the capital of Iceland, was the locale of the encounter between Boris Spassky and Bobby Fischer. For over two months the attention of the world was focused on that tiny city in that tiny island. The match captured the imagination of the man in the street all over the globe; the quiet pushing of Pawns and pieces created some kind of logarithmic response that even pushed the tribulations of Senator McGovern and Senator Eagleton off the front pages of American newspapers. Words like poisoned Pawn, Nimzo-Indian, Alekhine's Defense, and Ruy Lopez entered the international consciousness. Hitherto unknown names, such as that of Shelby Lyman, who covered the entire match for educational television in the United States, suddenly became famous. The on-the-scene estimates and evaluations of such grandmasters as Larsen, Gligorić, Janošević, and Iceland's own Fridrik Olafsson were taken as seriously as the pronouncements of a Greek sibyl after the study of the entrails of a chicken. In New York bars, gamblers and other sports were betting vast sums on each move made by Fischer or Spassky. All over the world action seemed to come to a halt as moves were relayed over the wires and through the air into city rooms and television stations.

With all due deference to Spassky, this was all Bobby Fischer's doing. He and he alone brought the match to fever pitch and made of it a thrilling drama that far transcended a mere chess match: first by not showing up in Reykjavik; then by appearing and starting his usual round of threats and complaints; by being party to the most hysterical theatrics since the great days of King Lear; then by losing the first two games (the second on a forfeit), yet coming from behind and convincingly smashing the champion. Of such deeds are legends made. For a delirious period of time, chess was front-page news in any civilized section of the world. People who previously did not know a Pawn from the rear end of a Knight would sit entranced while two great players fought each other, tried to outmaneuver each other, tried to dominate and psychically destroy each other. Willy-nilly, this chess match between Boris Spassky of the Soviet Union and Robert James Fischer of the United States became much more than a match between two players. It became an international incident, a struggle between two societies, a symbol of the confrontation between East and West. Both players denied any political implications. "I can only say that while seated at the chessboard I am a chess player and not a politician," said Spassky. "I am interested only in the best move," said Fischer. But the world ignored these remarks. Russia was facing America in the persons of these two players.

Reykjavik was a compromise location. When the bids for the match were opened in Amsterdam on January 3, 1972, it was found that Belgrade—where Fischer is idolized—had offered a purse of $152,000 to be host to the match. Other cities offered nearly as much. Reykjavik's bid was $125,000—about fifty cents for every man, woman, and child in that island. And this was only for the purse. Much more money would have to be put up before the match was even started. There were the personal expenses of the players and their entourages. There was the money needed to prepare a hall for a chess match. And so on. Fischer wanted Belgrade, or so he said. Spassky wanted Reykjavik. He said its climate was closest to that with which he was most familiar and most comfortable (Spassky, it will be remembered, came from Leningrad). On January 18, Dr. Euwe, as president of FIDÉ, invited Fischer and Spassky to Amsterdam for a discussion of the playing site. Euwe said that "if the order of preference of both lists is not the same, the President has the right to decide which offer shall be accepted." Fischer's list was headed by Belgrade, Sarajevo, Buenos Aires, and Montreal. Spassky's preferences were Reykjavik, Amsterdam, Dortmund, or Paris. Edmund B. Edmondson, Executive Director of the United States Chess Federation, arrived in Amsterdam on January 20, and Fischer came the following day. Edmondson formally handed over to FIDÉ Fischer's preference of sites. Edmondson was, in a way, Fischer's surrogate father. He had accompanied Fischer to many of the Candidates' Matches, handled all of his affairs, and smoothed out things to his satisfaction.

The Russians did not come to Amsterdam. They claimed that procedure had been violated. Euwe disallowed the protest. The Russians refused to send a spokesman for Spassky. Fischer went home. Edmondson, acting (so he thought) for Fischer, visited Iceland, then Moscow, then Belgrade. All of a sudden, Fischer, in the United States, acted up. He denied being a party to any negotiations, saying that Edmondson had no authority to act for him and hence no authority to sign as his representative. "I never signed anything," said Fischer, which was true. Fischer never signs *any* documents.

After some thought, Euwe decided to resolve the dispute by dividing the match between Belgrade and Reykjavik. That, he thought, would make both players, if not entirely happy, at least mollified. Belgrade telegraphed acceptance. Euwe announced that the match would start there on June 25, shifting to Reykjavik after twelve games. The USSR objected, but Euwe held firm. At that moment in history, Dr. Euwe departed on a two-month tour of Asia and Australia, saying that Rafael Mendez of Puerto Rico, the deputy FIDÉ president, could act for him. On January 23 an agreement was signed in Amsterdam splitting the match between Belgrade and Reykjavik. Yefim Geller signed for the USSR and Edmondson for Fischer.

But Robert James Fischer had not been heard from. He sent a cable denying Edmondson's authority to act for him, and refused to accept the terms, demanding that Belgrade considerably improve its offer. Fischer wanted all the money over total expenses to be divided between him and Spassky. Otherwise, "I will not play your match in Yugoslavia." Or Iceland, for that matter. Another cable followed: "Your financial offer is out of the question and I will not play Spassky in Belgrade."

Belgrade, understandably confused and put out, demanded

that the United States Chess Federation and the Soviet Chess Federation each put up a bond for $35,000 ensuring the appearance of the Belgrade sponsors. Belgrade, after all, had put up an immense sum, as chess purses go, far in excess of the previous record, the $20,000 raised for the Capablanca-Lasker match. But that was not enough for Bobby Fischer. The Russians gloated, writing about money-hungry Bobby, *nyekulturny* Bobby, that representative of capitalist culture who thought money was more important than art. The Russians, knowing very well the condition of the United States Chess Federation's bankroll, hastened to put up the $35,000 bond. Edmondson said something to the effect that the Belgrade demand was unconstitutional, immaterial, irrelevant, and that anyway the United States Chess Federation could not raise the money. He also said that Fischer had fired him. Fischer had decided to handle all negotiations personally. At that point FIDÉ cabled Fischer, who was in training at Grossinger's, a summer resort in the Catskill Mountains, that a guarantee of his appearance was requested. If Fischer did not answer by April 4 he would be disqualified. Just before that deadline, FIDÉ did get a wire from Fischer that said he would play—under protest. Fischer also made some disparaging remarks about Iceland, mentioning among other things that it had no facilities for international coverage—a remark that was to appear hilariously funny a few months later.

By this time, however, Belgrade had had enough. The sponsors pulled out, saying there was not enough time to organize Belgrade's part of the match. That left Reykjavik, which offered to stage the entire match. FIDÉ accepted. The Russians had won a victory of sorts; that had been their preferred choice from the beginning. Fischer had outsmarted himself.

Reykjavik: population of about 80,000. A charming little city on an island in the North Atlantic, just under the Arctic Circle, halfway between England and Greenland. Reykjavik, where in June and July there are twenty-four hours of daylight, and golfers tee off at midnight. Reykjavik, a city mostly of small white houses with gaily painted roofs; a city surrounded on three sides by water; a city with no pollution problems, no crime problems, no fuel problems (geysers heat the city). Reykjavik, which went to "war" with England over fishing rights a few years ago. Iceland has a navy of three ships, tugboat-size. The fleet steamed out to engage the enemy, loaded its guns with potatoes, and sprayed the British flagship with a barrage of mashed spuds. (Iceland is a civilized country; when she goes to war she does not want to *kill* anybody.) Reykjavik, with its Viking and Danish heritage, its Old Norse language (FISCHER FELLST EKKI A AD DÉMA-RARNIR SÉU SKÁKMENN, ran a headline in the paper), its kind and considerate people, its 100 per cent literacy, its one-class society where nobody is very poor and nobody is very rich. Reykjavik, with its few tiny trees and lawns, on the outskirts of a lunar landscape where the land bulges in spectral lava conformations and not a house is seen for miles, and where, outside the city, the transportation network consists of bumpy, one-way dirt roads going from nowhere into nowhere.

The Spassky-Fischer match was scheduled to start on July 2. Spassky arrived on June 21, to give himself plenty of time to acclimatize and get his biological clock in order. He was accompanied by his second, Yefim Geller; by a grandmaster psychologist, Nikolai Krogius; and by a chess-playing trainer, Ivo Nei from Estonia. They were lodged on the seventh floor of the Hotel Saga. Spassky settled down to playing tennis, jogging, and exercising. On June 26 he held a press conference and handled himself as smoothly as a diplomat, capturing all Iceland with his charm and *politesse*. Spassky speaks fluent English, but spoke in Russian with a translator putting his words into English. (In Iceland nearly everybody is trilingual—Icelandic, Danish, and English.) Spassky said that he looked forward to the match, that he liked Iceland, that he was perfectly happy with the rules and playing conditions. Questions from the press were neatly parried, with a dead-pan face but with a twinkle in the eye.

Meanwhile, Exhibition Hall, the site of the match, was being rushed to readiness. The Russians inspected it and pronounced themselves well satisfied. Visiting grandmasters agreed that the Iceland sponsors had put every effort into making the hall quieter and more comfortable than had obtained for any previous match in history. Krogius and Nei said that they had never seen anything like it. Only one thing was missing—the presence of Bobby Fischer. His aide, Fred Cramer of Milwaukee, FIDÉ vice-president (representing Zone 5—the United States), arrived on June 27, without

Fischer. Nobody was worried. Fischer, after all, was a known eccentric. He would appear in due course. Cramer, acting as Fischer's personal representative, presented Gudmundur Thorarinsson, the president of the Icelandic Chess Federation and the chief organizer of the match, with a list of Fischer's demands—the first of many which were to drive Thorarinsson and everybody else to desperation. This list contained Fischer's requirements for lighting and the containment of the audience. These were expected. Not expected was an explosive demand that the referee was unacceptable. Lothar Schmid, the amiable and debonair German grandmaster who seldom appeared in international tournaments, and who had been the referee of the Fischer-Petrosian match in Buenos Aires, had been named by FIDÉ. Fischer objected. Active grandmasters, he said through Cramer, are subject to pressure by the Russians. A nonplaying referee, such as Paul Klein of Ecuador (who had been the referee for the Fischer-Larsen match in Denver), was Fischer's choice. Fischer kept on making demands. He *never* ceased making them during the match. A partial list would include:

A demand for a new Mercedes-Benz automatic to be placed at his disposal for the duration of the match.

A demand for thirty per cent of the gate receipts in addition to the winner's share of the $125,000 purse.

A demand that the loser's share of the purse be placed in escrow for him.

A demand, constantly repeated during the match, that the chessboard and pieces be changed. (The Icelandic Chess Federation had engaged an artisan to make a heavy table with inlaid marble squares between $2\frac{1}{4}$ and $2\frac{5}{8}$ inches wide. Fischer wanted the size to be exactly $2\frac{1}{8}$ inches. Spassky also agreed that the squares were too large in relation to the size of the chess pieces. Experienced chess players have a spatial relationship between the pieces and the squares they rest on, much as pianists have a tactile relationship with the size of the piano keys. An unorthodox size can be disconcerting in both instances.)

Spassky in Iceland. He charmed everybody by his aristocratic manner.

A demand that the first ten rows of seats be removed from the auditorium.

A demand for improved lighting.

A demand for removal of the television cameras. (This was one of the key squabbles of the match.)

A demand for a private room to continue the match.

A demand that children in the hall be forbidden candy with noisy wrappers.

A demand that children be confined to the balcony.

A demand that children be barred from the hall entirely.

A demand that wooden boards be substituted for the marble ones.

A demand for additional restaurants for his meals.

A demand for a new car halfway through the match.

A demand for an indoor tennis court.

A demand for a new suite in the Loftleidir Hotel.

A demand for his pocket money to be paid in advance.

A demand that the swimming pool of the Loftleidir Hotel be closed to the public at all times and reserved for the exclusive use of Bobby Fischer.

A demand for a better flow of periodicals and other reading matter in the hotel.

A demand that Chester Fox, who was in charge of filming the match, be refused admittance to Exhibition Hall.

A demand that Chester Fox be deported from Iceland.

A demand that there should be better contrast between the light and the dark squares of the chessboard.

A demand that the table on which the board was resting be cut down.

A demand, toward the end of the match, that seven additional rows of seats be removed.

A demand that the cafeteria and demonstration rooms of Exhibition Hall be soundproofed or emptied.

A demand that the Icelandic Chess Federation show Fischer a copy of the medical certificate when Spassky took the option of a postponement.

A demand, after Spassky had resigned the final game by telephone, to see the resignation in writing.

Some of these demands were reasonable, and some had been promised by the Iceland organizers. Others were outrageous and made the sponsors of the match throw up their hands in dismay and sputter incoherently.

But this is getting ahead of the story. Spassky was ready to play. Cramer kept saying that Fischer was due any day. Every morning, starting at five o'clock, the press corps raced out to the airport at Keflavik to greet all arriving aircraft. The city had more foreign journalists—almost one hundred fifty members of the working press, at its peak—than had ever assembled in the history of the island. Desperate journalists would be crisscrossing the city at an unseemly hour in the morning, most of them lost, trying to find the road to the airport. Each day saw them stationed en masse at Keflavik, and each day saw the nonarrival of Fischer. Icelanders were amused. "Is there really a Bobby Fischer?" they kept asking, pronouncing it "Bubby Fissa." Newspapermen had a field day. They started the war-of-nerves theory. Bobby, they wrote, was doing all this to upset and undermine Spassky, to make him nervous and incapable of his best concentration. Would it work?

On June 30, Fischer was indeed at Kennedy Airport in New York, en route to Iceland. Newspapermen spotted him there and he fled. His lawyer charged that "the press" had kept him from getting on the plane. (Throughout the match the Fischer group looked upon the press much as the White House regards the Eastern Establishment newspapers.) Officials of Loftleidir, the Icelandic airlines, told a different story. Their account of that incredible evening was that Fischer had been taken to Kennedy Airport by a private limousine. He would be transported to the plane through a back entrance. Nobody would see him. On the plane he would have an entire front section reserved for himself. (Normally Loftleidir does not have a first-class compartment; it flies tourist only.) Just as Fischer was ready to be led onto the plane, he changed his mind, went into the terminal, and disappeared. After some search his friends located him in a store, where he was buying an alarm clock. At this point, Fischer demanded that his luggage be removed from the plane, saying that he would take a later flight. During all this, the plane and its passengers were held up far past the scheduled departure time. Fischer then decided to go to a restaurant. Of course the reporters and photographers found him there. They advanced and Fischer rushed from the terminal building. Later he was located by security guards at a motel outside the airport. Then he decided to return to New York. "Fischer *wanted* to be found by the press," said a Loftleidir official.

The official ceremony to open the match was held on the evening of Saturday, July 1, at the National Theater in downtown Reykjavik. But the stiff-upper-lip proceedings did not hide the fact that one seat in the auditorium was conspicuously vacant. It was a sad, sad ceremony. The Icelanders had tried so hard to do everything right, and everything was going wrong. Brave speeches were made by Russians, Icelanders, Dr. Euwe for FIDÉ and the American chargé d'affaires. The United States Embassy was wringing its hands. "This is no way to make friends for America," said one official.

July 2, the official start of the match, came and went without Fischer. The Icelandic Chess Federation and Dr. Euwe, desperately trying to keep the match alive, announced a two-day postponement on grounds of Fischer's health. The United States delegation said that two telegrams from Fischer's physician had been sent but had somehow got lost. Nobody ever did see those telegrams. Fischer, in New York, was adamant. He wanted the two players to share thirty per cent of the gate receipts or there would be no match. This the Icelandic Chess Federation would not do. Every day saw three, four, five meetings and press conferences. Dr. Euwe was in despair. Chess buffs from Europe and the United States were furious; they had come to Reykjavik on their vacations to see the Match of the Century. ("*What* century?" they were asking.) Spassky and the Russians remained quiet through all the turmoil. The champion mildly suggested that Fischer was afraid to play. At one point, Dr. Euwe told Spassky that FIDÉ was prepared to disqualify Fischer immediately. Spassky said no; do not do that; he had come to play and wanted to play. The purse did not interest him. "I am not here for the money." Nevertheless, Euwe ruled that if Fischer were not present by noon of July 4 he would be disqualified.

On Monday, July 3, a chess-loving British industrialist, James D. Slater, put up $125,000 to match the purse. He said that he was eager to follow the match and that he wanted to eliminate

Fischer's money problem. If Fischer did not appear after that, he was a coward. The next morning Fischer was in Reykjavik. He came off the plane visible only from a distance, like the ghost of Hamlet's father ("Look, my lord, it comes!"), ignored the press and dignitaries waiting for him, rushed to a car, raced to Reykjavik, and went to bed. Nobody was able to see him, much less speak to him. That was his pattern for the rest of the match. He slept during the day, got up in the late afternoon, played his game, and spent the early morning hours bowling at the United States base at Keflavik, or playing ping-pong and tennis. Nor did Spassky give any interviews, though he at least spoke to the press and gave some off-the-cuff statements.

Fischer was now in Reykjavik but, as everybody immediately learned, that did not mean that a chess match would take place. The next few days saw a series of mixups that threatened to stop the match before it got started. Now it was the turn of the Russians to do some objecting. Claiming that the rules of the agreement had been breached, the Russians refused to hold the drawing ceremony (at which Fischer and Spassky would draw to see who would have the White pieces in the first game). The tall, elderly, courtly, soft-spoken Dr. Euwe was in despair. "It's difficult," he told the press. "I don't understand it. You don't understand it." Was it psychological warfare? "I don't know." The Americans, augmented by Father William Lombardy, Fischer's second, held a press conference that managed to alienate every journalist in Reykjavik. The Americans had their problems; trying to defend Fischer was trying to defend the indefensible; but wisecracking and evasion were not ways to take care of the situation. One American chess patron, at the end of the press conference, stood up and roundly denounced the American presentation. The Russians held a press conference. The Americans held another press conference. Fischer wrote an apology for his behavior. The Russians rejected it, saying that the statement was not even signed by him. Finally a meeting to arrange for a drawing ceremony was held. Spassky arrived, to find Lombardy representing Fischer, who had not cared to come. Fischer was within his legal rights, but it was an insulting gesture nevertheless, and Spassky took it as such. The furious Spassky charged that Fischer had maligned not only him but also the Russian people, and that

Fischer arriving in Iceland on July 4, 1972. This was virtually the last time anybody was to see him in public except during the actual games.

his behavior had made it doubtful whether he had a moral right to play the match. "If there should be any hope for the match to be held, Fischer must bear a just penalty." But what kind of penalty did the Russians have in mind? A linguistic hassle developed. In the official Russian text, the word was *nakazanyia*. Shades of meaning were weighed. What was the meaning of *nakazanyia?* Penalty? Punishment? Reprimand? A telegram from the Soviet Chess Federation clarified the *nakazanyia;* it demanded that the first game be forfeited by Fischer.

At a meeting on July 5 there was a still further clarification. Geller, speaking for the Russian delegation, demanded three things: Bobby Fischer must apologize; the president of FIDÉ had to condemn the behavior of the challenger; and the president of FIDÉ had to admit that his granting of a two-day postponement to Fischer had violated FIDÉ rule. An agitated Dr. Euwe stood up and admitted that he had no excuse for Fischer's behavior. "It is inexcusable. Fischer is living in another world. I am quite prepared to condemn Fischer's behavior not only in the last two days but all through the negotiations." As for the third part, Euwe admitted that the Russians were correct. "I violated the rules. There are reasons. If I had not violated them, there would be no match." He promptly signed a statement to the effect that he had violated FIDÉ rules "on the basis of assumptions proved wrong."

The American delegation immediately held another press conference. "Bobby doesn't feel that he has violated any rules," said Cramer. In a remarkable soliloquy, Cramer said that Fischer was having his pants pressed, eager to play. He also defended Fischer's ban on photographers in the hall by saying that "It wouldn't be nice if the camera caught Bobby picking his nose or reaming out his ears." He said that Fischer was so eager for battle that he insisted on an immediate drawing ceremony. Bobby was the one who had broken the rules in favor of the Russians; if there was any apologizing to be done, "*we* want an apology from Euwe." Cramer's remarks were received with stunned incredulity and a rush to the exit. One American said it was the greatest American disaster since Pearl Harbor. It was clear that the American delegation was working not only under direct orders from Fischer; it was also frightened to death of him. "I'm authorized only to complain and not to approve," Cramer blurted out at one point.

Paul Marshall, who was one of Fischer's attorneys, told a journalist that his (Marshall's) role was simple: "We insist on whatever Fischer wants us to do." It was felt by many that Fischer's attitude was megalomania bordering on actual insanity. "He's finally flipped his lid," said one American grandmaster.

But Fischer personally delivered a letter of apology to Spassky (not to his actual bedside in the dead of night, as some reports had it, but to the desk of the Hotel Saga). Spassky was appeased. "Now it looks good," he said. Dr. Euwe quietly left for Amsterdam, muttering that new FIDÉ rules would have to be written to cover the Bobby Fischers of this world. He did not return until the last game of the match. The Russians stopped talking about a forfeit of the first game. The Americans stopped talking about replacing Schmid as referee. On Thursday, July 6, Fischer and Spassky finally met on the stage of Exhibition Hall for the drawing ceremony: Spassky suave, confident-looking, elegant; Fischer with his usual shambling gait and looking ill at ease. Spassky arrived on time. Fischer was twenty minutes late. It was announced that the match would start on Tuesday, July 11. Spassky drew the White pieces for the first game of the twenty-four-game match. He would thus be playing White in all odd-numbered games.

There were still a few rumbles. Fischer did not like the chair provided by the Icelandic Chess Federation and had a $470 black leather swivel chair flown in from New York. (Later the Icelandic Chess Federation provided Spassky with its mate.) There were quibbles about the size of the chessboard, and the artisan got to work cutting new marble squares. Fischer also demanded that a check for the loser's share of the prize money (40 per cent) be put in escrow for him at the American Embassy. Other incidents ruffled the surface. Schmid's son was injured in a bicycle accident and he hastily rushed to Bamberg, saying that he would probably miss the first game of the match (he didn't, however). Fischer was asked to inspect the playing area. An appointment was made, but Fischer didn't show up, and after waiting in vain for an hour or so the officials of the Icelandic Chess Federation went home. The day of the match, at 1:00 A.M., Fischer finally made a thorough inspection of the hall. He complained that the lights were not bright enough, that the marble squares of the board were still too big, that the audience was too close to the stage (the distance was measured and turned out to be 40 feet, exactly what the specifications of the contract called for). Nobody seemed to take Fischer's complaints too seriously. The Icelandic Chess Federation was beginning to get the idea: Fischer was a compulsive complainer, a connoisseur of complaints, unhappy and unfulfilled unless he was complaining. Little did the officials of the Icelandic Chess Federation know what was in store for them.

21 ♕

Psychic Murder

When it was all over, on September 1, 1972, the world had a
new chess champion. Robert James Fischer, who for years had
been saying he was the best, had proved so by decisively beating
Boris Spassky. But *had* he really proved so? Had he won on his
chess alone, or had he "psyched" Spassky out of the title? Spassky,
a gentleman to the end, said nothing and took his defeat in his
best form, like Samuel Pepys's flayed gentleman. Others had no
hesitation saying that no player could be expected to operate at
his best while also having to contend with the crazy antics swirl-
ing around Fischer. Tal stated that Spassky "had suffered not so
much a chess setback as a psychological defeat. I believe that the
unprecedented kaleidoscope of events at the start of the match
had a fatal effect on his play in the first half. . . . All the commo-
tion threw him off balance, and made it impossible for him to
wage the struggle with the attention it needed."

Everything was controversial about the match, including the
very first game. The two players faced each other on July 11, at
long last, and for twenty-eight moves the game was uneventful.
Then, without thinking very long over it, Fischer made his no-
torious twenty-ninth move, seizing a poisoned Pawn, and shortly
thereafter losing his Bishop and the game. Was it a blunder or a
deep conception that misfired? Grandmasters present could not
believe that so precise a technician as Fischer had failed to see
some sort of continuation. Yet apparently that is what had happened. A source close to Fischer admitted that Bobby had

"goofed." He was so anxious to win the first game that he impulsively tried to force a dead-drawn position into a win. Fischer admitted as much after the game. "I played like a fish," he told a friend, white-faced and nervous.

Then there followed a Fischer eruption. He said that he would not continue playing unless the television cameras were removed from the hall. In all truth, they had been noisy during the first game—noisy for Fischer and his superacute hearing, at any rate. Spassky had not been bothered. What to do? The Icelandic Chess Federation had made a contract with Chester Fox for film and television coverage, and were relying on the proceeds to help reduce the estimated $200,000 deficit. All concerned tried to work out a compromise. The television towers were removed and the camera equipment was hidden in a well adjoining the stage. That did not suit Fischer. He talked darkly about Commies and plots against him; reputedly he was, at times, actually raving. Both Lothar Schmid and Paul Marshall tried to get Fischer to go to Exhibition Hall and see what actually had been done with the equipment. Fischer refused. "We tried for twenty-four hours to contact Fischer," said Schmid, "to ask him to come to the hall. Fischer has not come. I cannot break the rules." Fischer was demanding that all equipment be physically removed or else he would not show up for the second game. Schmid's position was that he was a referee, not a policeman. Spassky did arrive promptly at 5:00 P.M. to begin the second game. Fischer was in his hotel room with the telephone torn out of the wall. Lawyers for both sides were running frantically around. Gudmundur Thorarinsson was white-faced. Fischer refused to budge from his room, and Schmid had no alternative but to forfeit the game after an hour had elapsed. "It is a great pity," Spassky murmured.

For the next three days there were rounds of conferences. It was pointed out to the United States delegation that now the cameras were hidden and inaudible. Tests in the hall without the cameras measured fifty-five decibels. Tests with the cameras in operation also measured fifty-five decibels. The cameramen had removed their shoes and any change in their pockets. Surely that would satisfy Fischer's supersensitive ear. No, said Fischer. The cameras must go. The mere knowledge that they were present, whether or not he could hear or see them, would be enough to annoy him, he maintained. Fischer also demanded that the forfeit be revoked.

The date of the third game was Sunday, July 16. Fischer had booked reservations on all the flights out of Reykjavik that day. His entourage admitted that Fischer had made up his mind to leave. But at the last minute Fischer indicated that he would play the game if it were held in a private room upstairs in Exhibition Hall—a room used for ping-pong matches—and if television equipment were removed. Schmid got in touch with Spassky, and the Russian agreed to the terms. Chester Fox and his cameramen had no choice but to agree. Spassky arrived first, as usual, made his move and started his clock. Fischer came in a few minutes later and started complaining. Spassky then became irritated and demanded that the game be removed to the main room downstairs. Fischer was under severe emotional strain, Spassky was equally upset, and Schmid did his best to mediate. "Boris," he pleaded, "you *promised* to play here. Bobby, please be kind." Schmid thought that Fischer "would collapse on the floor." Finally both players quieted down, Fischer apologized for his hasty words, and the game started, Fischer "looking like death." To Schmid, that twenty minutes was the worst moment of the match. Fischer gathered himself together and won the game:

	WHITE: SPASSKY	BLACK: FISCHER
1.	P-Q4	N-KB3
2.	P-QB4	P-K3
3.	N-KB3	P-B4
4.	P-Q5	PxP
5.	PxP	P-Q3
6.	N-B3	P-KN3
7.	N-Q2	QN-Q2
8.	P-K4	B-N2
9.	B-K2	O-O
10.	O-O	R-K1
11.	Q-B2	N-R4
12.	BxN	PxB
13.	N-B4	N-K4
14.	N-K3	Q-R5
15.	B-Q2	N-N5

16.	NxN	PxN
17.	B-B4	Q-B3
18.	P-KN3	B-Q2
19.	P-QR4	P-N3
20.	KR-K1	P-QR3
21.	R-K2	P-N4
22.	QR-K1	Q-N3
23.	P-N3	R-K2
24.	Q-Q3	R-N1
25.	PxP	PxP
26.	P-N4	P-B5
27.	Q-Q2	QR-K1
28.	R-K3	P-R4
29.	R(3)-K2	K-R2
30.	R-K3	K-N1
31.	R(3)-K2	BxN
32.	QxB	RxP
33.	RxR	RxR
34.	RxR	QxR
35.	B-R6	Q-N3
36.	B-B1	Q-N8
37.	K-B1	B-B4
38.	K-K2	Q-K5ch
39.	Q-K3	Q-B7ch
40.	Q-Q2	Q-N6
41.	Q-Q4	B-Q6ch
	Resigns	

Fischer's final move was sealed. Spassky came to Exhibition Hall the following afternoon, took one look at it when Schmid opened the envelope, and resigned. He and his second had analyzed all night, and Spassky immediately knew that Fischer had sealed the winning move. One possible continuation might have been: 42. K-K3, Q-Q8; 43. Q-N2, Q-K8ch; 44. K-B4, P-B6; 45. Q anywhere, Q-K4 mate. Or if Spassky played 42. K-K1, then QxPch is an easy win for Fischer. In any variation Spassky was lost. He immediately told Schmid so, and left the hall. Schmid addressed the small audience: "I am sorry. The game is over. Mr. Spassky resigns." Fischer arrived on the stage of Exhibition

Hall, breathless, about fifteen minutes after Spassky had left. "What happened?" he wanted to know. Schmid told him that Spassky had resigned upon seeing the sealed move. Fischer signed his score sheet and rushed out. It was the first time that he had conquered Spassky.

Spassky could not have known it, but this third game was the beginning of the end. Had he not assented to Fischer's demand for a private room, Fischer would have gone home and Spassky probably would still be world champion (he would have played Petrosian instead of Fischer). Had not Fischer overcome his hysteria and played such a brilliant game, he might have found Spassky's two-point advantage too much to overcome. But now Fischer knew he could take Spassky's measure. And he did. Spassky seemed to collapse. The fourth game was a draw. Fischer won the fifth and sixth. The seventh and ninth were draws; Fischer won the eighth and tenth. Thus in ten games, Spassky could win only two, and one of those by a forfeit. There were all kinds of surprises. Fischer did *not* invariably open with his usual 1. P-K4. He mixed his openings, throwing Spassky completely off balance. It seemed clear to the assembled grandmasters that Spassky and his team had prepared against King-Pawn openings only and were startled and upset when Fischer departed from his normal routine.

Spassky was suffering, and it showed in his mannerisms. Even his poker face occasionally broke. Chess players, like prizefighters, are trained to accept and absorb punishment without showing any sign of strain or stress. But Spassky began to show his inner misery. As the match went on and Fischer drew inexorably ahead, Spassky seemed more and more in a private world. Fischer would sit directly facing Spassky, in profile to the audience. Spassky played much of the five-hour sessions with his back to the audience, head tilted toward the pieces, his chair swiveled at right angles to the table. Often he would stare at the rear wall of the stage even while he was on the move. Never did he look at Fischer. When he got up to stretch his legs, his body no longer had the elasticity and confident movement it had shown at the beginning of the match. His handsome, intelligent-looking face was drawn. Often his lips would compress as though he were in physical pain. His formerly impassive expression began to hint at signs of deep emotion. His mind was no longer responding alertly, and he was beginning to make blunders of an almost elementary nature. Boris Spassky, the chess champion of the world, the player supposedly without nerves, the representative of Soviet culture, the suave gentleman admired by all who came into contact with him, was being torn apart and psychologically ground down by the rude, inconsiderate, ego-crushing savage from the United States.

Spassky was suffering from Fischer-fear. Perhaps the weight of the Soviet bureaucracy was too much for him to bear. Probably Fischer was too strong for him to begin with. Whatever it was, the Spassky mind-style was being swamped by the Fischer mind-style. When the Fischer aura envelops an opponent, terrible things happen, and Spassky was finding that out much as Petrosian, Larsen, and Taimanov previously had found it out. Combinations turn out faulty. Exchanges are lost. Players end up in *Zugzwang*. Well-tested openings develop flaws. Outright blunders are made.

It is hard to describe the Fischer aura, but there it was, and fascinated followers of the match all over the world began to get an idea of its potency. The Fischer aura is palpable in its presence, reaching over the board to embrace the opponent, reaching beyond the stage to seize the audience. Relentless, monomaniacal, and pitiless, it is the aura of a killer. It is there in Fischer's face. He sits at the board, lips slightly parted, his deep-set and bleakly expressionless eyes scanning the sixty-four squares. He knows more about the openings that his opponents do, and can see a little deeper into the possibilities of a position. He mercilessly takes immediate advantage of the opponent's slightest inaccuracy, and he can nourish a minute positional advantage into a won end game, and he always seems to have plenty of time on his clock while his opponents are in desperate time trouble. But terrifying as all this may be to Fischer's opponents, that is not what scares them. That is not the essence of the Fischer aura.

No. The Fischer aura goes deeper than that, deeper even than his insatiable will to win, and Spassky received it full blast. Basically, the Fischer aura is the will to dominate, to humiliate, to take over an opponent's mind. A player losing to any other player shrugs and walks away. He has lost, and all chess players lose at one time or another, and there will be another day, another game. But a loss to Fischer somehow diminishes a player. Part of him has been devoured, and he is that much less a whole man. It is psychic murder that Fischer represents, far more than any other player in history. Spassky, winning a hard-fought game, like as not will feel sorry for his opponent. He will smile at him, pat him on the back, sympathize. Fischer, winning a game, exults in it whether or not it shows in his face. His ego has been fed, the blood has been licked and savored. Other grandmasters play for points. Fischer plays to obliterate another mind. What he had said in the past was true. He really *does* like to see them squirm.

In the process of tearing Spassky apart, Fischer became one of the most famous men in the world. From being the Mozart of chess he had developed into the Beethoven of chess—a surly, cantankerous genius with the notion that the world had to accommodate itself to *his* wishes. Like Beethoven, he has insisted on respect for his uncommon creative ability. Like Beethoven, he has cultivated one talent to the exclusion of everything else. Like Beethoven, he has broken away from the Establishment, refused to remain a lackey, and has demanded handsome payment for his services. Like Beethoven, he must have his own way and he goes into rages when he is crossed or thinks somebody is taking advantage of him. Like Beethoven, he is impractical, unworldly, sloppy, suspicious, not always ethical in his business dealings, totally lacking in the social graces.

Reykjavik established the fact that Fischer cannot really be happy and play at his best unless he is terrorizing people, making them jump, making them rush to obey his whims. That builds up his own ego. As over the board, so it is in life. Bobby Fischer feeds on other egos, and his own grows correspondingly fatter and hungrier. This boy from a broken family, who never had much money up to now, who has lived mostly alone in cheap hotel rooms surrounded by copies of girlie magazines—this boy is, by God, going to show everybody who's boss.

Through the match he had his way in almost every particular. The television cameras were permanently removed, to the infinite grief of the Icelandic Chess Federation, who were thus assured of a financial loss. Lawyers came and went; the American Broadcasting System sent their smoothest operators to deal with Fischer. He was adamant. Through the entire match he continued to complain about playing conditions. The Russians were on record as saying that the Iceland sponsors had provided the finest ambience ever created for a chess match. Fischer thought differently and kept bombarding the officials with furious letters about the "intolerable" conditions under which he was forced to play. As late as August 21 he was addressing to Lothar Schmid such *billets doux* as:

> Sir:
>
> You have received four letters and many urgings from us during recent weeks, yet playing conditions at Exposition [*sic*] Hall continue to worsen. They have now reached the point where I do not intend to tolerate them further.
>
> I shall expect you to schedule play in the private room beginning with game 17 and continuing there, unless or until the corrections to the auditorium, as requested by my representatives, have been completed to my satisfaction.
>
> Should your failure to do this produce another forfeit, I shall consider the match summarily terminated and there will be no further play under any conditions.
>
> The decision is now in your hands. I and the chess world expect you to reject the present travesty and to give us playing conditions worthy of a world's championship match.
>
> Yours truly,
>
> *Bobby Fischer*

Between the third and twenty-first games, Spassky was able to win only a single one outright—the eleventh. Games 14 to 20, however, were all draws. Spassky had found unexpected resources. Perhaps it was the presence of his wife, who arrived on August 11 and stayed until the end of the match. Spassky moved out of the Saga Hotel, away from the Russian delegation, and was his own man for the first time. That may have helped his frame of mind. But still he could not beat Fischer, though he threw at him everything he had. Half point by half point Fischer edged into the title. To the Russians, Spassky's play was inexplicable. There had to be a reason. Spassky himself, who for the first time in his career was looking at the board without any ideas coming to mind, actually came to believe that some kind of external force was working to keep him from concentrating. Gas?

Poison? Finally some bright minds in Moscow, presumably follow-ing up Spassky's theory, issued a statement. Fischer and the Amer-icans were cheating. They were using chemical and electronic warfare. On August 22 Geller had to release, under his own name, a statement carrying those charges.

It was the funniest moment of the match. In effect the state-ment said that the hall was Bobby-trapped. Why had Fischer in-sisted on lighting according to his own specifications? Why did Fischer always insist on his own chair, even though both chairs were identical? What were the Americans doing so often in Exhibition Hall at the dead of night, when all honest, respect-able chess players should be in bed happily dreaming of the Exchange Variation of the Ruy Lopez?

Everybody thought that the Russian charges were the funni-est thing since Snorri Sturlsson signed away Iceland to Norway. Even the Russians went around with suppressed grins. But so spectacular a charge of cheating and trickery could not be dis-missed out of hand by the organizers. Straight-faced, they brought in a chemist and an electronics engineer. The lighting was in-spected and all that could be found in the world were two dead flies. ("Are you *sure* they are dead?" purred Ivo Nei, equally straight-faced.) Wags said that the flies should be dissected. Had they died a natural death? Or was their death a result of tasting the Poisoned Pawn Sicilian? Or had an American death ray put an end to them?

The chairs were X-rayed. A foreign object was discovered in Spassky's chair. Aha! The chair was field-stripped, prodded, un-glued, dismembered. The stage looked like an operating room in the Presbyterian Hospital. Pieces of chair were strewn all over the arena. An upholsterer was picking at its insides. A policeman was on duty in case the unknown object was a bomb. Worried officials of the Icelandic Chess Federation were standing by, wringing their hands, wondering if the *membra disjecta* could ever be reassembled. Nikolai Krogius of the Russian delegation was standing aloof, looking inscrutable.

The foreign object in Spassky's chair turned out to be wood filler.

The chemist was busy. If Spassky was being chemically manipulated, the chemicals could enter his body through food

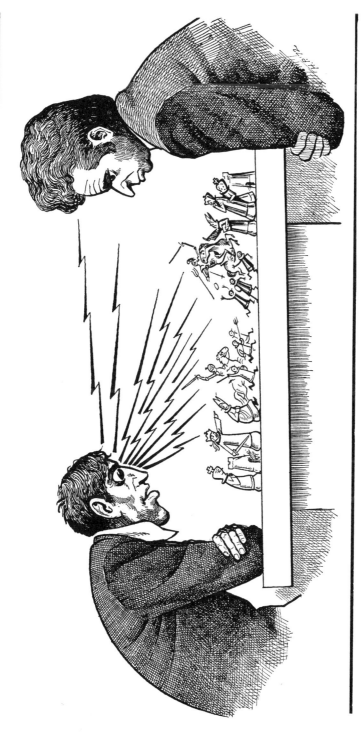

The Morgunbladid, Reykjavik's largest newspaper, had a long series of caricatures by Halldor Petursson. For those who believed that Fischer was hypnotizing Spassky, Petursson drew this cartoon.

Bobby Fischer by Harold C. Schonberg.

and drink, through the air, or by injection through the skin. Air samples were tested. Negative. Scrapings were taken from the chairs and analyzed by gas chromatography. Negative.

In one grand gesture, the Russians had undercut all the sympathy that had been built up by Spassky. Everybody had admired his sportsmanship and his grace under pressure. Now he was associated with a preposterous excuse to explain away his bad showing in the match. The Icelanders were now saying that the Russians were poor losers. One American in Reykjavik, thinking of mighty Russia and mighty America glaring at each other across the ocean, could only say: "Thank God they're dumber than we are."

Slowly, inexorably, draw by draw, the match approached its end. At the twenty-first game Fischer needed one more point to win. The game went to an adjourned position, easily a draw for Fischer, most likely a win, depending on Spassky's sealed move. Spassky sealed 41. B-Q7, and overnight analysis demonstrated to him that it was not the best move (41. K-R3 would have offered much more resistance). He therefore telephoned his resignation to Schmid at 12:50 P.M., Friday, September 1. But before the announcement was officially made, there was the kind of infuriating hassle that had disfigured so much of the match. Fischer refused to come to Exhibition Hall and take Schmid's word for the resignation. He demanded that Spassky submit it in writing. Dr. Euwe, who had come from Amsterdam to make the official presentation, was torn between laughter and tears. "Fischer *has* to be here," he said. "Officially he doesn't know that Spassky has resigned." Fischer was finally persuaded to go to Exhibition Hall. He arrived forty-seven minutes late, and Schmid addressed the audience of 2,500:

"Ladies and gentlemen, Mr. Spassky has resigned by telephone at 12:50. This is a traditional and legal way of resignation. Mr. Fischer has won this Game No. 21, and he is the winner of the match." Fischer, busy signing the score sheet, nodded, glanced at the audience out of the corner of his eyes, and rushed from the stage. The final score of the match was 12 1/2 to 8 1/2 in favor of Fischer (seven wins, three losses, eleven draws).

Two days later there was a final ceremony at which Fischer received $78,215 and Spassky $46,875. An equal sum awaited both players in London. At the ceremony Fischer was true to form. He kept Spassky and about 1200 people waiting almost an hour for their dinner. They could not start without the guest of honor, and he took his time arriving. One statement of Fischer's from the stage of Exhibition Hall, when Dr. Euwe gave him his medal, somewhat startled the audience. Fischer looked carefully at the medal. "It's so small," he said.

After the match Gligorić interviewed Spassky, who insisted that he was convinced that he had a chance even up to the twenty-first game. But in the final result, said Spassky, "I lacked the nerves and the energy." He had wasted, he said, his nervous energy "terribly stupidly" sometime earlier. As for Fischer's play, Spassky estimated it as "very economic. He solved no great problems of the world; he just played. If he saw a good or even average move on the board, he played it right away and—finish!" Spassky described it as pragmatic rather than creative chess. He cited Fischer's health, tremendous chess energy, and burning desire to win every time. "He is an extraordinary chess player in all ways—straightforward in his chess, like a child."

On his return to the United States, Fischer remained true to himself. His business agents said that there were, waiting for his signature, millions of dollars in endorsements, lectures, exhibitions, and books. But as far as anybody knows, Fischer did not sign anything. This backed up the belief of some Bobby-watchers that he does not really know what money is. He is not the money-grubbing capitalist the Russians make him out to be. He wants money, but only as a symbol of success. That is something he had figured out years ago: if you are a success, you have money. Bobby had his match money; that was enough.

Fischer made a few television appearances, then disappeared into his lodgings in Pasadena. Before the match Fischer had said that he would not be like the champions of the past, and especially he would not be like those Russians. *He* would defend his title twice, thrice a year "if the price is right." But from Pasadena came a dead silence. Over a year had passed since he had become the chess champion, and he had not played a single game of competitive chess, much less a match. Reports had it that Fischer had been offered $1,400,000 by a Las Vegas hotel for a rematch with Spassky or, failing that, any player of his choice. Fischer did not act. One rumor says that Fischer asked for $10 million. There

Bobby Fischer by Harold C. Schonberg.

also was a report of a possible match with young Mecking of Brazil. Fischer could not be reached to confirm or deny the report. Perhaps, despite all his previous talk, he was not anxious to risk a title that meant so much to him. He would wait, many began to believe, three years and then meet the FIDÉ challenger. Some wondered if he would even do that; but, assuming that he did, who might the FIDÉ challenger be? Tal in 1972 and 1973 had found new life and was winning every tournament in sight. The prospect of a Fischer-Tal match had hearts going pitapat. Or there was the new Russian threat, the twenty-one-year-old Anatoly Karpov, who played a solid, old-man's game and was being talked about as the one young player who could give Fischer some real competition. Great things were expected of this young man.

But neither he, nor Tal, nor even Spassky, had anything near the Fischer charisma. While Bobby Fischer was around, chess would continue to be what it was in those delirious Reykjavik days —big-league competition for big-league stakes for the first time in its long history. Bobby Fischer was more than a chess player; he was a force of nature. If he stopped playing for some reason, chess very likely would revert back to the $2500 purses of yore. If he continued to play, chess would remain a glamorous, intoxicating, internationally publicized sport/art/science/game. It was Bobby Fischer who had, singlehandedly, made the world recognize that chess on its highest level was as competitive as football, as thrilling as a duel to the death, as aesthetically satisfying as a fine work of art, as intellectually demanding as any form of human activity. If for no other reason Bobby Fischer was and would be the greatest chess champion who ever lived.

Bibliography

BOOKS AND MAGAZINE ARTICLES

Abrahams, Gerald: *The Chess Mind.* London 1951.

Alekhine, Alexander: *My Best Games of Chess, 1908–1923.* New York 1966.

———: *My Best Games of Chess, 1924–1937.* New York 1966.

———: *The World's Chess Championship 1937.* Philadelphia 1938.

Alexander, C. H. O'D.: *Fischer v. Spassky.* New York 1972.

Allen, George: *The Life of Philidor.* Philadelphia 1863.

Barden, Leonard: "Portrait of a World Champion [Spassky]." In *Chess Life and Review,* Jan., 1970.

Botvinnik, Mikhail: *One Hundred Selected Games.* Drexel Hill, Pa., 1951.

Brady, Frank: *Profile of a Prodigy—The Life and Games of Bobby Fischer.* New York 1965.

Capablanca, José R.: *Chess Fundamentals.* New York 1967.

———: *Last Lectures.* New York 1966.

———: *My Chess Career.* London 1920.

Carroll, Charles Michael: "Philidor in London." In *British Chess Magazine,* 1961.

Chernev, Irving: *The Bright Side of Chess.* New York 1948.

———: *The Chess Companion.* New York 1968.

———, and Fred Reinfeld: *The Fireside Book of Chess.* New York 1949.

Cheshire, Horace F.: *The Hastings Chess Tournament 1895.* New York 1962.

Clarke, P. H.: *Mikhail Tal's Best Games of Chess.* New York 1961.

————: *Petrosian's Best Games of Chess 1946–1963.* New York 1964.

Cluley, William: *The Philosophy of Chess.* London 1857.

Coles, R. N.: *Dynamic Chess.* London 1956.

Davidson, Henry Alexander: *A Short History of Chess.* New York 1949.

Devidé, Charles: *A Memorial to Wilhelm Steinitz.* New York 1901.

Edge, Frederick: *The Exploits and Triumphs in Europe of Paul Morphy.* New York 1859.

Euwe, Dr. M.: *The Development of Chess Style.* New York 1968.

————: *Meet the Masters.* London 1940.

Fine, Reuben: "Chess and Music." In *Notes,* Sept., 1944.

————: *Psychoanalytic Observations on Chess and Chess Masters.* Psychoanalysis Monograph 1, 1956.

————: *The World's a Chessboard.* New York 1948.

————: *The World's Great Chess Games.* New York 1951.

Fischer, Bobby: *My 60 Memorable Games.* New York 1969.

Fiske, Daniel Willard: *The Book of the First American Chess Congress.* New York 1859.

————: *Chess Tales and Chess Miscellanies.* New York 1912.

Franklin, Benjamin: *The Complete Works.* 3 vols. London 1806.

Gligorić, Svetozar: *Selected Chess Masterpieces.* New York 1970.

————, and R. G. Wade: *The World Chess Championship.* New York 1972.

Golombek, Harry: *Capablanca's Hundred Best Games of Chess.* New York 1965.

Graham, P. A.: *Mr. Blackburne's Games at Chess.* London 1899.

Hannak, Dr. J.: *Emanuel Lasker.* New York 1959.

Harkness, Kenneth: *The Official Blue Book and Encyclopedia of Chess.* New York 1956.

Hayden, Bruce: *Cabbage Heads and Chess Kings.* London 1960.

Horowitz, I. A., and P. L. Rothenberg: *The Personality of Chess.* New York 1963.

Horton, Byrne J.: *Dictionary of Modern Chess.* New York 1959.

Jones, Ernest: "The Problem of Paul Morphy." In *Essays in Applied Psychoanalysis.* London 1951.

Karpman, Ben: "The Psychology of Chess." In *Psychoanalytic Review*, vol. XXIV, no. 1, Jan., 1937.

Kennedy, Hugh A.: *Waifs and Strays*. London 1876.

Keres, Paul: *The Complete Games of Paul Keres*. New York 1972.

Kmoch, Hans: *Rubinstein's Chess Masterpieces*. New York 1941.

Knight, Norman: *Chess Pieces*. London 1949.

Koltanowski, George: *Adventures of a Chess Master*. New York 1955.

König, Imre: *Chess from Morphy to Botwinnik*. London 1952.

Kotov, A., and M. Yudovich: *The Soviet School of Chess*. Moscow 1958.

Lambe, Robert: *The History of Chess*. London 1764.

Lasker, Edward: *The Adventure of Chess*. New York 1949.

————: *Chess Secrets I Learned from the Masters*. New York 1951.

Lasker, Emanuel: *Common Sense in Chess*. New York 1910.

————: *Lasker's Manual of Chess*. New York 1927.

Lawson, David: "The Life of Paul Morphy." In *Chessworld*, Jan.–Feb., 1964.

Liddell, Donald, and G. A. Pfeiffer: *A History of Chessmen*. New York 1937.

Liepnieks, A.: *The Chess Psychologist—World Champion Tal*. Lincoln, Neb. 1961.

Löwenthal, J.: *Morphy's Games of Chess*. London 1876.

MacDonnell, G. A.: *Chess Life-Pictures*. London 1883.

Marshall, Frank: *Chess Masterpieces*. New York 1928.

————: *My Fifty Years of Chess*. New York 1942.

Matthews, Kenneth: *British Chess*. London 1948.

Murray, H. J. R.: *A History of Chess*. Oxford 1913.

Napier, William Ewart: *Paul Morphy and the Golden Age of Chess*. New York 1957.

Nimzovich, Aron: *The Praxis of My System*. New York 1962.

Prins, Lodewijk: *Master Chess*. London 1950.

Purdy, C. J. S.: The Return of Alekhine. Sydney 1937.

Reinfeld, Fred: *Great Moments in Chess*. New York 1963.

————: *The Human Side of Chess*. New York 1952.

————: *The Joys of Chess*. New York 1961.

————: *Tarrasch's Best Games of Chess*. London 1947.

————: *A Treasury of British Chess Masterpieces*. New York 1962.

————: *The Treasury of Chess Lore*. New York 1951.

Reinfeld, Fred, and Reuben Fine: *Dr. Lasker's Chess Career*. New York 1935.

Reshevsky, Samuel: *Reshevsky on Chess*. New York 1948.

Réti, Richard: *Masters of the Chessboard*. New York 1932.

————: *Modern Ideas in Chess*. London 1924.

Richards, D. J.: *Soviet Chess*. Oxford 1965.

Salzman, Jerome: *The Chess Reader*. New York 1949.

Sarratt, J. H.: *The Works of Damiano, Ruy-Lopez and Salvio*. New York 1813.

Sergeant, P. W.: *Championship Chess*. New York 1963.

————: *Charousek's Games of Chess*. London 1919.

————: *Morphy Gleanings*. Philadelphia, 1932.

Sergeant, P. W., and W. H. Watts: *Pillsbury's Chess Career*. New York 1966.

Smyslov, Vasily: *My Best Games of Chess 1935–1957*. New York 1972.

Soltis, Andrew: *The Best Chess Games of Boris Spassky*. New York 1973.

Stahlberg, G.: *Chess and Chessmasters*. New York 1955.

Staunton, Howard: *Chess Praxis*. London 1860.

————: *Staunton's Chess-Player's Handbook*. London 1935.

————: *The Chess Tournament*. London 1852.

Sunnucks, Anne: *The Encyclopaedia of Chess*. New York 1970.

Tartakower, S. G.: *My Best Games of Chess (1905–1930)*. London 1953.

————: *My Best Games of Chess (1931–1954)*. London n.d.

Wade, R. G.: *Soviet Chess*. New York 1968.

————: *The World Championship 1963*. New York 1963.

————, and Kevin J. O'Connell: *Bobby Fischer's Chess Games*. New York 1972.

Walker, George: *A New Treatise on Chess*. London 1833.

————: *Chess and Chess Players*. New York 1850.

Wellmuth, Francis J.: *The Golden Treasury of Chess*. New York 1943.

Windisch, Gottlieb de: *Inanimate Reason; or a Circumstantial Account of That Astonishing Piece of Mechanism, M. de Kempelen's Chess-Player*. London 1784.

Winkelman, Barnie: *Modern Chess*. Philadelphia 1931.

Winter, William: *Kings of Chess.* London 1954.
————, and R. G. Wade: *The World Chess Championship 1951.*
    London 1951.
Wood, Baruch H.: *The World-Championship Match Between Dr.
    Machgielis Euwe and Dr. Alexander Alekhine, Oct.–Dec.,
    1937.* Sutton Coldfield 1938.
Yates, F. B., and W. Winter: *Modern Master-Play.* London 1929.

MAGAZINES

American Chess Bulletin
American Chess Journal
American Chess Magazine
American Chess World
British Chess Magazine
Chess Amateur
Chess Life and Review
Chess-Monthly
Chess Monthly
Chess Player's Chronicle
Chess Review
Chess Weekly
City of London Chess Magazine
International Chess Magazine
Lasker's Chess Magazine
Westminster Chess Club Papers

Index

Italic page numbers indicate illustrations.